Karl Friedrich SCHINKEL

THE DRAMA OF ARCHITECTURE

EDITION AXEL MENGES

Karl Friedrich SCHINKEL

1781 - 1841

THE DRAMA OF ARCHITECTURE

Edited by

JOHN ZUKOWSKY

With Essays by

KURT W. FORSTER

WOLFGANG PEHNT

MITCHELL SCHWARZER

DAVID VAN ZANTEN

BIRGIT VERWIEBE

CHRISTOPH MARTIN VOGTHERR

THE ART INSTITUTE OF CHICAGO

WASMUTH

This book was published in conjunction with the exhibition "Karl Friedrich Schinkel, 1781–1841: The Drama of Architecture," organized by The Art Institute of Chicago and presented October 29, 1994, through January 2, 1995.

Copublished by:
The Art Institute of Chicago,
111 South Michigan Avenue,
Chicago, Illinois, 60603-6110,
and by Ernst Wasmuth Verlag,
Fürststraße 133, D-72072 Tübingen,
Germany.

The exhibition and book were made possible by the support of:

The National Endowment for the
 Humanities
Lufthansa German Airlines
The Federal Republic of Germany
Commerzbank Aktiengesellschaft
 Chicago Branch
Kimball International, Kimball Office
 Furniture Company
The Benefactors of Architecture at
 The Art Institute of Chicago

This book is a publication of the Ernest R. Graham Study Center for Architectural Drawings at The Art Institute of Chicago.

Edited by Robert V. Sharp
 Associate Director of Publications

Design concept by Joseph Cochand
 Senior Designer, Department of Graphic Design and Communication Services

Essays by Wolfgang Pehnt and Birgit Verwiebe were translated from the German by Matthew Heintzelman, Chicago

Type composition by Fotosatz Fritz, Fellbach, Germany

Printed in Korea

Library of Congress
Cataloging-in-Publication Data

Schinkel, Karl Friedrich, 1781–1841.
 Karl Friedrich Schinkel, 1781 to 1841: the drama of architecture / edited by John Zukowsky; with essays by Kurt W. Forster…[et al.].
 p.   cm.
 Published in conjunction with the exhibition organized by the Art Institute of Chicago and presented Oct. 29, 1994, through Jan. 2, 1995.
 Includes index.
 ISBN 0-86559-105-9 : $29.95
 1. Schinkel, Karl Friedrich, 1781 to 1841—Exhibitions. 2. Neoclassicism (Architecture)—Germany—Exhibitions.
 I. Zukowsky, John, 1948–
 II. Forster, Kurt Walter. III. Art Institute of Chicago. IV. Title.
 NA 1088.S3A4   1994
 720'.92—dc20   94-5313
                       CIP

FRONT COVER

Perspective view of a Doric temple, possibly a set design for *Olympia* (detail), 1821 (cat. no. 95).

BACK COVER

Perspective view of an Indian scene, a set design for *Nurmahal*, 1822 (cat. no. 98).

FRONTISPIECE

Perspective view of the theater within the Schauspielhaus, looking toward the stage, 1821 (cat. no. 54).

Contents

Foreword

In 1987 I had the pleasure to escort Wolf-Dieter Dube, General Director of the Staatliche Museen zu Berlin, Preußischer Kulturbesitz, through the most recent addition to the Art Institute, the classically inspired Rice Building, designed by Thomas Beeby, which was then under construction. Professor Dube was accompanied by the architect Christoph Sattler, designer of the new museum buildings going up in the area of Berlin known as the Kulturforum, very near Ludwig Mies van der Rohe's famous Neue Nationalgalerie of 1962–68. Little did I know then that we at this museum would have the pleasure of working with Professor Dube and one of his institutions to bring the masterworks of architectural drawing by Karl Friedrich Schinkel to an American audience for the first time. When we began exploring this project in 1988, Schinkel's works themselves were the victims of a divided Berlin. His paintings were largely in public collections in the West, while his drawings remained in his archive in the East. His buildings could likewise be found on both sides of the infamous Berlin Wall. With the collapse of the Berlin Wall in 1989, and the subsequent reunification of Berlin and Germany, Berlin's museum collections came under the jurisdiction of one agency headed by Professor Dube. It is he who deserves our gratitude for expediting this important project, along with the cooperation of Alexander Dückers, Director of the Kupferstichkabinett, and the persistence of the Art Institute's Curator of Architecture, John Zukowsky, and the exhibition's guest curator, Kurt W. Forster, professor of architecture at the Eidgenössische Technische Hochschule, Zurich.

But Chicago's connections to Berlin and Schinkel go deeper than these recent interchanges. More than a century ago, Prussian émigré architects and Schinkel disciples Frederick and Edward Baumann were among those who laid the foundations of the Chicago School of commercial architecture with simple, classicist detailing on their early skyscrapers. In addition, Mies van der Rohe had a significant role in reshaping Chicago's skyline and architectural education in this, his adopted city, after he left Berlin in 1937–38. It is also noteworthy that while Mies was still at the famed Bauhaus in 1932–33, he trained Chicago architects such as Howard Dearstyne, William Priestley, John Barney Rodgers, and perhaps best known among them, Bertrand Goldberg. The disciples of Mies and his colleagues at the Illinois Institute of Technology include German-born architects who practice in Chicago, among them Dirk Lohan and Helmut Jahn, as well as German architects such as Christoph Sattler and Peter C. von Seidlein who came to study at IIT and then returned home to practice. More recently, in 1981, a team of young Chicago architects composed of Kenneth Hazlett, Stephen O'Malley, and Christopher Rudolph prepared a limited-edition reprint and English translation of Schinkel's famous portfolio, *Sammlung architektonischer Entwürfe (Collection of Architectural Designs)*.

With this background in mind, it is only appropriate that the Art Institute's Department of Architecture should organize an exhibition of drawings by Schinkel. Although Schinkel's work is well known to architectural professionals in Chicago and the United States, the average architectural enthusiast may be more familiar with the importance of Mies and Walter Gropius than with Schinkel. Yet, of Berlin's and Germany's great architects, Schinkel has proved to be as influential, through subsequent generations, as those modernist masters, if not more so. We are also extremely pleased that Kurt W. Forster and the other scholars who have contributed to this volume have offered us a new way to see Schinkel's work through the theme of theatricality. We are grateful as well to Stanley Tigerman, who through his creative installation has enabled us to view these spectacular drawings within a theatrical framework. Finally, I am especially pleased that our own Department of Architecture and its curator, John Zukowsky, assisted by the various support departments within this museum, were able to overcome numerous hurdles over the past seven years to make this unique exhibition a reality in Chicago.

JAMES N. WOOD
Director and President
The Art Institute of Chicago

mong the many people who cooperated with us over the years to make this Schinkel catalogue and the exhibition that accompanied it a success, the first and foremost to be thanked is our guest curator, Kurt W. Forster, founding Director of the Getty Center for the History of Art and the Humanities and currently professor at the Eidgenössische Technische Hochschule (ETH), Zurich. We owe much to his insight and creativity in recognizing the viewpoint of theatricality inherent in Schinkel's work, the subject that became the theme of this project. We are also grateful for his perseverance in working with us over an almost seven-year span, during which time we witnessed the fall of the Berlin Wall, the reunification of Germany, and enormous changes in society, east and west.

The Art Institutes's director, James N. Wood, gave the initial plans for this exhibition his enthusiastic endorsement in early 1989, when he contacted both Günther Schade, then General Director of the East Berlin museums, and Peter Betthausen, then Director of the Nationalgalerie in the East, to propose this Schinkel exhibition for our museum. Following the reunification of Germany and the corresponding consolidation of the Berlin museum administration, Wolf-Dieter Dube, the General Director in the Staatliche Museen zu Berlin, Preußischer Kulturbesitz, helped in numerous instances to simplify complex decisions and pave the way for a speedy realization of this project, as did Alexander Dückers, Director of the Kupferstichkabinett, where Schinkel's archive has been housed since 1993. Through these often complicated changes of administration, the curator of the Schinkel archive, Gottfried Riemann, has remained constant in his control over these irreplaceable artifacts.

Beyond Berlin, many people recognized the importance of this project and gave us their generous support. Foremost among them are those whose financial contributions made it possible for us to implement the exhibition and produce this catalogue. In 1991 Heinz Wirth, the former Consul for Cultural and Economic Affairs in the Consulate of the Federal Republic of Germany, assisted us in obtaining funds for this endeavor, as did his successor, Renate Friedemann. Additional thanks for their continued support on the part of the German government go to Gabrielle von Malsen-Tilborch, the German Consul General in Chicago, and Andrea Moehwald, their Vice Consul for Cultural, Economic, and Public Affairs. In 1992 we received further financial assistance from the Chicago Branch of Commerzbank AG, and we thank Rainer H. Wedel, then Executive Vice President, and his successor, Helmut R. Töllner, for their faith in our enterprise. In 1992 Hans-Georg Knopp, the Director of the Goethe-Institut in Chicago, introduced us to Gernot Hübl, then Vice President for the Central Region USA of Lufthansa German Airlines and now a Vice President with their main office in Frankfurt, and Bahman (Bob) Armajani, the Marketing Manager for the Central Region USA of Lufthansa. We are very thankful for those introductions, which ultimately resulted in the support we received from Lufthansa for the transport of Schinkel's drawings and related courier travel. This base of corporate and German government support was enhanced with funding from the Benefactors of Architecture at The Art Institute of Chicago: J. Paul Beitler, John Buck, Charles Gardner, Lee Miglin, Sandi Miller, Stuart Nathan, Harold Schiff, and Richard Stein. Together, these grants and funds were able to help match the major grant for implementation provided in 1993 by the National Endowment for the Humanities. The N.E.H.'s Director of the Museums Program, Marsha Semmel, and Program Officer, Fred Miller, gave us invaluable advice for the preparation of our grant proposal. After receipt of these funds, we were very fortunate that Kimball International decided in 1994 to be an American corporate sponsor for this exhibition, and we thank Jeff Blackwell, Vice President of Marketing, for this support. Two people at the Art Institute helped to obtain the funds from these various public and private sources, and they deserve our thanks for their tireless efforts. Linda Noyle, Director of Corporate Relations, helped secure the Commerzbank and Lufthansa contributions, while Karin Victoria, Director of Government Relations, prepared the extensive grant application submitted to the National

Endowment for the Humanities. Other museum staff involved with the financial and administrative responsibilities of this exhibition should be thanked, as well, especially, Robert E. Mars, Executive Vice-President for Administrative Affairs, and Dorothy Schroeder, Assistant to the Director for Exhibitions. The Art Institute's Committee on Architecture, chaired by David C. Hilliard, rendered invaluable assistance and support throughout this process.

With that firm financial backing in place, we were able to implement this project with the assistance of a number of people in, and outside of, Chicago. Our six catalogue authors from Germany and the United States are to be thanked for their contributions to this book and for their promptness in submitting their essays under a tight deadline. The publisher Ernst Wasmuth and especially his agent, Axel Menges, merit our gratitude for their diligent enthusiasm throughout this project. We particularly thank Robert V. Sharp, Associate Director of Publications, for his precise editing of these essays under a very restricted schedule. He was assisted in his editorial and photographic researching tasks by Carol Jentsch Rutan, Elisabeth Dunn, Cris Ligenza, and Jason Greenberg. Joseph Cochand, Senior Designer in the Art Institute's Department of Graphic Design and Communication Services, created a striking design for this book, and for the installation's graphics. Translation services for the essays were provided by Matthew Heintzelman of Chicago.

The transportation of these rare objects required special care beyond the efficient and secure transatlantic transportation provided by Lufthansa. Jack Lewin and Scott Pfeifer, both of Jack Lewin and Associates, Inc., arranged their swift clearance through customs and shipment to the museum. Mary Solt, Executive Director of Registration, and Darrell Green, the Assistant Registrar for Loans and Exhibitions, coordinated the complexities of moving these important pieces. Reynold V. Bailey, the Manager of Art Handling, and his staff carefully installed the objects within the creative installation superbly designed by Stanley Tigerman with the assistance of his staff at Tigerman McCurry Architects, particularly Melany Teleen, Mark Lehmann, and Bruce Johnson. Gary Heitz of Chicago Scenic Studios, Inc., supervised the elaborate construction of the installation itself in conjunction with staff of the Physical Plant Department of the Art Institute, headed by its Executive Director George T. Preston, with the assistance of Ron Pushka. Other staff members who devoted their time to promoting and interpreting this project include John Hindman, Associate Director of Public Affairs, and the Executive Director of that department, Eileen Harakal; Jane Clarke, Associate Director of Museum Education, and Mary Sue Glosser, Senior Lecturer for Performance Programs. Staff members within the Department of Architecture also assisted in the creation of this project, and I would like to especially thank Department Secretary Linda Adelman and Technical Specialist Luigi Mumford for their extensive help. They and the Art Institute staff, in general, deserve our appreciation for the splendid job they did in realizing this project.

Finally, a mention should be made of one of the people who was present when Kurt Forster, Robert Sharp, Axel Menges, and I first assembled in Berlin in 1988 to discuss this exciting project—Helga Menges. Helga shared in our experiences that day, including our fascination with Kurt Forster's explanation of the themes inherent in Schinkel's striking drawings and the artistic power of his simple classicist buildings there. She was an informal advisor and witness to our painstaking preparations for this exhibition and catalogue. We grieved to hear of her premature death in 1993 and are especially saddened that she did not see our long-term efforts come to fruition.

JOHN ZUKOWSKY
Curator of Architecture
The Art Institute of Chicago

Introduction

JOHN ZUKOWSKY

Karl Friedrich Schinkel. Who was he? Why is his name so little recognized in America? Why is it that more than 150 years after his death, Schinkel and his achievements as an architect, draughtsman, painter, and designer retain a central place in the cultural life of Berlin while across the Atlantic he is virtually unknown? Clearly, the Berlin Wall effectively isolated Schinkel and his accomplishments from the West. In addition, the body of his work is in East German territory that was largely off-limits to Americans since the Second World War. Yet, even after the enormous upheaval of political and social conditions in Germany during the past century, Schinkel is revered as a supreme artist in his native land.

The basis for Schinkel's reputation in Germany becomes apparent if one visits Berlin to examine his work, as I was fortunate enough to do in September of 1988 when I met with the publisher Axel Menges and his wife, and Robert Sharp, my colleague from the Art Institute at the Friedrichstrasse Railroad Station checkpoint prior to entering East Berlin, the capital of the German Democratic Republic. Along with the legendary Checkpoint Charlie, the Friedrichstrasse station was one of the major entry points for Westerners to visit East Berlin. The four of us made our way through immigration and customs checkpoints and continued on past the stone-faced border police, to the other side. The goal of our pilgrimage that morning was the famed Altes Museum of 1822–30 designed by Karl Friedrich Schinkel. During our walk we examined some of Schinkel's masterpieces, such as the Neue Wache (New Guardhouse), from 1816–18. This tiny jewel of a building had served as a war memorial since 1931, and since 1960 had been designated as a Memorial to the Victims of Fascism and Militarism. Just as an honor guard stood outside Lenin's Tomb in Moscow, so here sentinels from the East German Peoples Army stood watch *(fig. 1)*.

Continuing along the legendary Unter den Linden—the historic boulevard of linden trees—we crossed

FIGURE 1

The Neue Wache (New Guardhouse) of 1816–18 (later designated a Memorial to the Victims of Fascism and Militarism), on Unter den Linden, Berlin. (Photo 1988.)

Schinkel's Schloßbrücke (Palace Bridge) of 1821–24 (see Vogtherr, *fig. 12*) to reach the Altes Museum. It was at the side entry to the Altes Museum that we joined Kurt Forster, then the director of the Getty Center for the History of Art and the Humanities, and we were soon greeted by Gottfried Riemann, the long-time curator of the Schinkel Archive. With Forster and Riemann as our expert guides in a rather spartan basement study and storage room, we were shown a dazzling collection of the architect's drawings, many of them exquisite renderings in watercolor and gouache. As we were shown box after box of drawings from the archive—including travel sketches, large-format pen-and-ink drawings, delicate watercolor landscapes, and highly dramatic and vibrantly colored gouaches—we all realized how little of Schinkel was known in the West and how exciting an exhibition of these spectacular drawings would be. A selection of these very drawings, more than six years later, now constitutes the exhibition represented in this catalogue.

The world has witnessed a dramatic turnabout in German politics and geography in recent years. At the time this exhibition was conceived, of course, it fit well within the ongoing programs of museum officials in the German Democratic Republic. Schinkel was one of their most

FIGURE 2

View looking east over the Berlin Wall along Niederkirchnerstraße toward the former Preußischer Landtag (Parliament), 1892–1902, designed by Friedrich Schulze. (Photo 1988.)

FIGURE 3

View looking east over the Berlin Wall along Niederkirchnerstraße showing the Martin-Gropius-Bau (formerly Kunstgewerbemuseum [Museum of Decorative Arts]) of 1877–81 on the right. (Photo 1990.)

important cultural commodities, his drawings having already been used for exhibitions in Berlin (1981), Hamburg (1982), and Venice (1982), with others planned for Madrid (1989) and London (1991). (The commodification of Schinkel could even be seen in a champagne named for him in the latter days of the German Democratic Republic: "Schinkel Sekt," a luxury product available for Westerners with hard currency at high-style East Berlin restaurants.) Considering the numerous precedents for our own exhibition, we were hoping to make our project distinct from these other European shows in some thematic way, though we also knew that this exhibition would be a landmark as the first time Schinkel's striking drawings would be seen in the United States. The theme of this exhibition gradually took shape as our guest curator, Kurt Forster, eloquently pointed out how Schinkel used various graphic techniques in his compositions to create dramatic works of art that were linked, in many ways, to the popularity of German theater in Berlin during the nineteenth century.

Schinkel's first involvement with popular theater began in 1807, when he undertook the production of perspective optical pictures for dioramas presented in Berlin. By 1815 he had moved from these to the design of stage sets for operas such as Mozart's *Die Zauberflöte (The Magic Flute)* and Gaspare Spontini's *Fernando Cortez* and *Nurmahal* and plays like Friedrich Schiller's tragedy *Die Jungfrau von Orléans (The Maid of Orleans)* (see *pls. 13–34*). He continued to produce stage sets, over one hundred in all, for some forty-five plays and operas, until 1828. The sets were mounted in either the National Theater (designed by Carl Gotthard Langhans; see Schwarzer, *fig. 9*) or the Königliches Opernhaus (designed by Georg Wenzeslaus von Knobelsdorff; see Schwarzer, *fig. 2–4*), and following the fire that destroyed the National Theater in 1817, in the new Schauspielhaus (see Schwarzer, *fig. 1*) that Schinkel was commissioned to design, which opened in 1821.

As Kurt Forster made clear that day in East Berlin—and as he argues in his essay in this catalogue—Schinkel's experience with stage design is evident in the very way he represents his own actual and ideal building projects. In his drawings and in the plates of his magnificent *Sammlung architektonischer Entwürfe (Collection of Architectural Designs)*, Schinkel structures the design as a setting for a highly inventive drama—to be played out across the history of architecture (see, for example, Forster, *fig. 14*, or Vogtherr, *figs. 3, 9*, and *15*). The principle of theatricality that consistently informed Schinkel's drawings and buildings quickly became the overriding theme of our proposed exhibition and projected catalogue. Having completed our assignment for that day, we returned to West Berlin via tourist stops at sites that included other Schinkel buildings such as his famed Schauspielhaus and the nearby Friedrichswerdersche Kirche (see Pehnt, *fig. 4*), a Schinkel museum that was unfortunately closed for renovation (much like an item on a menu in a Socialist restaurant in those days that was listed but never really available).

Upon returning to our respective homes, we continued to plan our exhibition. Kurt Forster and I made several subsequent trips to Berlin, both alone and in concert, to visit with museum officials in order to make our proposal a reality. On one such trip in the first days of November 1989, I sensed that a change was indeed in the air, as the various protest marches against the East German government in Berlin, Dresden, and Leipzig made so perfectly clear. Border guards and immigration officials seemed a bit more relaxed as I passed through Checkpoint Charlie during one of these day trips to the East. This time I had brought along a copy of one of our recent publications on Chicago architecture as a gift for one of the East German museum officials. The guard looked through it inquisitively as with everything one brought through customs, but this time his questions actually centered on the photographs of Chicago past and present and what Chicago and America were really like. In this conversation, as in other casual encounters with East Germans during that trip, there was a surprising willingness to talk with a Westerner. Little did I know how drastically the world would change when, only a few days later, on November 9, 1989, the infamous Berlin Wall was scaled and eventually toppled, as East met West for subsequent and continued reunification (see *figs. 2–4*).

My next trip in February 1990 brought me face-to-face with an exciting new world ripe for exploration. Border guards now strolled atop the Berlin Wall while souvenir seekers removed its precious concrete chips. I was fascinated by what was happening, but I also had to wonder what this new sense of freedom would mean for our Schinkel project. For the moment, the potential reunification brought numerous questions and almost paralyzing confusion, especially about which museum officials would retain their jobs. Therefore, 1990 and 1991 saw little progress on our project, although the East Berlin staff fulfilled their commitments to a 1991 Schinkel exhibition organized by the Victoria & Albert Museum in London, a retrospective exhibition that did not travel to another venue.

FIGURE 4

View looking east along Niederkirchnerstraße showing the newly restored Berlin Landtag on the left and the Martin-Gropius-Bau on the right. (Photo 1993.)

FIGURE 5

Abandoned cafe on a Soviet Army base near Elstal, west of Berlin. (Photo 1992.)

Nikolai Wassiljewitsch Tomski, Statue of Vladimir Ilyich Lenin, 1970, in Leninplatz, Berlin. (Photographed in November 1991, shortly before its removal.)

But this hiatus in detailed planning permitted me to see a range of monuments, both official and unofficial, in this and subsequent trips to Berlin: trips to other Schinkel sites in Potsdam and Berlin to see the Charlottenhof of 1826–28 (see Vogtherr, *figs. 5* and *6*), Schloß Babelsberg of 1834–35 *(fig. 6)*, the Charlottenburg Pavilion of 1824 *(fig. 7)*, and the gardens of Klein Glienicke of 1816–50 by Peter Joseph Lenné, with Schinkel's Schloß of 1824–1827, and other structures such as the Casino of 1824–25. The Glienicke park and palace, known to Westerners, were situated nearby where the local tour buses made regular stops at the infamous "Spy Bridge" of Potsdam, where East met West during the Cold War, the most notable exchange being the swap of U-2 pilot Francis Gary Powers for Soviet spy Rudolf Abel on February 10, 1962. Despite my forays into Prussian environments of the early nineteenth century, one could not escape other landmarks of Berlin's recent past, relics of the postwar Soviet occupation (see *fig. 5*). While the London exhibition was under way in mid-September 1991, I returned yet again to meet with Kurt Forster and Gottfried Riemann to make our initial selection for the exhibition from the Schinkel archive. Over the next two years, during which time we worked to raise the funds necessary to implement this proposal, we also watched the Schinkel drawings and their curator move to another institution in a new building within the Kulturforum near the Neue Nationalgalerie, designed by Ludwig Mies van der Rohe.

At the time of my last visit in the fall of 1993, Gottfried Riemann, now on the staff of the Kupferstichkabinett, the new home of Schinkel's drawings, and his Director, Alexander Dückers, met with Kurt Forster, our editor Robert Sharp, our exhibition designer Stanley Tigerman, and myself to make the final selection of the works to be displayed. Berlin monuments had come and gone (see *fig. 8*), newly accessible landmarks had been restored (see *fig. 9*), and Schinkel buildings had been renamed, but Schinkel's work still loomed large in Berlin. Together we looked at these drawings again with the same sense of awe and wonder that we had experienced five years before. And, although these documents and our experiences with them are just a small footnote to the dramatic events of international politics over the past five years, the drawings themselves are, individually and collectively, theatrically composed and strikingly rendered objects in the history of art and architecture—powerfully delineated works that we are pleased to present and interpret for the first time to an American audience in this catalogue and exhibition. Schinkel's work may be known to some architects and architectural historians in Chicago, but neither these professionals nor lay enthusiasts have ever enjoyed the opportunity to examine these important original drawings in relation to those principles of theatrical design that he seems to have consistently employed in his delineations. It is our hope that the essays included in this catalogue and the works represented in it, as well as the accompanying exhibition, will still project that spirit of theatricality to the catalogue reader and museum visitor that we felt when we first encountered them in another time in history, less than a decade ago.

Carl Gotthard Langhans, Brandenburg Gate, 1788–91, Pariser Platz, Berlin. (Photo 1991.)

"Only Things that Stir the Imagination": Schinkel as a Scenographer

KURT W. FORSTER

Eidgenössische Technische Hochschule, Zurich

Karl Friedrich Schinkel characterized his passionate preoccupation with things theatrical[1] in a letter to the actor and director August Wilhelm Iffland in 1813 as "an inclination I have felt since adolescence for the pictorial treatment of the stage."[2] When he claimed that following his inclination "had given him much insight," Schinkel obviously wished to persuade Iffland that it was not a passing fancy for the stage that had prompted his unsolicited letter, but rather the conviction that he possessed a particular aptitude for seeing the world from a theatrical point of view.

Schinkel conceived of the visual arts less as a representation of the world as it appears, than as a means of "viewing nature with a certain disposition."[3] Such ideas, vaguely idealist but definitely affective, would naturally seek their arena of experimentation on the stage. Hence, it seems only fitting that Schinkel made his debut in the annual exhibition of the Akademie der Künste of 1802 with a set design for the last scene from Christoph Willibald Gluck's opera *Iphigenia in Tauris*. The commentaries on his entry in the catalogue, and the recollections of his friend Johann Gottfried Schadow, laid emphasis on Schinkel's depiction of the story's ending in a heroic setting at daybreak.[4] Not content with the design of a landscape or an architectural subject, Schinkel had extended its scope to include the action on the stage. His interest in images that told stories—not only the grand events from the course of civilization, but also intimate ones of a psychological kind—became the subject of much comment throughout his life, as well as the object of friendly competition with writers such as Clemens Brentano, a virtuoso of Romantic poems and novellas.[5]

That Schinkel had chosen to exhibit a set design in the first place, and that he ventured into the domain of pictorial narrative rather than remaining in the realm of imaginary views, clearly conveys his attitude toward these two genres. Architecture, Schinkel argued, always finds its place within a specific setting, just as "landscape painting elicits a special interest, if it contains traces of human occupation."[6] "Pure landscape," he wrote, "with no signs of human presence, may appear grand and beautiful, but causes a sensation of the uncanny."[7] On the other hand, Schinkel viewed architecture as the result of the profound transformation of nature through human action, and he therefore considered architecture to be fraught with the "dramatic meaning … of destruction and creation."[8]

In Schinkel's hands, landscape painting was less an exercise in picturing the sublime than in imagining the sites of human history. For all their similarities with Caspar David Friedrich's paintings, Schinkel's landscapes take their viewers to other times, rather than transporting them into a transcendent realm of belief. No matter whether he chose actual or imaginary localities, whether he based them on archaeological or purely poetic notions, Schinkel always treated them with human events in mind. He painted landscapes in order to locate events, to situate a story, or to embed the particular view *(Gesinnung)* of his approach in the topography of the earth. His locales transcend geography *because* of history, not in spite of it. When history carries as strong a connotation of the imaginary as it does for Schinkel, then imagining events in their time and place becomes one of its essential tasks. With historical imagination as its basis, Schinkel could apply his idea of landscape painting directly to the problems of set design and explain the main effect that the stage exercises upon the viewer as the forcible dislocation *(Ortsversetzung)* of the audience,[9] achieved solely with the powers of artifice.

Schinkel's strategy thus turned the stage into a place of poetic displacement: the rising curtain suddenly reveals a moment in the ceaseless process of cultural transformation, confronting the audience with an image of that very process, "at a glance and with a grand impression,"[10] as was explained by his contemporary E.T.A. Hoffmann—himself a resident of the capital (1814–22) during Schinkel's involvement with the stage. Like Hoffmann, Schinkel recognized in the human imagination a native tendency to extend the transformation of nature into history beyond its time-bound order, to expand the process into the internal realm of desire. He found that "pure landscapes leave us with a sensation of

FIGURE I

Panoramic view of Rome from Schinkel's apartment
window, c. 1803–04 (cat. no. 20).

longing and dissatisfaction," that is, they leave us desiring something beyond themselves,[11] whereas the new art, although it is the offspring of landscape painting, will need to meld figure and landscape. In this way, it would be able to create an image of the *character* of a country, and, at its most imaginative, a view of an entire culture.[12]

Such *Charakterbilder* are nothing if not narrations of history, images of action at once externally concrete and internally fantastic. Precisely because they are rent by a conflict, these new poetic images are fit for the stage: their palpable observations rivet attention; their imaginary transformations invite the mind to wander. They engender a state of divided attention in the audience, a disposition that allows the spectators to follow the course of action, whatever it may be, and simultaneously submit to the currents of fantasy, wherever they may lead. As the arena of such experiences, the theater sought to deploy the techniques of atmospheric evocation with all the pictorial and illusionistic means at its disposal. Schinkel had acquired a considerable knowledge in these

fields, and he felt no compunction about putting it to use in the sphere of popular entertainment, or volunteering his services as a set designer to Iffland, the director of the Berlin National Theater. For Schinkel, the stage represented one thing above all others: an instrument to transport the audience into the realm of imagination. In order to bring this about, Schinkel found it necessary to take on more than the problems of sets, lighting, orchestra, and costumes. As he analyzed the mechanisms of optical illusion and studied the psychology of performance, he wound up redesigning the entire theater.

For Schinkel and his contemporaries, the discovery of such illusory but irresistible experiences as theater still held a deep fascination. Other, more short-lived fads in visual entertainment had begun to cater to a new appetite for "dislocating" the viewer's sensations, but they also called attention to the technologies of illusion. Although Schinkel was not involved in the invention of new optical and illusory techniques as such, he nonetheless picked them up wherever he could find them and applied this knowledge to any task that might benefit from it. Recently returned to Berlin after an extended stay in Italy in 1803–04 *(fig. 1)*,[13] Schinkel found himself without professional engagements, but nonetheless eager to make a name as an architect. Despite his auspicious beginnings after the turn of the century, he was forced to make do with odd jobs and small assignments for almost a decade, until the French were driven from Prussia and the monarchy reestablished itself in Berlin. A fair share of his income came from the design of shopwindow displays, in which famous places such as the interior of Saint Peter's in Rome (see Verwiebe, *fig. 8*), the Duomo in Milan (see Verwiebe, *fig. 5*), and sites in Venice and elsewhere were illusionistically represented and theatrically lit at set hours after nightfall.[14] Moveable figures, effects of backlighting, moonlight, and musical accompaniments, greatly enhanced the popularity of these presentations.

FIGURE 2

Schinkel on the summit of Mount Etna with the sunrise in the distance, 1804 (cat. no. 12).

The grand panoramas, with which Schinkel otherwise occupied himself, required speculative investments and special buildings. Panoramas had been patented by Robert Barker in 1787, and within a few years they became sensational commercial attractions.[15] They presented an uninterrupted view, unfolding all around the spectators, who observed these "endless" images from an elevated central platform inside a cylindrical structure. Indirect, and often changing, lighting helped create effects that flabbergasted the public. Comparable to the popularity of cinema in the twentieth century, the panorama and its descendant, the diorama, leveled the traditional distinction between cognoscenti and laymen, overwhelming both by the sheer size and precision of their images.

A committee appointed by the French government investigated the phenomenon when it first appeared on the continent, and it produced a characterization so lucid that it is worth quoting: "The first panorama to be seen in Paris... represents a view of this immense city: the spectator is seemingly raised on the roof platform of the central pavilion of the Tuileries; from this vantage, the spectator's gaze encompasses an immense horizon containing not only Paris but also part of its surrounding countryside; he dominates everything, seems to glide over it, his eyes follow the embankments of the Seine, move through the trees of the Tuileries Gardens, or wander through streets and squares; and wherever he fixes his gaze he is struck by the truthfulness with which the whole ensemble and the details of its immense perspective have been rendered. ... Upon entering the enclosure of a panorama, the first impression one gains is that of an immense, but confusing view in which all points overwhelm the eyes at once and without apparent order; this effect is inevitable for it is brought about by the brusque and instantaneous transition of the appearance of nature to that of its image."[16]

This analysis of a brand-new phenomenon cut to the heart of the matter: it recognized in these optical sensations a dizzying and boundless experience induced by novel images.

In fact, the language in which the impact of panoramas has been captured by the French report can be matched by some of Schinkel's own observations in nature, as he recorded them in his travel diaries.[17] The simulation of *Stimmung* (sentiment or feeling) so characteristic of the panorama, did not remain an in-house experience, as it were, but instead became one whose affective powers had the ability to alter the viewer's perception of nature. After the panorama, neither the status of images, nor the visual experience of nature remained quite what it had been before. The French panoramas Schinkel visited in Paris must have confirmed his interest in producing such *Stimmungsbilder* of his own, and his affinity for their effects sprang from his underlying desire to explore the means of achieving this aesthetic displacement of the viewer. That he so quickly embraced the new medium shows how keen he was to adopt its means, but the true intelligence of his grasp lies in its application to the stage, and even to the cityscape of central Berlin, where Schinkel later operated as a kind of urban scenographer.[18] In 1807, Schinkel entered into collaboration with the firm of Wilhelm Gropius, the fabricators of stage sets and masks, in an effort to produce a series of panoramas. These ventures laid the basis for a lasting association between Schinkel and the Gropius family, whose capable execution of many of his stage sets helped secure his later success with the genre (see the essay by Birgit Verwiebe in this book).

During his recent Italian journey, Schinkel had experienced the sweeping landscape under serene skies as a widening of his own horizon. He committed one such sublimely dislocating experience to paper when he sketched himself and his travelling party ascending the icy rim of Etna *(fig. 2)*. Schinkel had endured a strenuous climb through the night, but then watched as the sun rose over the sea and gradually brought a boundless panorama into view. This natural spectacle affected him deeply, for he felt overwhelmed by an almost physical experience of dislocation that altered the very sense of his own body: "I felt able to encompass the earth below me at a glance, so small appeared the distances, the breadth of the sea to the shores of Africa, the expanse of southern Calabria, the island itself, everything submitted to my overview, so that I felt disproportionately large myself."[19] This experience may have endowed him with a less fettered perception of himself, along with the indelible memory of a boundless view from one of the ridges of the world. In effect, for Schinkel, the vast depth and scope of the view seemed to seek its vanishing point not at the farthest horizon, but in the eye and mind of the observer. The image of infinite nature required a threshold in time, a frame on which to fasten itself in history, just as Goethe and Wilhelm Tischbein had felt it before him, and Christoffer Wilhelm Eckersberg, J. M. W. Turner, and Jean-Baptiste Camille Corot would seek it after him.[20]

On the slopes of the volcano at Taormina, geology appeared to be an active agent, while the ruins of the ancient theater provided a ledge or viewing platform onto the re-

FIGURE 3

View of the ancient theater at Taormina, 1827.

FIGURE 4

Perspective sketch of the Champs-de-Mars, Paris, after Friedrich Gilly, c. 1798–1800 (cat. no. 4).

moteness of time. With a paradoxical twist, Schinkel noted in his diary: "Entering into the theater moved me more powerfully than ever: I saw the proscenium near me, and above it, and through its apertures, an immense distance."[21] With the ancient stage so near and the present world so far, Schinkel's mind turned to the effect this theater must have had on its audience. His sketch of the site prefigured for him a finely detailed rendering, a painting, and, back in Berlin, that sketch served as the subject of a perspective optical display in 1810 and 1812. As late as 1827, Schinkel drew the scene anew *(fig. 3)*, and much enlarged, as a gift to his Parisian colleagues, the architects Percier and Fontaine. In 1810, the poet Joseph von Eichendorff had visited the backlit display of Schinkel's "forlorn view" of the volcano and remarked in his diary on its affecting *Stimmung*. Eichendorff's jottings read as if the poet had just fixed the barest outline for the opening scene of one of his own Romantic tales and poems, such as "Sehnsucht" ("Yearning"),[22] as when he recorded the impression of Mount Etna "at sunrise, with the deserted ruin of the theater at Taormina in the foreground and the sounds of a hunting horn echoing" in the distance.[23]

A cache of drawings from his journey, many of them panoramic in scope rather than archeological in focus, sup-

FIGURE 5

Perspective study of proposed mausoleum for Queen Luise, 1810 (cat. no. 29).

FIGURE 6

Gothic cathedral behind a massive tree, 1810 (cat. no. 28).

plied the subjects and ideas Schinkel tapped for his commercial work in Berlin during the lean years of the Napoleonic occupation. On his return trip to Germany, he had spent several weeks in Paris, where the new panoramas were all the rage, and where he was impressed by the public pomp and theatrical displays (see *fig. 4*) of the young empire. Back in Berlin, it was as a painter of panoramas and displays with special perspective optical effects that he came to the attention of the Prussian court and secured a commission for the fittings of the queen's bedroom at Schloß Charlottenburg.[24] His strikingly theatrical designs for a mausoleum dedicated to Queen Luise *(fig. 5)*, who died tragically in 1810, were conceived as a private counter-project to the sternly classical temple the king had erected for his wife in the park of Charlottenburg.[25] Displayed in the Academy exhibition of the same year, Schinkel's mausoleum project blurred the conventional distinction between architectural rendering and stage design, and in its accompanying description he clearly invoked yet again the experience of aesthetic transport, as the beholders are asked to imagine "a porticus, shadowed by the darkest trees," before ascending the steps and "entering, with a feeling of mild dread, into its darkness, where they behold the recumbent effigy of the queen, surrounded by heavenly figures, resplendent in the clear light of the morning."[26]

Such atmospheric evocations seek to trigger the senses all at once, conjuring the synaesthetic experience of opera, and appealing to a kind of sentiment that is both calculatedly induced and Romantically naive. They hover on the verge of kitsch, a category almost coincident with the purveyance of induced sentiment, and they seem redeemed only by their exquisite execution. An eerie chill surrounds the luminous transparency of these tempera sheets, whose character is far more explicit—even stagy—than, say, the canvases of Caspar David Friedrich that were also shown in the Academy exhibition of 1810. Yet the artistic impurity of Schinkel's works betrays his true intentions: He strove above all for effect, for *Empfindung* (sentiment), of the kind only the musical theater could achieve.

In the same year, 1810, Schinkel also experimented along similar lines with the new medium of lithography. He drew a view of a tree-shrouded Gothic church and captioned it on the stone with a poetic line that moves from description straight to evocation: "An essay to express the sweet melancholy, replete with yearning, which fills the heart upon hearing the sounds of worship ringing out from the church" *(fig. 6).*[27] The very notion of such sentiments issues from

FIGURE 7

Schloß am Strom (*Palace on the River*), 1820. Oil on canvas,
70 x 94 cm. SMB-PK, Nationalgalerie.

Schinkel's conviction that a painting can match the poetic power of language and even assume the burden of speculative ideas. True, this instance stood as an experiment, a mere "essay," as its title readily admitted; but the idea of a *paragone* among painting, poetry, and music remained vivid in Schinkel's mind and may have prepared him for the challenges inherent in theatrical work. As Schinkel was not in the habit of making sharp distinctions between his private and professional life, he did not hesitate to test his aesthetic theories in a parlor game of his own invention. In the company of close friends who regularly gathered for an evening's conversation in his apartment, Schinkel asked Clemens Brentano to improvise a story.[28] While the poet captivated the guests with his Romantic tale, Schinkel sketched—and later executed in painting *(fig. 7)*—Brentano's narrative in an attempt to prove that painting was every bit as eloquent and capable of conveying a tale—locale, mood, action, and all—as was the language of the poet. Ironically, this one example of Schinkel's exercises in this particular genre of *peinture parlante* has survived, but Brentano's tale has come down to us only in the chronicler's sketchy account.

In his 1813 memorandum to Iffland, Schinkel had volunteered his ideas for modernizing the stage. He proposed to do away with the remains of the Baroque tradition,[29] which was based on elaborate sets and soffits whose artificiality Schinkel considered an obstacle to modern theatrical illusion. Instead of the cumbersome coulisses, whose silhouettes fragmented the scenery and disrupted the atmos-

pheric unity of the stage with their bulky shapes and creaky mechanisms, Schinkel wished to extend the proscenium deep into the stage and thereby frame the actors before a highly pictorial backdrop. His vision of the new stage was essentially atmospheric in nature, employing lighting and painterly *Stimmung* as the main devices for the creation of theatrical effects. At least with respect to the latter, the popular panoramas and shopwindow displays had served as a kind of laboratory for the development of lighting and atmospheric effects. The techniques of transparent images *(Transparentbilder)*, lit from behind and preferably accompanied by music for sentimental affect, had become an irresistable popular attraction.[30] The idea of the relatively shallow proscenium as the fulcrum of action had long been on Schinkel's mind: a set of pictorially finished drawings from his trip to the Salzkammergut in 1811,[31] perhaps intended as a suite for publication, combined this theatrical concept with the idea of the *Stimmungsbild.* These magnificent sheets, especially the views of the Königsee near Berchtesgaden, the Paß Lueg near Salzburg *(fig. 8)* and of the Traunsee near Gmunden *(fig. 9)* would have lent themselves to immediate transposition onto theatrical backdrops. They may also be key to understanding why Schinkel proved eminently fit, once the occasion presented itself, to design for the stage with no apparent difficulties.

At the outset, Schinkel had planned to advance his modest proposal to Iffland in the hope of garnering a commission for stage sets; in the end, his radical rethinking of theatrical practice led him to propose major changes in the architecture of the existing playhouse, the National Theater designed by Carl Gotthard Langhans (see Schwarzer, *fig. 9*). The guiding idea throughout, and one he would put to the test a few years later, was the achievement of psychological dislocation by means of stagecraft. Schinkel's intention to transport the audience into other places and times must be reckoned one of the most astonishingly sophisticated conceptions and one of the wellsprings of our current preoccupation with simulated realities. With this goal in mind, Schinkel couched his proposal to Iffland in the terms of a new aesthetic of the stage, explaining its technical requirements and even arguing for its financial advantages. He went to great length, densely covering two folio sheets with a collage of drawings and explanatory texts, and drafting a virtual mini-treatise on the reform of the stage (see *fig. 10*).[32] He argued in favor of an extended proscenium for the actors, lighting from the sides as well as from above, a unifying pictorial backdrop, and an orchestra sunk to near-invisibility in

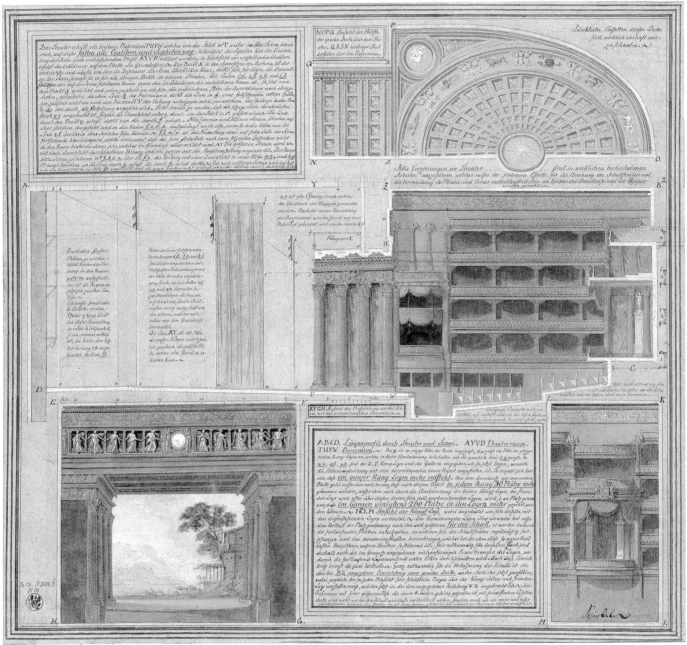

FIGURE 10

Perspective views, elevations, details, and sections
of a proposed national theater, 1813 (cat. 49).

FIGURE 11

Perspective view of a mausoleum on an island in the Nile
River, a set design for *Die Zauberflöte (The Magic Flute)*, 1815.
Hand-colored aquatint etching, 22.7 x 34.7 cm.

FIGURE 12

Perspective view of an Egyptian temple, a set design for
Die Zauberflöte (The Magic Flute), 1815.
Hand-colored aquatint etching, 23.7 x 36.7 cm.

FIGURE 13

The Hall of Stars in the Palace of the Queen of the Night,
a set design for *Die Zauberflöte (The Magic Flute)*, 1815.
Hand-colored aquatint etching, 22.8 x 34.9 cm.

the pit. Gone were the creaky machinery and the many complex coulisses that were moved up and down on the Baroque stage. In their place, Schinkel devised a backdrop that evoked the calm and focus of the ancient theater, where, he argued, "the stage was nothing but a lens, gathering the image of action in one place and thereby removing it from the surroundings."[33] He strenuously opposed blatant illusion on the grounds that it could succeed only for a small number of privileged spectators; instead, he found the psychological effect of poetic *Stimmungsbilder* could achieve far greater satisfaction than the fragmented sets of the traditional stage could afford. The key to his concept lies in an example of such a backdrop, which Schinkel illustrated in the lower left corner of the very sheet he sent to Iffland *(fig. 10)*, a prealpine landscape with a humble building shaded by a tree on the shore of a lake, an idyllic scene suffused with light in the manner of Claude Lorrain.

The unifying idea that links his observations on acoustics and architecture, scenery and stage, is precisely the notion of poetic suffusion. Its achievement enables the spectator to internalize the heterogeneous impressions emanating from the stage, and to project them onto an image, which, in turn, will "liberate the spirit for the pure contemplation of art."[34] Schinkel's new poetics of the theater owed a good deal more to the paintings of Caspar David Friedrich, and to the poetics of Berlin playwrights such as Ludwig Tieck (1773–1853), than it did to the contemporary practice of stagecraft in the Royal Theater. He was also deeply in tune with the synaesthetic experiments of a Philipp Otto Runge (1777–1810),[35] who held views of landscape painting very similar to those expressed in the poetic quest of the principal character of Tieck's novel *Franz Sternbald*.[36] Tieck's itinerant medieval artist expressed his yearning for an art of *animated* landscape painting in which, "when the sun goes down and when the moon tinges the clouds with gold, I want to capture the fleeting spirits." Schinkel, who was well versed in the creation of such effects, went further and imagined a grand fusion of landscape and history painting, a theatrical *Gesamtkunstwerk* of visionary dimensions. Little wonder then, that his proposal met with incomprehension from an old hand like Schauspieldirektor Iffland. It was not Iffland but rather his successor, Count Karl von Brühl, who proved to be receptive to Schinkel's new ideas and immediately commissioned a number of sets from him for the Königliches Opernhaus (Royal Opera House) on Unter den Linden.[37]

Schinkel's debut as a set designer, while long in the making, thrust him onto the Berlin stage with a sensational production of Mozart's *Die Zauberflöte (The Magic Flute)* during the coronation festivities of January 1816. It may be unfair to the dozens of other productions Schinkel designed in less than a decade, but it is surely justified to single this one out for its inventiveness and poetic cunning. Teeming with ideas he had tested many times before, and masterful in their cadence of images and contrasting moods, the backdrops for the scenes of *The Magic Flute* remain the capstone of Schinkel's accomplishment as an inventor—not just a designer—of theatrical imagery (see *pls. 13–16).*

The range of locales and their characterization are extraordinary, even encyclopaedic, as they move from prehistoric cave to celestial sphere, from fiery abyss to Andean jungle, and concluding the drama with the prospect of an awesome Egyptian temple *(pl. 16).* As this stunning panorama unfolds before the audience, they find themselves transported to the most diverse sites that humans have occupied, and abandoned, in the course of time. In every instance, albeit in greatly varying degrees, the natural setting and its cultural transformation direct attention to Schinkel's ideas about the meaning of architecture for the course of civilization. The extremes of an all-powerful nature and a self-sufficient architecture are established by an alpine jungle and a cryptlike mausoleum, whose oppressive darkness stands in contrast to a moonlit scene of an island in the Nile *(fig. 11).*

The opera opens with a view of a misshapen temple, grotesquely adorned with chimeras and lying in the shade of a gigantic cliff *(fig. 12).* Through a rock-arch, the spectators already catch a glimpse of the star-studded firmament under which the Queen of the Night will appear in the following scene. The opera's closing set leaves such lugubrious sites behind and radiates with the eternal harmony of an imaginary sun-city. It was his clever handling of theatrical effects that helped Schinkel achieve popular success with his inaugural sets and secure a string of further commissions, although his artistic ambition was no doubt fixed on something else. Many of his theoretical efforts turned on the relationship between aesthetic ideas and artistic practice, and most of these ideas had yet to be formulated when Schinkel created his *Magic Flute.* But their poetic surfeit hints at his desire to turn the object of pictorial imagination into a construct of ideas.[38]

In 1808, and again in 1812, Schinkel had garnered high praise for an artificially illuminated night view over Sorrento on the Gulf of Naples, in which captivating optical effects were underscored by piano accompaniment. This combination of an evocative landscape display with a musical *notturno* was described by the *Berlinische Nachrichten* as unsurpassed in its power to "transport the viewers"[39] through its suggestion of a balmy summer night at the moonlit scene, effects that were no doubt magnified when Schinkel brought them onto the musical stage. The newspaper critic of the *Berlinische Nachrichten* attempted to cast into words an experience that by its very nature defies descriptive logic. Schinkel had tried to do much the same with the title of his lithograph of 1810, and he later touched on the mystifying dimensions of such moments when he articulated a distinction between the domain of history and the realm of sentiments *(Stimmungen).* He found the subject of a work of art to be different, and largely separate, from "the sensations, or, more precisely, the sentiments" *("Empfindungen oder vielmehr Stimmungen")* that pervade it and affect its perception by the viewer.[40] By dint of their particular *Stimmung,* the new pictorial scenes struck their viewers in powerfully affective ways that are more akin to music than to words. Because music has the power to render affective states *("Seelenzustände")* through no other medium than sound itself, Schinkel considered music to be the "main ingredient" of all the arts.[41] When the sites and topics of opera moved beyond the familiar, or when they touched on states of dread and bliss, Schinkel welcomed the insinuations of fantasy and, in several instances, achieved dreamlike figments that were, in the parlance of their time, almost pure *Stimmungsbilder.* The undiminished popularity of some of Schinkel's scenographic ideas, such as those for the Queen of the Night *(fig. 13),* certainly derives from their affinity with music insofar as they work only with the materials that constitute their subject. The firmament is made of light and dark,[42] and this is the subject of the set, while, in the second act of *The Magic Flute,* the distant radiance of the moon casts a ghostly pallor over the island, where mortality has assumed immovable form *(fig. 11).* The effect of stillness that results from a slight rippling motion may be a purely musical sensation, and Schinkel's scenes that aim to render motion and change within the context of static images belong to some of his most affecting work, both on and off the stage. Their pictorial medium is light, their radiance pure *Stimmung.*

Schinkel's latest sets for E. T. A. Hoffmann's Romantic opera *Undine* had already been prepared when his career as an architect, then still in its early stages, was suddenly propelled forward by the conflagration of Berlin's National

FIGURE 14

Perspective view from the northeast
of the Schauspielhaus, Berlin, 1821
(cat. no. 51).

Theater. Hoffmann himself witnessed the fire from his apartment on the corner of the *Gendarmenmarkt*, opposite the theater. He informed his friends with fantastical descriptions and sketches of the event, drowning out his disappointment over the loss of the sets for *Undine* and the cancellation of his opera with grotesque cartooning.[43] *Undine* marked a high point in Schinkel's Romantic refashioning of the stage, and the production more than fulfilled the expectations of its quixotic composer Hoffmann. As Schinkel's first biographer, the Berlin museum director Gustav Friedrich Waagen, recalled, "the sets are said to have surpassed everything in their fantastic and genial effects,"[44] based as they were on a libretto full of enigmatic action and haunted characters (see *pls. 17* and *18*).

The fire in the National Theater broke out during rehearsals around midday on July 29, 1817, and, by nightfall, had burned the building to the ground. The superintendant of the theater dispatched his report to the king in Karlsbad

within forty-eight hours of the conflagration, making proposals for a new building and soliciting approval for his plans. The alacrity of this initiative, which already named Schinkel as one of the candidates for the work of redesigning the building,[45] was countermanded by many setbacks. Augmented by Schinkel's own willpower, however, Count von Brühl's efforts brought off a new and splendid structure within four years. The new house was inaugurated with courtly pomp on May 26, 1821. By this time, Schinkel was well on his way to becoming the premier architect of Prussia. Examples of his achievements as a set designer had been gathered together for publication, and first appeared in a lavishly printed suite of plates in 1819.[46] The fascicle of his *œuvre complète*, the *Sammlung architektonischer Entwürfe (Collection of Architectural Designs)*,[47] emerged within months of the theater's inauguration and spread the design for the new building over twelve plates (see frontispiece and *fig. 15*, and Schwarzer, *figs. 10–12* and *14*). Among all of his works, only

Schinkel's Altes Museum was to receive similarly copious treatment.

The architect had been honored with the Order of the Red Eagle, but after the flush of the first season in the new theater had subsided, certain features of the building began to come in for niggling critical comment. He drafted a lengthy rebuttal in a letter to Goethe's friend Zelter, blaming such petty complaints on those "particularly boring creatures of habit *("Gewohnheitsmenschen")*, who are dissatisfied with everything that is different from the way they have known it for years."[48] Undaunted, and, one may fairly say, largely unaffected by grudging criticism, Schinkel confirmed his professional status with a move to better quarters on Unter den Linden, where he and his family resided for fifteen years before taking up residence in a splendid apartment below his offices in the new Bauakademie (Architectural Academy). While the Schauspielhaus stood as a grand and logical conclusion to Schinkel's fascination with the stage and with its literary and musical repertoire, his subsequent professional obligations left less and less room for the kind of artistic indulgence that had enabled him to invent set designs and to conceive of a new theater building in the first place. Yet this does not imply a complete disjuncture, for Schinkel had begun early on to apply the lessons of the stage to the dramatic visualization of architecture in general.

Any assessment of Schinkel's ideas on theater architecture must take as its point of departure the famous plate he published in his *Sammlung architektonischer Entwürfe* (see frontispiece). To celebrate the inauguration of the Schauspielhaus, Schinkel had designed a special proscenium curtain, and his idea for the occasion literally brought the house down. According to the *Berlinische Nachrichten*, "At six o'clock precisely, the orchestra struck up. The curtain rose and we had before us, faithfully and brilliantly executed by Gropius, a view of the splendid building itself within which we were gathered, as well as of the stately spires flanking it on both sides. It is difficult to describe how deeply this struck the audience, how proudly they enjoyed the view of this imposing part of the city, and what waves of enthusiasm they gave forth."[49]

This spontaneous effusion of delight may have had as its basis a certain parochial pride, but it must also have owed something to the spellbinding aesthetic of Schinkel's idea. The architect had created much more than an attractive representation of the building that the audience was occupying at the moment of its inauguration. He put before their eyes his very conception of the Schauspielhaus and its presence in the city. While a view of the building in which performances were being staged could be enjoyed on painted curtains in other theaters, such as, for example, the imperial theater at Schönbrunn, Vienna, Schinkel's representation had other and more speculative purposes than merely to delight the public.

Above all, the theater "needed to be an aesthetically ordered whole, for which a perfect expression of its character was indispensable,"[50] as Schinkel had argued in his first proposal to Count von Brühl. Beyond the seemingly endless list of specific requirements Brühl had submitted to the architect, Schinkel paid special attention to the matters of fire safety, circulation, heating, and optimal sight lines.[51] His true criterion for the building's success, however, remained the perfect manifestation of its "character." To this end, the Schauspielhaus was to "rise above ordinary urban buildings"[52] and be "plainly recognizable as a theater and nothing else."[53] Because it needed to accommodate not only the theater proper, but also numerous subsidiary workshops and offices, along with a concert hall *(fig. 15)*, festive foyers, and elaborate technical equipment, the architect argued that a building of such complexity and multiplicity of use could only be judged on the basis of precise knowledge of all of these conditions.[54] His own description of the Schauspielhaus, appended to the *Sammlung architektonischer Entwürfe*, is by far the longest of his published elucidations, longer even than his commentaries on the Altes Museum. The sheer complexity of the enterprise generated a flood of internal memoranda comprising the proposals, replies, and counterarguments that characterized the tenacious exchanges between Count von Brühl and Schinkel, not to mention scrupulous accounting records, and nearly daily site supervision reports. In sheer complexity, this enterprise must be ranked among the weightiest of Schinkel's entire career.

The perspective view of the Schauspielhaus, and a rather unusual lateral prospect of the building in Schinkel's *Sammlung* deliberately assume a pedestrian's point of view and thereby confirm the architect's intention to exalt the theater "above ordinary urban buildings" *(fig. 14)*. He could not attribute to the modern theater what he felt to have been its ancient distinction as a "religious institution,"[55] but he wished to secure its urban status with the modern means of siting and architectural decorum. The Schauspielhaus thus enjoys undeniable pride of place on the Gendarmenmarkt. It rises over a rusticated pedestal that is markedly higher than the platforms of the two flanking churches, and it overshadows their porches with a grandiose stylobate and steep

FIGURE 15

Perspective drawing of the concert hall in the
Schauspielhaus, Berlin, 1821 (cat. no. 58).

flight of stairs (see Schwarzer, *figs. 1* and *14*). Despite the constraints of site and budget,[56] the building received a great deal of sculptural and pictorial ornamentation. Among the panoply of ornaments, Apollonian imagery barely prevails over the strains of Dionysian revel. Schinkel's rendering, and others based on it, make clear that the public gained entry chiefly through the carriageway beneath the porch, while the elevated facade of the building served as a kind of set piece on the square.

One is justified to look at the Schauspielhaus as both theater and set piece in an urban tableau. This larger *mise-en-scène* embracing the building itself gained resonance on the

proscenium curtain Schinkel furnished for its inauguration. Here, the viewer enjoys a nearly ideal vantage, seeing the theater in the far distance, below the level of the stage floor, and at a slightly oblique angle, so that the flanking churches appear distinctly uneven in size. Since this perspectival representation has been carefully constructed, and the dimensions of the building are precisely known, the assumed vantage point can easily be deduced: What appears on the painted backdrop corresponds exactly to the prospect one would have had from the royal Schloß, if no other buildings blocked the view of the theater. It is, in effect, *the* royal view of the Königliche Schauspielhaus, a view that suggests that

FIGURE 16

Perspective view, plan, and section of Schloß Babelsberg,
Potsdam, c. 1838. Photo: *Sammlung architektonischer Entwürfe*
(Berlin, 1866).

the king never left his residence to reach the royal box! Schinkel had thus applied his idea about the psychological effect of the theater—to wit, its power to effect a dislocation in the viewer—to the *topography* of the city itself. From the royal box, the theater appears deeply embedded in the Friedrichstadt, whereas on the Gendarmenmarkt, it is the Schauspielhaus that dominates its precinct and towers over its neighborhood. That Schinkel insisted on these two aspects, indeed, that he calculated his representations of the building in order to establish their distinction, also goes to show how completely the institution of the theater was caught up in the polarity of commoner and court.

Schinkel represented his concept of the Schauspielhaus in three distinct, but fundamentally related, aspects: the *stage* as a locus of internal *Stimmung*, the *building* as an urban centerpiece, and, finally, the *institution* of the theater as a monument within the ambit of the crown. While the nature of the urban set piece addresses itself to the pedestrian's point of view, the ideally constructed vantage from the royal residence at once distances and dominates its object. Each of these aspects results from a special condition of

viewing and therefore implies a different audience. And, each vantage point correspondingly throws other qualities of the building into high relief: the internalized experience of the spectacle initiated flights of fancy and engendered psychological displacement from the ordinary; for the population at large, on the other hand, the theater remained a closed world, whose majestic frame lent authority to what it concealed; and, as the king himself was an avid theatergoer,[57] it placed another royal hallmark within the topography of the capital. Considered one by one, these three domains are those of theater artists, of the public at large, and of the courtly elite—or, put another way, those of affective experience, cultural perception, and political power. While their differences were definitive for the evolving concept of the theater, the decision to make each a prime factor of his edifice enabled Schinkel to produce a container of collective significance.

To be sure, the significance of his work could not have been secured by the qualities of either his architecture or his scenography alone. That significance remains intimately bound up with the theatrical and operatic works themselves.

The years of Schinkel's activity as a set designer witnessed new productions of those works that were just beginning to become the classics that most of them have remained ever since: works by Friedrich Schiller, including *Don Carlos*, *Die Braut von Messina (The Bride from Messina)*, and *Die Jungfrau von Orléans (The Maid of Orleans)*, Goethe's *Iphigenie auf Tauris*, Kleist's *Käthchen von Heilbronn*, Mozart's *The Magic Flute*, Gluck's *Alceste*, Gaspare Spontini's *Olympia* and *La Vestale*, as well as new operas such as Carl Maria von Weber's *Der Freischütz* and *Oberon*, E. T. A. Hoffmann's *Undine*, and Rossini's *Othello*.[58] Not only did these productions meet with resounding critical response in German theaters, but they also helped to firmly establish German drama and opera in theaters throughout Europe, thus paving the way for the successes of figures like Giacomo Meyerbeer and Richard Wagner, as well as diffusing German opera and production practices in general.

The brilliance of Berlin's dramatic seasons was greatly strengthened by the engagement of a lively press. The pages of newspapers and fashionable journals provided a ready forum for the debates carried on by writers, composers, and producers. Their critical reception of plays and operas cemented a long-standing perception of the stage as the preeminent arena of urban culture. Both creative and critical responses to the dramatic and musical stage brought ideas into play that were by no means restricted to their traditional practice. On the contrary, set design began to be recognized more for its dramaturgical significance than its baroque values of entertainment and surprise, and stage direction was newly appreciated for its power to effect tableaux and arresting figurations. Moreover, as Count von Brühl pointed out in his introduction to the first publication of the set designs in 1819, "Schinkel stands out as a great and noteworthy architect because he has avoided one-sidedness by studying all kinds of edifices with equal attention and by following their evolution, as well as the changes of taste, across all times and climes."[59] He went on to praise Schinkel's talent as a landscapist and credited the widening recognition of the Schauspielhaus to Schinkel's uncanny ability to render on stage the historic and poetic vastness of the world. The strength of Schinkel's scenographic design derived largely from his synthetic conception of architecture and its poetic capacities. As a matter of fact, Schinkel had sought to deploy on stage all of his fundamental ideas about the evolution of architecture in highly varied renderings of the principal human habitats of cave, tent, and house in their gradual evolution across the ages.

Initially, it had been Schinkel's own musical gifts[60] and his experiences as a painter that qualified him for the theater; in later years, it was his accomplishments as a scenographer that amplified the poetic power and range of his architectural works. The differences are therefore slight between his designs for operas staged in ancient or Gothic settings, and the plates of his late *Werke der höheren Baukunst (Works of Advanced Architecture)*, published posthumously in 1845–46 (see *pl. 10*). His characteristic perspective views rarely aligned principal facades with the picture plane, but expanded the scope of vision so as to open views into depth while generously yielding to wide lateral horizons. He peopled his architectural representations with human figures who are often gathered together in groups or captured in moments of intimate conversation. They act both as vicarious agents of the viewer inside the picture, like characters on a stage, and as commentators who stand outside and apart from the architecture. In short, Schinkel virtually staged his architectural ideas in his drawings and on the pages of his *Sammlung architektonischer Entwürfe* (see *fig. 15* and Vogtherr, *figs. 3, 9* and *15*).

Some of his most pictorially accomplished plates orchestrate the various aspects of architecture with the geology and climate of a site, preparing the stage for a drama that plays itself out across history (see *fig. 16* and Pehnt, *fig. 18*). Moreover, in the ambit of his Berlin Bauakademie, where the range of architectural knowledge kept expanding daily, Schinkel came to understand its formal variety and cultural characteristics in new terms and categories, and along lines charted by natural scientists.[61] On the last day of his professional life, before a severe stroke immobilized him on September 9, 1840, Schinkel approached Wilhelm Gropius with the idea of returning once more to the medium of his early success in Berlin: he envisaged a vast picture-in-the-round that would embrace the "main monuments of many countries, from Asia, Egypt, Greece, Rome, and Germany of the middle ages, each sited in its most ideal and appropriate landscape."[62] The epic drama Schinkel envisioned for this vast theater was, of course, that of the struggle of human history, in which architecture had played a central role. Embracing all of his experience in designing and building for the stage, Schinkel thus returned at the end to *staging buildings* as true protagonists of culture.

1. Schinkel's maxim "Nur was die Phantasie anregt, soll in der Kunst aufgenommen werden" puts the highest premium on imaginative rather than on analytical faculties; see *Romantische Kunstlehre*, ed. Friedmar Apel, *Bibliothek der Kunstliteratur*, vol. 4 (Frankfurt, 1992), p. 183.

2. Paul Ortwin Rave, *Berlin, Erster Teil* in *Karl Friedrich Schinkel: Lebenswerk* (1941; rev. ed., Berlin, 1981), p. 81: "eine von Jugend auf gefühlte Neigung für die malerische Behandlung der Szene, welche mich auf manche Erkenntnis führte." Rave's history of the Schauspielhaus, although partially augmented by later studies, remains fundamental to an understanding of Schinkel's accomplishment as an architect and scenographer. All English translations of original texts, documents, inscriptions, and titles are my own. While they differ little, in some cases, from those found in other publications, in other instances, they seek to render the meaning of frequently archaic or peculiar German expressions more precisely.

3. See Alfred von Wolzogen, *Aus Schinkels Nachlaß. Reisetagebücher, Briefe und Aphorismen*, 3 vols. (Berlin, 1862–63; reprinted 1981). Schinkel's philosophical reflections have been frequently quoted, usually out of context and often in partial form, but their autographs survive in albums, entitled *Klebehefte*, which are preserved in the Schinkel archive at the Staatliche Museen zu Berlin, Kupferstichkabinett, Sammlung der Zeichnungen und Druckgraphik. For the latest publication of these highly significant aphorisms and notations see: *Romantische Kunstlehre* (note 1), p. 195: "Alles beim Kunstwerk liegt darin, daß die Natur mit einer bestimmten Gesinnung gesehen werde."

4. For this, and many other aspects of Schinkel's work as a designer of stage sets, see the latest comprehensive treatment by Helmut Börsch-Supan, *Karl Friedrich Schinkel: Bühnenentwürfe. Stage Designs*, 2 vols. (Berlin: Ernst & Sohn, 1990), vol. 1, p. 6. Johann Gottfried Schadow's recollection of the exhibition, published in his *Kunst-Werke und Kunst-Ansichten Berlin* (Berlin, 1849), p. 71, is worth noting: "Alles bis dahin Gesehene in diesem Kunstfache wurde dadurch so sehr übertroffen, daß er allgemeine Bewunderung erregte."

5. See note 28 below.

6. See Wolzogen (note 3), vol. 3, p. 367.

7. *Romantische Kunstlehre* (note 1), p. 196f.

8. Ibid. p. 196.

9. Rave (note 2), p. 84: Schinkel stated that the ancient theater could be greatly surpassed by modern stage design, which, following his recommendations, would effect "a total physical illusion solely with the means of art" ["Wenn wir daher unsere Szene in den mehrsten Fällen mit einer einzigen großen Bildwand verzieren könnten, so gingen wir schon unendlich weiter als die Alten, indem auf einer solchen selbst die vollkommenste physische Täuschung einer Ortsversetzung durch Mittel der Kunst erzwungen werden kann"].

10. See the exhibition catalogue *E.T.A. Hoffmann—Ein Preuße?* (Berlin: Berlin Museum, 1981), p. 186.

11. *Romantische Kunstlehre* (note 1), p. 196f.

12. In 1825, in the wake of his greatest successes as a scenographer, Schinkel painted such a sweeping historical *Kulturlandschaft* with his *View of Greece in Its Prime* (destroyed): see Kurt W. Forster, "Schinkel's Panoramic Planning of Central Berlin," *Modulus* 16 (Charlottesville: University of Virginia School of Architecture, 1983), pp. 63–77, esp. p. 65; and Adolf Max Vogt, *Karl Friedrich Schinkel: Blick in Griechenlands Blüte* (Frankfurt: Fischer, 1985).

13. See Karl Friedrich Schinkel, *Reisen nach Italien*, ed. Gottfried Riemann (Berlin: Rütten & Loening, 1979).

14. Börsch-Supan (note 4), esp. pp. 26ff., gives a detailed account of Schinkel's activities in this popular genre.

15. See, especially, Heinz Buddemeier, *Panorama, Diorama, Photographie: Entstehung und Wirkung neuer Medien im 19. Jahrhundert* (Munich, 1970).

16. My translation after the French text in Buddemeier (note 15), p. 166f.

17. Compare the emphatic language in which Schinkel describes his experiences of alpine landscapes, both during his first and on the occasion of his second trip to Italy, with the observation of visual *Entrückung*, or transport, in the French government report on the first panoramas. Atmospheric effects in the morning and at sundown come in for particularly detailed observation and illustrate to what extent Schinkel experienced them as a "spectacle" ["Ein schöneres Schauspiel kann man nicht leicht sehen," *Reisen nach Italien* (note 13), p. 148].

18. See Forster (note 12).

19. "Ich glaubte, die ganze Erde unter mir mit einem Blick zu fassen, die Entfernungen erschienen so gering, die Breite des Meers bis zu den Küsten Afrikas, die Ausdehnung des südlichen Kalabriens, die Insel selbst, alles lag so überschaulich unter mir, daß ich mich selbst fast außer dem Verhältnis größer glaubte," *Reisen nach Italien* (note 13), p. 89f.

20. See also Kurt W. Forster, "Wandlungen des Rom-Bildes um 1800," in *Stil und Überlieferung in der Kunst des Abendlandes, Akten des 21. Internationalen Kongresses für Kunstgeschichte in Bonn 1964* (Berlin, 1967), vol. 1, pp. 207–17.

21. *Reisen nach Italien* (note 13), p. 90.

22. Joseph Freiherr von Eichendorff, *Sämtliche Werke*, ed. Wilhelm Kotsch and August Sauer (1908), vol. 2 ["Es schienen so golden die Sterne / Am Fenster ich einsam stand / Und hörte aus weiter Ferne / Ein Posthorn im stillen Land."] Walther Killy has discussed Eichendorff's evocation of landscapes as a series of magical set pieces through which the narrator moves, as in a maze, along the path of an endless quest; see: "Der Roman als romantisches Buch," in Walther Killy, *Wirklichkeit und Kunstcharakter. Neun Romane des 19. Jahrhunderts* (Munich, 1963).

23. Eichendorf (note 22), vol. 2, p. 257: "Die einsame Ansicht des morgenrothen Aetnas (im tiefen Vordergrunde die öde Ruine) das römische Theater von Taormina mit Waldhornsecho."

24. For this highly theatrical design, see Margarete Kühn, *Schloß Charlottenburg. Die Bauwerke und Kunstdenkmäler von Berlin* (Berlin, 1970), pp. 114–16. Schinkel's first design envisaged a kind of *lit de parade* with flanking alcoves, all shrouded in *voile* draperies, and adorned with carved owls and swans, a veritable stage set that included a ceiling painting of purely coloristic effect: "Der Plafond wird in Öl gemahlt und zwar in der Mitte dunkelblau, welches nach den Seiten sich in sanfteres Violet verliert und so den Effect des Himmels macht."

25. See, especially, the exhibition catalogue *Karl Friedrich Schinkel, 1781–1841* (Berlin: Altes Museum, 1981), pp. 53ff.

26. As reprinted in the *Katalog der Berliner Akademie-Ausstellungen 1786–1850*, ed. Helmut Börsch-Supan (Berlin, 1971): "Vor dieser Halle ist eine Vorhalle, die von den dunkelsten Bäumen beschattet wird; man steigt Stufen hinan und tritt mit einem sanften Schauer in ihr Dunkel ein, blickt dann durch drei hochgewölbte Bogenöffnungen in die liebliche Palmenhalle, wo in hellem morgenroten Lichte die Ruhende, umringt von himmlischen Genien liegt."

27. The autograph inscription on the stone reads: "Versuch die liebliche sehnsuchtsvolle Wehmut auszudrücken welche das Herz beim Klange des Gottesdienstes aus der Kirche herschallend erfüllt, auf Stein gezeichnet von Schinkel."

28. Wolzogen (note 3), vol. 2, p. 40. Schinkel later fashioned a painting, *Schloß am Strom* [Berlin, Staatliche Museen, Preußischer Kulturbesitz, Nationalgalerie, on loan to the Schinkel Pavilion], after the drawings he made while listening to Clemens Brentano's tale. See also Helmut Börsch-Supan's commentary on this painting, and the circumstances of its genesis, in Helmut Börsch-Supan and Lucius Grisebach, eds., *Karl Friedrich Schinkel: Architektur, Malerei, Kunstgewerbe* (Berlin: Verwaltung der Staatlichen Schlösser und Gärten und Nationalgalerie, 1981), p. 58f.

29. See Hans Christian Wolff, *Opern Szene und Darstellung von 1600–1900, Musikgeschichte in Bildern*, vol. 4 (Leipzig, 1968); and Ekhart Berckenhagen and Gretel Wagner, eds., *Bretter, die die Welt bedeuten. Entwürfe zum Theaterdekor und zum Bühnenkostüm in fünf Jahrhunderten* (Berlin, 1978).

30. Again, see the accompanying essay by Birgit Verwiebe in this catalogue.

31. See also Helmut Börsch-Supan, "Schinkels Landschaft mit Motiven aus dem Salzburgischen," *Zeitschrift für Kunstgeschichte*, 32 (1969), pp. 317–23.

32. Rave (note 2) pp. 79–87. The early draft of a shorter version was followed by a second, more extensive one addressing all aspects of the extant building which Schinkel proposed to alter. His reasoning brings technical and historical arguments into play, and proposes specific measures so that "the stage set may be treated in every way as a work of art."

33. Ibid., p. 82: "Die Szene selbst war damals nichts weiter als das Sammlungsglas, welches das Bild der Handlung auf einen Punkt zusammenzog und dadurch der physisch umgebenden Welt entrückte."

34. Ibid., p. 82: The poetic *Stimmung* of the stage made it possible for the "ungestörte frei gewordene Geist in dem reinen Antlitz der Kunst eintauchen und jeder höheren Freude teilhaftig werden [zu können]."

35. See Jörg Traeger, *Philip Otto Runge und sein Werk. Monographie und kritischer Katalog* (Munich, 1975), and *Runge in seiner Zeit*, ed. Werner Hofmann, exh. cat., Kunsthalle Hamburg (Munich, 1977).

36. See Oskar Bätschmann, *Entfernung der Natur: Landschaftsmalerei 1750–1920* (Cologne, 1989), pp. 301–04.

37. Franz Kugler, "Die Dekorationsmalerei der Bühne und Schinkels Entwürfe," *Zeitschrift für Bauwesen*, 15 (1855), pp. 396ff. Paul Mahlberg, "Schinkels Theater-Dekorationen" (Diss., University of Greifswald, Düsseldorf, 1916); Ulrike Harten, "Die Bühnenbilder K.F. Schinkels 1798–1834" (Diss., University of Kiel, 1974). Max Ewert, "Karl Graf von Brühl," *Zeitschrift des Vereins für die Geschichte Berlins*, 55 (1938), pp. 1–7; Börsch-Supan (note 4).

38. For a fairly detailed account of Schinkel's published set designs, see Börsch-Supan (note 4).

39. *Berlinische Nachrichten. Von Staats- und gelehrten Sachen*, November 21, 1812.

40. *Romantische Kunstlehre* (note 1), p. 184.

41. Ibid., p. 176: Since Schinkel considered it a prime purpose of works of art to give expression to affective states, he concluded that "es ist dann Musik die

Kunst im allgemeinsten Sinne, die Kunst, die in allen übrigen Kunstformen wieder enthalten und ihren Hauptbestandteil ausmachen muß."

42. Ibid., p. 195: "Das Firmament ist von den Naturgegenständen das Erhabenste, weil die rein sinnlichen Einflüsse darauf am geringsten sind; es steht in seinem Urtypus vor uns, keine oder sehr geringe Einwirkung von Heterogenem wird von uns darin wahrgenommen, —nicht so die Gegenstände auf der Erde."

43. *E. T. A. Hoffmann* (note 10), p. 209.

44. Gustav Friedrich Waagen, "Karl Friedrich Schinkel als Mensch und als Künstler," *Berliner Kalender* (Berlin: Koniglichen Preußischen Kalendar Deputation, 1844).

45. Within days of the fire, Schinkel's friend Bettina von Arnim wrote to her husband on 8 August 1817: "Schinkel ist sehr begierig zu wissen was der König dazu gesagt hat, ob er Lust hat ein ganz neues oder eins auf die Fundamente des alten gegründetes [Theater] zu bauen, was ihm nicht behagen würde; ich glaube nicht, daß er den ganzen Bau allein übernehmen dürfte, denn schon jetzt spricht man davon, daß alles, was er je erfunden habe, viel zu phantastisch sei, und daß er keinen Kuhstall erbauen könne, wo er seine Ideale nicht anbringen würde." *Achim und Bettina in ihren Briefen, Briefwechsel Achim von Arnim und Bettina Brentano,* ed. Werner Vordtriede (Frankfurt, 1961), vol. 1, p. 84. Two aspects of this report reveal how Schinkel was viewed even by his closest friends: His imagination is considered "fantastic," in the romantic sense of the term, and his dedication to architecture ambitious and almost fanatical. Bettina von Arnim's doubts about whether Schinkel would be allowed to design the new theater all by himself may refer to Count Brühl's heavy hand in the task.

46. Karl Friedrich Schinkel, *Dekorationen auf den Königlichen Hoftheatern zu Berlin,* ed. Count Karl von Brühl (Berlin: Ludwig Wilhelm Wittich, 1819). A suite of six colored aquatints on loose sheets, with a preface by Brühl. A second installment appeared in 1822, a third in 1823. The third fascicle was dedicated entirely to the sets for *The Magic Flute.* Five fascicles were published altogether, the plates of the last two in a larger format but without color, accompanied by a second preface of Brühl, dated 1824. The subsequent republications pose some fairly difficult problems, as the series was augmented, as well as technically altered. In effect, it remains a torso of Schinkel's work for the stage. See also Börsch-Supan (note 4), esp. pp. 54ff.

47. The fascicle devoted to the Royal Theater appeared as the second installment in the serial publication of Schinkel's *Sammlung architektonischer Entwürfe* (Berlin, 1821). For a reprint of the entire *Sammlung,* see that of the 1866 edition, *Collection of Architectural Designs,* trans. Karin Cramer (Princeton: Princeton Architectural Press, 1989).

48. Rave (note 2) p. 124.

49. Quoted in Rave (note 2), p. 121.

50. Ibid., p. 90.

51. Ibid., p. 94. Schinkel explicitly recommended English models for an iron curtain, a safety feature hitherto unknown in Berlin, and he also argued in favor of slender iron colonnettes in the interior of the theater so that the view from the boxes and upper ranks would not be impeded. Similarly, he proposed and built a heating and ventilation system which included cast-iron *torchères* as radiators in the concert hall (see Schinkel's plates and explanations in the *Sammlung architektonischer Entwürfe*).

52. Rave (note 2), p. 94.

53. Ibid., p. 90.

54. Schinkel's comments in the *Sammlung architektonischer Entwürfe* open with the following observation: "Judging a building of significant size must be predicated on an awareness of the conditions from which its external and internal forms emerged. For the present plans of the new Schauspielhaus in Berlin, I consider an enumeration of these conditions all the more important since it is a rare case indeed that so many, and such complex ones, come together in a single building."

55. Rave (note 2), p. 82: "Im griechischen Altertum war das Theater als ein religiöser Gegenstand ein reines Ideal."

56. Essentially for budgetary reasons, the king insisted on building over the existing foundations, and allowed major extensions only for the new porch. As it turned out, the foundations on which Langhans Sr. had erected the first Royal Theater at the turn of the century, proved to be inadequate, partly weakened by the fire, causing a grievous accident, and requiring partial replacement; see Rave (note 2), p. 101.

57. See Thomas Stamm-Kuhlmann, *König in Preußens großer Zeit* (Berlin, 1992), p. 520ff.

58. C. Schäffer and C. Hartmann, *Die Königlichen Theater in Berlin; Statistischer Rückblick vom 5. December 1786 bis 31. December 1885* (Berlin, 1886).

59. The preface is reprinted in Börsch-Supan (note 4), p. 77: "Herr Schinkel ist deshalb als Architekt vorzüglich groß und ausgezeichnet, weil er sich vor Einsei-

tigkeit bewahrt, alle Arten von Baukunst mit gleicher Theilnahme aufgefaßt, und das Fortschreiten, so wie die Veränderung im Geschmack der Baukunst, durch alle Jahrhunderte und durch alle Länder mit Fleiß studirt hat."

60. See Eva Börsch-Supan, "Die Bedeutung der Musik im Werk Karl-Friedrich Schinkels," *Zeitschrift für Kunstgeschichte,* 34 (1971), pp. 257–95.

61. Schinkel was, of course, intimately familiar with the travels and writings of Alexander von Humboldt, having rebuilt the estate of the Humboldt brothers in Tegel after a design of 1820. Moreover, it is fair to say that Schinkel's dual interest in the systematic study of architecture and its history, and in the affective power of buildings and their settings, coincided with contemporary scientific explorations of geography, physics, and psychology. For "*Ortsversetzung*" of a scientific kind, see, especially, Barbara Stafford's comprehensive study *Voyage Into Substance; Art, Science, Nature, and the Illustrated Travel Account, 1760–1840* (Cambridge, Mass., and London, 1984). She argues that extreme natural phenomena "had the capacity to elicit a sentiment that lies at the heart of scientific curiosity: astonishment" (p. 264).

62. Waagen (note 44), p. 240.

Schinkel's Perspective Optical Views: Art between Painting and Theater

BIRGIT VERWIEBE

Nationalgalerie, Staatliche Museen zu Berlin

erlin architect Ludwig Catel wrote in December 1808, "This era's thirst for knowledge produced this fondness for travel which has spread over all the cultured nations of Europe."[1] "This need has produced numerous inventions, whose goal it is to provide the curious with deceptive illusory images of those distant objects."[2] Writing in a Berlin newspaper, Catel went on to announce that Karl Friedrich Schinkel, an excellent artist guided by his genius, had invented a new type of illusory image that—in comparison with the panorama—achieved the same desired effect and indeed surpassed it in many ways. Over a period of only four weeks, Schinkel—then twenty-seven years old—had been able to depict four of the most interesting sites in foreign lands and to display them to the public in a room at house number 16 on Berlin's Spittelmarkt.

"Here one can see the greatest and most admirable work of modern architecture, St. Peter's in Rome with its adjoining immense colonnade and its 400-foot-high dome illuminated by lamplight. Another presentation shows the greatest and most beautiful work of early German and Gothic architecture, the famous Cathedral in Milan. The innumerable towers and peaks rise up boldly into the air like pious prayers to the Divine. Moonlight gently surrounds the exalted construction. A ceremonial procession by torchlight entices the gaze into the illuminated church and forces the imagination to freely reconstruct the interior of the church. In a third presentation, the softer illumination of the moon must give way to columns of fire and lava flows from the Erupting Vesuvius. Naples appears, illuminated by the glow of the volcano.

In order to distract the viewer from these images of the horrors of natural devastations and to moderate their effect, the painter closes with a fourth presentation that has the opposite result. The rays of the morning sun illuminate a peaceful Swiss Valley at the foot of Mont Blanc which rings a lake. The transfigured white-haired head of the colossus looks out over gentle shadows in lower areas that breathe a profound peace; next to him other colossal sculptures, his brothers, form a row into the blue distance."[3]

Catel also provided information on the technical details of Schinkel's achievement. "A powerful illumination by lamp, both in front of the image and behind it for the transparencies, increases the illusion of the whole."[4] The size of these "transparencies" was quite remarkable: they measured approximately 13 x 20 feet (4 x 6 m). The viewers stood at a distance of about 30 feet (9 m) and looked at them through a darkened row of columns, "before which was exposed the magical mirror upon which the magical deception was painted."[5]

Between 1807 and 1815, Schinkel created more than forty such "magical mirror" paintings, works that he himself called "perspective optical views." As artistic spectacles, these paintings were greatly admired and they achieved extraordinary popularity. Their fascination was essentially based upon three factors. First, the magic of real light dominated in the dark surroundings. Light—as a giver of life and as a stimulus—was not painted into the images, but it was nonetheless present. It flowed from them, and the experience of this light was sensually stimulating and entrancing. In addition, by increasing and decreasing the light, it was possible of course to make the depictions appear and disappear. Music was often played as accompaniment to these presentations and it also added to the totality of the artistic experience. Finally, the whole event took place in a social context, accompanied by the exchange of viewers' impressions of what they had seen. Drawing all these qualities together, Schinkel's image presentations came close to the idea of a *Gesamtkunstwerk*, the complete work of art. The combined effects of the magic of lighting, of metamorphosis, of music, and of a communicative social atmosphere, cast their spell over the viewers completely, both physically and mentally.

Unfortunately, none of Schinkel's perspective views have survived, although some preliminary drawings and designs do exist. These activities began in the winter of 1807, when the young Schinkel became involved in the Christmas exhibits that were then extremely popular in Berlin. Contemporary critics found these Christmas exhibits nonetheless to be "a type of art-industry ... [that] had raised the greater public's sense for the creative arts one step, created pleasure in the art, and raised much that had previously been practiced as a craft to a degree of art."[6]

Only two years before, in 1805, Schinkel had returned from an extraordinarily fruitful trip to Italy. He was filled with impressions and ideas, but there were still, as yet, no opportunities for him to realize his architectonic ambitions. Thus, Schinkel seized a favorable moment, and he worked in the years that followed with great success on public presentations of his spectacular images. This activity did more than support him financially. His entire artistic yearning was brought to life in creating these perspective views, for here Schinkel could develop his architectural ideas, along with his mastery of painting, his knowledge of history, and his very clear sense of the stage.

Schinkel's involvement arose in collaboration with Wilhelm Gropius and later with Gropius's son, Carl. As early as 1806 Gropius had owned a mask factory and a theater with mechanical figures, for which Schinkel created numerous views. In addition, Schinkel held exhibitions in the Gabain House, at Breite Straße 22, where he also lived and shared the third floor with two of Gropius's sons. All of this smoothed the way for his fruitful collaboration with Carl Gropius, who was later the court theater painter. In 1807, during the French occupation of Berlin, Schinkel created his first perspective view, of the Ponte Molle near Rome: "a small image, approximately 10 cm wide and 6 cm high in distemper on paper. ... A sketch was not prepared for this, but rather the image was drawn directly from the idea. Nothing remains of this."[7] In the same year, Schinkel also displayed in Gropius's Mechanical Theater views of Constantinople (see *fig. 1*), Jerusalem, the Island of Philae, Apollinopolis, the Harbor of Genoa (see *fig. 2*), the Chamonix Valley, and a Norwegian, and a French Region.

In the spring of 1808, Schinkel began work on his first and only panorama: "In order to make the results of my journey through Italy more commonly available, I have undertaken to paint a panorama of the environs of Palermo."[8] His experiences in Italy not only influenced his decision to produce this panorama, but even more so determined the transparencies that he exhibited in the Christmas season of the same year—the ones described in detail by Catel for the newspaper *Spenersche Zeitung*. The sculptor Gottfried Schadow also remembered Schinkel's creations: "On the 25th, the Schillsche Korps [Schill Corps] paraded on Unter den Lin-

FIGURE 1

Perspective view of Constantinople, 1807 (22e.58). Pen and ink, 20.3 x 39 cm. SMB-PK, Kupferstichkabinett.

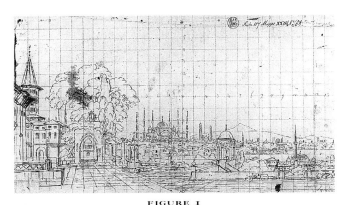

FIGURE 2

Panoramic perspective view of the harbor of Genoa, 1807 (4.12). Pen and ink, 25.3 x 59.4 cm. SMB-PK, Kupferstichkabinett.

den; at the same time there was the exhibition of Schinkel's perspectives, which surpassed everything one had previously seen of this genre. There were Vesuvius, Mont Blanc, St. Peter's in Rome, [and] the cathedral in Milan."[9]

In the following year, 1809, there were six transparent views on display in the royal stalls on the Breite Straße, which Schinkel advertised as "Representations of Noteworthy Buildings and Natural Objects." All the designs for this exhibition are extant. The views themselves included a View of the Baptistery, Cathedral, and Leaning Tower of Pisa (see *fig. 3*), the Theater in Taormina with a View towards Mount Etna (see *fig. 4*), the Interior of the Cathedral in Milan (see *fig. 5*), the Capitoline Hill in Rome (see *fig. 6*), the Ponte Sant'Angelo and Castel Sant'Angelo in Rome (see *fig. 7*), and the Interior of St. Peter's (see *fig. 8*). Once again, the review in the *Spenersche Zeitung* remained extremely positive; in particular, Schinkel's depiction of the interior view of the cathedral in Milan received detailed recognition: "The illusion that the artist has produced here on a flat screen is complete. One would like, if it were permissible, to go right up to it to be convinced that the columns depicted

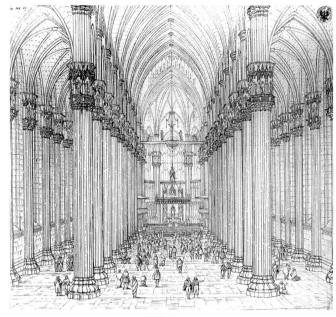

FIGURE 3
Perspective view of Pisa Cathedral and Baptistery, c. 1804
(cat. no. 19).

FIGURE 5
Interior view of Milan Cathedral, c. 1804 (4.10).
Pen and ink, 49 x 54.6 cm. SMB-PK, Kupferstichkabinett.

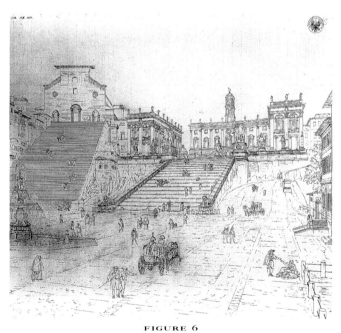

FIGURE 4
Perspective view of the theater of Taormina, looking
toward Mount Etna, c. 1804 (6a.15). Pen and ink with pencil,
48.4 x 54.5 cm. SMB-PK, Kupferstichkabinett.

FIGURE 6
Perspective view of the Capitoline Hill, Rome, c. 1803–04
(cat. no. 23).

FIGURE 7

Ponte Sant'Angelo, Castel Sant'Angelo, and St. Peter's
Cathedral, Rome, c. 1804 (4.57). Pen and ink,
48.5 x 55.7 cm. SMB-PK, Kupferstichkabinett.

FIGURE 8

Interior of St. Peter's Cathedral, Rome, c. 1803–04 (4.59).
Pen and ink, 48.5 x 54 cm. SMB-PK, Kupferstichkabinett.

are not actually physically present; one would like to try to go down the center aisle of the church, pulled so deceptively engrossed toward the high altar. The people, with whom one would like to mix, provide a measure for the colossal size of the building. It is a surprising view, which long captivates the eye."[10]

The Prussian royal couple, King Friedrich Wilhelm III and Queen Luise recently returned to Berlin, also visited this exhibit. The Queen later wished to receive Schinkel's explanation of the pictures in person, and according to Carl Gropius, who described the event to Schinkel's biographer Alfred von Wolzogen, this meeting was the opportunity "by which Schinkel's previously extremely limited situation was changed."[11] The commission to furnish rooms in the royal palace and his assignment to the Oberbaudeputation (Royal Office of Works) were results, in part, of Schinkel's successful presentations of his perspective views, and they certainly cleared the way for his career.

Among the guests at the exhibit, along with the representatives of the royal house, were numerous personalities from public life, intellectuals as well as artists. Even the famous Romantic poet Joseph von Eichendorff, who was staying temporarily in Berlin, visited the show of images—open since Christmas—together with the poet and dramatist Clemens Brentano on March 3, 1810. "In the evening we went to the theater of the talented painter Schinkel," Eichendorff recorded in his diary. "The sudden closing of the illuminated *avisos* [title cards] on both sides pleased Brentano. Several presentations (namely, the back wall, which was a magnificent perspective painting) with church music."[12]

In December 1810, Schinkel displayed in the Gabain House a rendering of the Square of St. Mark's in Venice and in the Mechanical Theater, in Brüderstraße 12, a view of a Region in the Harz Mountains with a Mine. There as well, in February 1811, he followed with a depiction of a Gothic Cathedral in the Morning Light.

"Right from the first, in fact, Schinkel's mastery is unmistakable. From a sea-town, lying on the edge of a cliff, one sees a Gothic church with two towers; in front of this a high-arched bridge built over the mouth of a river flowing into the sea. Each of the pillars is decorated with the chapel of a saint. Beyond this, one perceives through the arch openings the city, which reaches down from the cliff toward the shoreline along with a lighthouse at the furthest extreme. ... The scene is illuminated by the rising sun, in whose purple light the jagged and open-work construction of the Gothic towers is made all the clearer. The whole perspective view does not represent a real region, but rather it is entirely idealistic, while very poetically conceived and uniquely arranged for its intended purpose; it implies more than it actually depicts, and occupies the imagination in an interesting manner, especially at the end.[13]

The scene was reminiscent, the *Spenersche Zeitung* later wrote, of Schinkel's splendid depictions of years past, works that had created such diverse pleasure that the newspaper suggested they be revived annually.

If one follows the newspaper's descriptions of these transparencies, which are now lost, one can detect a similarity between such works and the oil painting *Cathedral (fig. 9)* that Schinkel created in the same year, 1811. It seems natural that Schinkel should test the theme and its effect in a perspective view, and after its success, decide to paint it in oil.

Schinkel's and Gropius's presentations were to continue for a few more years. Their collaboration proved to be extremely productive and brought sensational successes. "The art exhibitions, which Mr. Gropius has produced, have distinguished themselves laudably from others right from the beginning."[14] Even the transparency displayed in the following winter of 1811, which was combined with mechanical figures and musical accompaniment, continued the series of successes. A festive ball celebrated in the Palace of the Duke of Belfonsi was offered as a nocturne illuminated by its many "thousands of lights." "The dances performed on a well-played fortepiano along with the persons appearing at the windows of the palace, make it apparent that the ball is underway. Finally, however, the illumination is extinguished; the mass of people at the entrances to the palace vanish during the total darkness, and dawn breaks."[15] This type of metamorphic effect as well as the carefully selected musical accompaniment served to enhance the impact of the transparency. Carl Gropius recalled that "the arrangement was made that the pictures would be accompanied with song on one or two days per week. Grell, Rungenhagen and other leading quartet singers had undertaken this music accompaniment, which, combined with the pictures, produced an indescribable impression."[16]

When in 1812 the Sea Grotto near Sorrento, previously exhibited in 1808, was shown again, music again resounded, appropriately accompanying the moonlight transparency with great feeling.

"The perspective view of Sorrento in the Campania is a Romantic seashore with cliffs looking out over the sea; it is night and the full moon, which is reflected in the still, glowing tide, pours out a magical shimmer over the whole region.

This picture has a splendid effect; the cliff, on whose heights an old knight's castle serves as lighthouse for seafarers, is highly picturesque both in form and shading, and the horizon and the aerial perspective is unsurpassably beautiful. The viewer believes himself to be under a mild stretch of heaven, on a peaceful, calm summer night, on the bank of the sea; the music of the fortepiano, a highly melodic nocturne played by Mr. Detroit with feeling and tenderness, lulls the listener into such a sweet contentment that he surely wishes that the pleasure that is granted to him by the picture and music could be extended beyond the customary amount of time for such an individual presentation."[17]

Also in 1812, though not as a Christmas exhibit, Schinkel showed his mastery as both painter and architect, in two views of a Mine in Calabria (see *figs. 10* and *11*) and in the transparent pictures of the Seven Wonders of the World. The latter were again exhibited at Gropius's with the Mausoleum at Halicarnassus, the Egyptian Labyrinth, the Egyptian Pyramids, the Temple of Artemis at Ephesus, the Colossus of Rhodes, the Hanging Gardens of Babylon (see *fig. 13*), and the Zeus of Olympus.

"Schinkel had conceived the works in their climatic environment with complete poetic freedom," Franz Kugler wrote, "and treated them through diverse lighting effects in such way that they seemed to be directly present. Thus, the Egyptian pyramids, as is quite appropriate to their simple colossal size, were bathed in the twilight of the moon, from which in the foreground, to the side and half-hidden by palms, the giant figure of the Sphinx rose up; thus, for the Hanging Gardens, the illumination came from the setting sun, indeed from the background of the picture, so that the fiery rays of the sun broke through a part of the opened substructure towards the foreground; thus, the open interior space of the hypaethral temple at Olympia was illuminated by the nearly vertically falling rays of the mid-day sun, whose reflection playfully lit up the shadows of the colonnades."[18]

This phenomenon of the immediately self-adjusting illusory world of appearances, to which one surrendered passionately, was carried one step further by Schinkel in his next transparent picture. This time the artist had selected an event from contemporary history. On December 19, 1812, in Gropius's mechanical theater at its new location at Französische Straße 43, Schinkel's exhibit of the Fire in Moscow opened, creating an "uncommon stir [which] of course was especially provoked by the excitement of those days."[19] There was a huge crush of people. "Already at six o'clock in

FIGURE 9

Cathedral, 1811. Oil on canvas, 206.5 x 138 cm.
SSG Berlin, Schinkelpavillon.

the evening all the streets near the exhibit were filled with equipages, and only with a veritable risk to life could one reach the entrance."[20] With this show, Gropius and Schinkel reacted with impressive speed to the events of the Napoleonic war, which had so shaken all of Europe. On September 29, the first report of the burning of Moscow had appeared in the *Spenersche Zeitung*; on October 20, the twentieth bulletin of the Grand Army dated September 17 followed: "Moscow, one of the most beautiful and wealthiest cities of the world, is no more. On the fourteenth, the Russians set fire to the stock exchange, the stores, and the hospital. On the sixteenth, a violent wind rose up. ... There was a sea of fire. ... Nearly everything has been consumed. The Kremlin was saved."[21]

The man of the theater and his painter based their project on this information. Only a few months later, an extremely moving "fire-picture" was created, which "signified

the reversal of the world conditions"[22] and at the same time created horror and patriotic fervor in its viewers. A report in the *Spenersche Zeitung* provided further witness to this: "One sees on the left side the Kremlin with its many variously styled towers, in front of this the Moscow river with its beautiful bridge resting on a row of vaulting arches, and beyond this, the sprawling city in a sea of flames. The effect of the fire is stupendous and almost more beautiful are the masses of clouds of smoke reflecting the fire! The blaze rages in the parts of the city most removed from the viewer. ... On the bridge the people (small movable figures) surge back and forth in a great crowd, and in order to enhance the imaginary experience, one hears cannon fire occasionally during the fortepiano music, which whirls and rolls like the fire."[23]

Here, too, the original painting is not extant; however, an impressive, detailed pen-and-ink drawing does exist, which Schinkel only prepared after completing the perspec-

FIGURE 10

Exterior study for a diorama of a mine in Calabria, 1812
(cat. no. 68).

FIGURE 11

Interior study for a diorama of a mine in Calabria, 1812
(cat. no. 69).

tive view, at the request of the art dealer Gaspare Weich *(fig. 12)*.[24]

Schinkel's transparent views mark an important phase in his career. Here he schooled his abilities and developed ideas that became the essential basis for his subsequent work as an architect. As Kurt Forster has discussed in his essay in this book, Schinkel applied in 1813 for the position of stage painter to August Wilhelm Iffland, the director of the National Theater on the Gendarmenmarkt. Since he was rejected, Schinkel continued to work on the popular perspective views until 1815. At Christmas 1813, again basing his work on current events, he showed the Battle near Leipzig (see *fig. 14*), followed in 1814 by a depiction of the Island of Elba and in 1815 by one of St. Helena.

ON THE HISTORY OF TRANSPARENCY PAINTING

Schinkel's transparent views were a welcome experiment, for here he tested not only his own abilities but also the very concept of painting as theater. The presentation of theatrically staged picturesque events from all over the world fascinated with their enlivening light-magic. But Schinkel's light-images were not a unique invention. This special artistic genre was already forming in the 1780s, and in the second quarter of the nineteenth century it developed into a visual mass-media in the diorama. The development of the diorama occurred nearly simultaneously and mostly independently in various locations in Italy, France, Germany, England, and America. At first such works were referred to as "moonlight transparencies." By describing nature with emotion, these transparent paintings struck a nerve during the period around 1800, often called *Empfindsamkeit* (sentimentality), in which the stimulation of the senses through art played a major role.

The German landscapist and view-painter Philipp Hackert (1737–1807), who lived for fifteen years in Naples beginning in 1785 as painter to the royal court, was the first to occupy himself with transparent pictures. Moreover, Hackert has almost unreservedly been called the inventor of this technique, which "at that time was still kept secret."[25] Many contemporaries reacted positively, often effusively to this new medium. One observer claimed that it was possible to depict, as never before, natural phenomena, such as a nocturnal landscape in moonlight, in a very lifelike and illusory manner (see *fig. 15*). At the same time, such a charming view filled the viewer with sensations of melancholy such as could not be expressed in words.

FIGURE 12

Design for a perspective optical picture, *The Fire of Moscow*, 1812 (cat. no. 70).

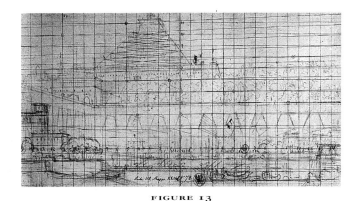

FIGURE 13

Gridded perspective sketch of the Hanging Gardens of Semiramis, for the *Seven Wonders of the World*, a perspective optical picture, 1813 (cat. no. 67).

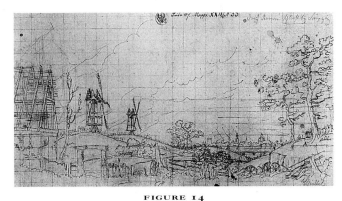

FIGURE 14

Battle near Leipzig, c. 1813 (22d.55). Pen and ink, 17.2 x 34 cm. SMB-PK, Kupferstichkabinett.

Philipp Hackert, *Moonlit Landscape*, c. 1785. Transparent
image with moon cut out. Watercolor and tempera on paper,
66 x 93 cm. Schloß Emkendorf, Schleswig-Holstein.

Andreas Nesselthaler, *Moonlit Landscape*, c. 1785.
Transparent image with moon cut out. Oil on paper,
48 x 66.5 cm. SMB-PK, Kupferstichkabinett.

FIGURE 17

Thomas Gainsborough, *Lonely Boat*, c. 1782.
Oil on glass, 27.9 x 33.7 cm.
Victoria & Albert Museum, London.

This at least was the description supplied by Friedrich Johann Lorenz Meyer, a canon, lawyer, and art-lover from Hamburg. In this description Meyer also reported about the transparent images of Andreas Nesselthaler (1748–1821). In 1786, during his stay in Italy, Meyer had acquired three works from the artist, who was then also living in Naples. Although Nesselthaler's works were smaller than Hackert's moonlight images, they were not of lesser beauty, according to Meyer's travel memoirs.[26]

The Kupferstichkabinett of the Staatliche Museen zu Berlin (National Museums of Berlin), which now contains the entire Schinkel archive, also possesses four transparent images by Andreas Nesselthaler. They are glued over with a white layer of cloth and thus are not visible under normal conditions. Only when illuminated from behind do the colorful lights of the moonlit landscapes appear from hiding. The secret of the image reveals itself through the power of the life-giving light that renders it visible (see *fig. 16*).

At about the same time as Hackert and Nesselthaler, the Frenchman Louis Carrogis Carmontelle (1717–1806), court artist in pre-Revolutionary Paris, was organizing presentations of transparent images. Painted on twelve- to eighteen-meter-long rolls of Chinese paper, Carmontelle's

transparencies were unwound in an approximately 50-cm-high box in front of a burning candle, so that illuminated images moved past. Seasons and times of the day as well as fire scenes could be seen. Carmontelle's "celebration for the eye and ear" was so popular at court, that he became famous as the "King of Illusionists."[27] Only a few examples of his creations are extant: they can be found in the Musée de l'Ile-de-France and the Musée Condé à Chantilly, as well as in private French and American collections.

In London, Thomas Gainsborough (1727–1788) had developed the so-called "Exhibition Box" in 1781, with which he could inspect his "transparencies." Gainsborough's nature scenes were painted on glass panes measuring 30 by 30 cm (see *fig. 17*). On social occasions, when friends were gathered to drink tea, the transparencies were shown as the high point of the evening. Aside from the entertainment value of these picture-events, the transparencies were another visual means of imagination for Gainsborough. Their influence on his landscape painting, in which the treatment of light played an important role, is evident in various paintings.[28]

Gainsborough's idea of the Exhibition Box had been inspired by Philippe Jacques de Loutherbourg's "Eidophu-

FIGURE 18

Charles Willson
Peale,
"A Descriptive
Catalogue of
Mr. Peale's
Exhibition of
Perspective
Views, with
Changeable
Effects; or
Nature
Delineated, and
in Motion,"
1786. American
Philosophical
Society,
Philadelphia.

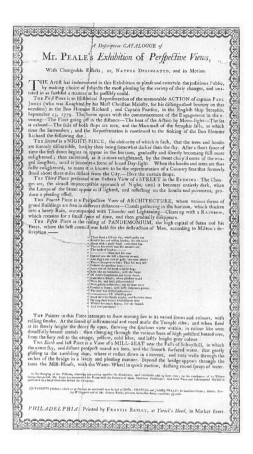

FIGURE 19

Franz Niklaus
König,
Mount Rigi,
c. 1815.
Transparent
image in a
display case.
Watercolor on
paper,
84.5 x 119 cm.
Kunstmuseum
Bern.

sikon" (literally, "image of nature"), which caused such a furor in London at the same time. De Loutherbourg (1740 to 1812) was a French-born painter who settled in London in 1771 and had an active career as a stage designer and painter for the Drury Lane Theater, before becoming a friend of Gainsborough's and a member of the Royal Academy. De Loutherbourg's creation was an illusory peep-show theater with mechanical figures and movable scenery, in which transparent paintings were also shown. As even the name Eidophusikon was supposed to express, de Loutherbourg was concerned with an effective imitation of nature. Celebrated as a sensation, the Eidophusikon was first shown in London in 1781 and continued there until about 1789, by which time it had become known worldwide.[29]

In America, it was Charles Willson Peale (1741–1827) who attempted the new medium. Peale possessed a universal mind, with interest and involvement in politics, science, crafts, and agriculture. He was also a collector, the founder of a museum, and a painter. In 1785 he opened an exhibition that introduced a new era in his artistic career. After altering the structure of his museum's building in order to install a "Moving Picture Room," he showed there his "Exhibition of Perspective Views, with Changeable Effects; or, Nature Delineated, and in Motion" *(fig. 18)*. Peale's transparent images with simulated movement were created under the influence of de Loutherbourg's Eidophusikon, which Peale himself had read about though never seen. The numerous descriptions in British newspapers and journals as well as verbal reports from travellers were the only available resources for his inspiration.

In Bern, almost contemporaneously with Schinkel's light-images in Berlin, could be seen the transparent paintings of the Swiss artist Franz Niklaus König (1765–1832). In 1815 König opened a public picture show in his apartment in Bern, which he called a "Diaphanorama." Primarily views of Swiss mountains and scenes from peasant life were displayed, which König commented upon with a lecture (see *fig. 19*). König had ordered a box built for the purpose of installing and illuminating the pictures. Starting in 1816, König undertook tours to Germany and France for many years. The success of these trips was remarkable. A Swiss newspaper, the *Aarauer Zeitung*, summarized the commentary of the German newspapers: "Painting is probably faced with the unresolvable task of representing with colors alone all objects with the true light of the sun, the moon, and fire …We must recognize that Mr. König's Swiss views stand at the point where art ends and beyond which truth begins."[30]

König himself shared this view of the relationship between reality and imitation, between being and appearance, of the transparency's power of simulation. He thought that the nature of Switzerland was so movingly unique, that it could only be convincingly depicted in the manner of transparencies.

Only two years after a year-long diaphanorama show by König in Paris, Louis-Jacques-Mandé Daguerre (1789 to 1851) opened his own diorama in 1822. Daguerre no doubt had seen König's exhibition and reworked the stimuli in his own project. His experiences as a celebrated stage designer for opera and theater, as well as his enormous energy and inventiveness, enabled Daguerre to achieve this. He also probably based the name of his own establishment on König's diaphanorama, which he shortened to diorama.[31] The popularity and influence of his picture show was immense. Daguerre's diorama was a cinema-like building made of stone, which could hold about 300 people *(fig. 20)*. The transparent paintings displayed within measured approximately 45 by 70 feet (14 by 22 m) and surpassed all previous ones in their optical power of illusion (see *fig. 21*). This illusionism experienced another improvement with the discovery of the so-called double effect in the year 1834, which made possible the illusion of movements in paintings that were themselves static. The depiction of Midnight Mass in the Church at St. Etienne-du-Mont, for example, was the most successful of all of Daguerre's images. Within only fifteen minutes, one could follow the course of a twenty-four-hour day: one saw the interior of a church, which was illuminated by entering light. Slowly twilight settled in, and at the same time the lights went on. Gradually the previously empty pews filled up with the faithful. Then midnight mass was rung in; and Haydn's Mass no. 1 was played on an organ. Afterwards the lights went out one by one until the church was as dark and empty as it had appeared at the beginning, and the approaching day announced itself.

Daguerre's creation exercised an enormous influence all over the world. In many European and American cities, buildings inspired by the Parisian model were constructed or transparent image presentations were organized in suitable existing houses.

Aside from these internationally fashionable public diorama productions, artists were inspired individually by the diorama for the purpose of their own private exercise of art. The important German Romantic painter Caspar David Friedrich (1774–1840) was one of those who occupied himself with the light experiments of transparency painting. As

FIGURE 20

The diorama building owned by Louis-Jacques-Mandé Daguerre in Paris, c. 1830. Color etching. International Museum of Photography at George Eastman House, Rochester, New York.

FIGURE 21

The diorama of the port of Boulogne as shown in Daguerre's diorama building. Color lithograph. International Museum of Photography at George Eastman House, Rochester. Photo: *Tableaux de Paris*.

FIGURE 22

Caspar David Friedrich, *Mountainous River Landscape in the Morning*, 1830/35. Double-sided transparent image. Watercolor and tempera on paper, 73.8 x 127 cm. Staatliche Kunstsammlungen Kassel.

FIGURE 23

Caspar David Friedrich, *Mountainous River Landscape at Night*, 1830/35. Double-sided transparent image. Watercolor and tempera on paper, 73.8 x 127 cm. Staatliche Kunstsammlungen Kassel.

in many of his oil paintings, Friedrich's preferred motif in transparency was the nocturnal moonlight scene. For Friedrich—as for all the Romantics—light, transparency, and moonlight possessed fully symbolic, world-signifying contents. Friedrich especially was fascinated by light shining into darkness. "To be able to annul the materiality of color" was essential for him.[32] At the beginning of the 1830s, Friedrich, at the suggestion of Wassilji Shukowski, the poet, state councillor, and educator of the prince at the Russian court, created four transparencies for the successor to the throne, Alexander. These four works constituted a cycle dedicated to an allegory of music, which was supposed to be staged with the accompaniment of music. Friedrich composed precise conceptions and lengthy letters on this project. The transparent images were sent to St. Petersburg and did indeed arrive there, but today are unfortunately lost.

One transparency, stemming from Friedrich's unpublished works, still does exist, however. This so-called double-effect transparency depicts a mountainous river landscape at first in the day and then on a moonlit night. The picture is painted on both sides in a mixed media of watercolors and tempera. Depending upon the location of the light source, one can choose between day and night views (*figs. 22* and *23*). Friedrich could encompass here on an experimental basis the course of a day in its temporality.

In the critical reception of Friedrich's transparencies there are negative and positive opinions. Emil Waldmann was among the critics who paid him homage: once the artist had placed a lamp behind the picture in the darkened room, the "miracle lamp [allowed] … the mountains to shine through gradually in the moonlit magical night, and made the universe deeper, and depending upon where one moved the lamp or whatever light source one used, it would become evening or night, and the world became more filled with details, and the total appearance [was] sometimes melancholically gloomy, sometimes mildly transfigured, … it is totally mysterious, and irresistible, like magic."[33]

SCHINKEL AND THE BERLIN DIORAMA

In the year 1827, five years after the foundation of the diorama in Paris, the Berlin diorama was opened by the theater painter Carl Gropius. Journeys to France and visits to Daguerre's establishment both by Gropius in 1822 and by Schinkel in 1826 had preceded this new venture. And Schinkel's architectural ideas probably had more influence than just in the creation of the building with its noble façade.[34] More than ten years after Schinkel's own transpar-

ent images had been shown in Berlin, the circle closed: his activities, already relegated to the past, subsequently inspired Gropius's diorama. Carl Gropius was, as already mentioned above, the son of Wilhelm Gropius, Schinkel's partner at the time of the earlier perspective view-painting. Twelve years younger than Schinkel, and living in the same house with him, Carl inevitably took part in Schinkel's works. In the shadow of the great master, he developed into a learned student and was able to fall back on Schinkel's experiences, especially for the diorama paintings.[35]

The building for the Berlin diorama was erected at the corner of Georgenstraße and Universitätsstraße, after the king had placed a spacious building site at their disposal (see *fig. 24*): "Entering through a portico artfully decorated in the ancient style, supplied with a beautiful fountain in the center, one ascends a spacious staircase up to the actual show-place. This was formed by a round, flatly domed hall with seats; at the same time it is a covered pavilion, which grants an unimpaired view only on one side, at first hung with a wide curtain.…Through the transparent cover, decorated with beautiful arabesques, a reddish light falls sparingly."[36]

On October 29, 1827, the diorama was opened, and it enjoyed enthusiastic popularity until May 31, 1850. Carl Seidel, a Berlin scholar and art critic, reported on a visit in February 1828 that in the viewers' rotunda, which could hold over 200 persons, a magical semi-darkness dominated, "preparing the eye, so to speak, for the artistic miracle."[37] The painting itself, executed in oil on white batiste, measured approximately 64 by 42 feet (21 by 14 m). From one side light fell through a large window onto the painting.

"The change in the lighting perceived here, from quiet twilight to the brightest sunshine, is … effected merely by opening and closing large window shutters, which, however, move easily and silently. These do not open to the sides, but rather come down from above, thus allowing the light to strike the picture at various angles."[38]

Carl Gropius himself wrote the first announcement of the diorama in October 1827. He reported that two oil paintings 2,500 square feet in size were being shown, depicting the Interior of the Church of Brou and a Cliff Ravine near Sorrento. How often the displayed images would be replaced with new ones, and "to what degree the selection of the displayed images [would] be able to include national interests by representing regions from the homeland," Gropius wanted to make dependent upon the level of support that the honored public would give the enterprise.[39]

The opening of the diorama building was a cultural event in Berlin that was appropriately celebrated. Thus, a critic in the *Spenersche Zeitung* announced his satisfaction with the fact that the German public finally had access to such a building, where in a tight space the gaze was directed into the greatest distance and where space and body as well as the atmosphere became visible through the changing appearances of light.[40] After the first two transparent paintings were exhibited for over a year, the diorama was reopened with two new pictures on June 20, 1829, after a four-week interim. Available for admiration were the famous View near Bacharach on the Rhine, Illuminated in Moonlight, and the Sea of Ice on the Grindelwald Glacier. Additional acoustic effects aided in completing the optical illusion. The preliminary announcement had already claimed that "A mechanism will also be added that is supposed to imitate the unique sound of the glaciers, the patter of the water, the bursting of ice blocks, the distant rolling of avalanches, etc., in the most illusory manner."[41] One year later, in 1830, a transparent image was exhibited in which Gropius followed an oil painting by Schinkel, *Gothic Cathedral in Morning Light*. Schinkel had painted the picture in 1813 and given it then to the Gropius family (see *fig. 25*).[42]

"While at first we see the cathedral in the dark morning light, the seemingly mobile clouds quickly change the scene and individual glances of the sun illuminate alternately various parts of the city, until a bright ray suddenly misses the darker clouds blindingly and displays the scene itself in the friendliest daylight…The distant sounds of bells and an organ contribute finally to the enhancement of pleasure primarily by completing the illusion in the most pleasant way, and thus lending the picture a lifelike quality."[43]

This diorama painting following Schinkel's model had a noteworthy response. It was exhibited without interruption for sixteen months and was advertised the whole time in the daily press as "new."

The business advertisements of Carl Gropius in the *Spenersche Zeitung* were directly next to those of the Königliche Schauspiele (Royal Theater) and Königstädtisches Theater (Royal Municipal Theater), which not least of all underscores the significance and estimation of this enterprise. In the "turbulent times of the crush of masses,"[44] above all during the Christmas season, more than 3,000 people streamed into the Gropius establishment on a daily basis, even though the entry fee was ten silver groschen. People even came to Berlin from a radius of up to ten miles just "to see the miracle."[45] Visits by King Friedrich Wilhelm III and his retinue were not uncommon, and the annual Christmas exhibits in particular, were well received by the royal house on occasion.

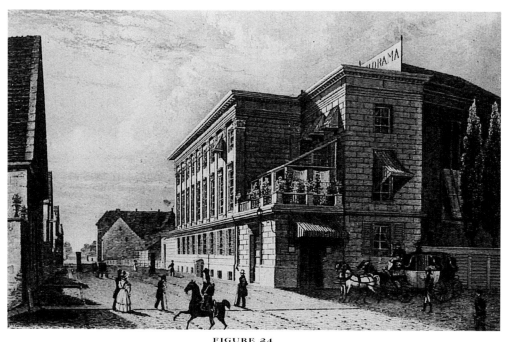

FIGURE 24

The diorama building owned by Carl Gropius, Berlin.
Etching, c. 1830.

FIGURE 25

Wilhelm Ahlborn after Karl Friedrich Schinkel, *Gothic
Cathedral in Morning Light*, 1813 (copy 1823). Oil on canvas,
80 x 106.5 cm. SMB-PK, Nationalgalerie.

Gropius's diorama, whose foundation was enthusiastically welcomed and highly treasured during its twenty-three-year existence, displayed a total of twenty-eight transparent paintings between 1827 and 1850. Among these were various interior and exterior views of churches, Swiss landscapes, city views, ravines, and grottoes, as well as views of Italian regions. According to the *Berliner Conversationshandbuch* of 1834, the transparencies gained "truth and life through the changing of lighting, which with the aid of an ingeniously invented installation creates nuances of color, and which is able to conjure up before us views of the sun, reds of evening and all other appearances of brighter and gloomier light." In this way, "a long series of highly interesting views"

was presented to the Berlin public.[46] As was the case already with Schinkel's perspective optical views, none of Gropius's dioramas are extant. Once the Gropius program ended in 1850 and the installation of the diorama was later sold to St. Petersburg, the building too lost its function. In 1876, it fell victim to the construction of the Berlin subway system.

Looking back, one can see that Schinkel's diorama works assume the outline of a pioneering feat. These works were path-breaking both for the development of transparency painting overall and for the art of stage designing. After the change of directorship from Iffland to Brühl in 1815, Schinkel's activity at the Königliches Theater immediately succeeded his diorama period. A magnificent beginning and simultaneously the high point in the Brühl era were Schinkel's decorations for Mozart's *Die Zauberflöte (The Magic Flute)*. The premiere took place on January 18, 1816, in celebration of the coronation and the peace festival. This production was immediately sold out twelve times.

As the production of *Die Zauberflöte* showed, Schinkel strove to reform the stage through simplification and technical functionalism. The Baroque decoration with its complex arrangement of staggered scenery gave way to a laterally confined stage space, which like the diorama was closed off with a large painting for a background. Greater clarity and space for the course of the plot were thus created.

Along with its significance for the stage, Schinkel's intermediate art experiment set the standard primarily for the development of the genre of the transparent image itself. Through him, as through other outstanding artists like Hackert, Gainsborough, C. D. Friedrich, and Daguerre, transparency painting progressed both artistically and technically. The illusions of transparencies, light, and change, were perfected step by step. Seen as a whole, this medium opens up perspectives into the twentieth century, already in the period of its genesis at the end of the eighteenth century. The transparent views made temporally and spatially distant worlds visible. They also reflected current events. Building upon the fantasy of the public, they brought what was distant within reach. It became possible to be an eyewitness to world events without actually being at the location of the event in real life. As a communication system typical of the nineteenth century, the diorama, also called the "permanent public art institute,"[47] prepared the way for the modern world of the media, especially film and television. The ability of these perspective views to illustrate, connect, and bring together the world was their great power.

All his life Schinkel was a protagonist of the art of the diorama, as well as the panorama. That fact may perhaps best be illustrated by the story of one of Schinkel's last artistic ideas, two days before he lost consciousness from a stroke. Gustav Friedrich Waagen has reported how deeply committed Schinkel was to such an artistic project: "He … took a stroll in the afternoon (on September 9, 1840) in the zoo, where he met the theater inspector, Mr. Carl Gropius, and suggested to him in a conversation that the most favorable subject for such a round painting would be to execute a panorama of Palermo from his sketches. In addition, however, he also informed him of the idea of combining the most important monuments from the most diverse lands from Asia, Egypt, Greece, Rome, and medieval Germany, each

within its appropriate natural surroundings, in a large panorama measuring ninety feet in diameter. He promised, when Gropius expressed the opinion that this hardly sounded feasible, that if he [Gropius] were not afraid of the costs of such an endeavor, that he [Schinkel] would gladly collaborate in such a project. Thus, one of his final thoughts was directed to joining together in a grand whole and a picturesque manner the spiritual culture of the diverse periods and nations, which he had so frequently addressed individually through their art, while preserving their most interesting contrasts and comparisons. And he was the man to fulfill such a promise."[48]

NOTES

1. Ludwig Catel, "Darstellungen von merkwürdigen Gegenden und berühmten Bauwerken in der Art der Panoramen," *Berlinische Nachrichten von Staats- und gelehrten Sachen*, also called *Spenersche Zeitung*, December 29, 1808.
2. Ibid.
3. Ibid.
4. Ibid.
5. Ibid.
6. *Spenersche Zeitung*, December 16, 1809.
7. Carl Gropius to Alfred von Wolzogen, February 1, 1862, Zentralarchiv der Staatlichen Museen Berlin, Autographensammlung.
8. Schinkel to Friedrich Wilhelm III, March 25, 1808; Alfred Freiherr von Wolzogen, *Aus Schinkels Nachlaß* (Berlin, 1863), vol. 3, p. 409.
9. Gottfried Schadow, *Kunst-Werke und Kunst-Ansichten Berlin*, ed. Goetz Eckardt (1849; new edition, Berlin: Deutscher Verlag für Kunstwissenschaft, 1987), vol. 1, p. 84.
10. *Spenersche Zeitung*, December 19, 1809.
11. Gropius to Wolzogen (note 7).
12. Joseph von Eichendorff, *Sämtliche Werke, Tagebücher*, ed. Wilhelm Kotsch and August Sauer (Regensburg, 1908), vol. 2, pp. 257–58.
13. *Spenersche Zeitung*, February 26, 1811.
14. Ibid., November 28, 1811.
15. Ibid.
16. Gropius to Wolzogen (note 7).
17. *Spenersche Zeitung*, November 21, 1812.
18. Franz Kugler, *Karl Friedrich Schinkel* (Berlin, 1842), pp. 148–49.
19. Ibid., p. 150.
20. Ibid.
21. *Spenersche Zeitung*, October 10, 1812.
22. Gustav Friedrich Waagen, *Karl Friedrich Schinkel als Mensch und als Künstler* (1844; reprint Düsseldorf: Werner, 1980), p. 348.
23. *Spenersche Zeitung*, December 24, 1812.
24. Gropius to Wolzogen (note 7).
25. Friedrich Johann Lorenz Meyer, *Darstellungen aus Italien* (Berlin, 1792), p. 304.
26. Ibid.
27. Pierre Francastel, "Les transparents de Carmontelle," *L'Illustration* (August 17, 1929), p. 159.
28. See, for example, *View toward the Harbor Exit of the Thames* (Melbourne National Gallery); *Landscape with Shepherd and Flock* (Neue Pinakothek, Munich); *Forest Landscape with a Bridge* (National Gallery, London).
29. See Ralph G. Allen, "The Stage Spectacles of Philip James de Loutherbourg" (Ph.D. diss, Yale University, 1960), and "The Eidophusikon," *Theatre Design and Technology* (December 1966), pp. 12–16.
30. *Aarauer Zeitung*, no. 40 (April 1, 1820), p. 158.
31. Helmut Gernsheim, *L. J. M. Daguerre: The History of the Diorama and the Daguerrotype* (London and New York, 1968), p. 14.
32. Werner Sumowski, *Caspar David Friedrich Studien* (Wiesbaden: F. Steiner, 1970), p. 223.
33. Emil Waldmann, *Caspar David Friedrich Almanach* (Berlin, 1941), p. 13.
34. Erich Stenger, *Daguerres Diorama in Berlin* (Berlin, 1925), p. 17.
35. In 1862, in a letter to Alfred von Wolzogen, Carl Gropius remembered having painted from memory copies of six of Schinkel's transparent paintings, which had made a lasting impression on him, to celebrate the artist's birthday. "Since these beautiful works still floated completely in my memory, I painted them once again in what I knew to be the Schinkel-style (in which I of course had provided a helpful hand at the time) and on his birthday these were illuminated and exhibited at the request of Stüler and Knoblauch." Zentralarchiv der Staatlichen Museen Berlin, Autographensammlung.
36. Carl Seidel, "Über Panoramen, Dioramen und Neoramen," *Berliner Kunstblatt*, 1 (1828), p. 64.
37. Ibid.
38. Ibid., p. 65.
39. Stenger (note 34), p. 31.
40. Ibid., pp. 31–32.
41. Ibid., p. 35.
42. In 1931, this picture was destroyed by a fire at the Münchner Glaspalast. There are two copies, however, one by Wilhelm Ahlborn (Nationalgalerie, Berlin), and another by K. E. Biermann (Neue Pinakothek, Munich).
43. *Spenersche Zeitung*, June 20, 1830.
44. Stenger (note 34), p. 26.
45. Ibid.
46. Leopold von Zedlitz-Neukirch, *Neuestes Konversations-Handbuch für Berlin und Potsdam* (Berlin, 1834), pp. 147–48.
47. Seidel (note 36), p. 68.
48. Waagen (note 22), p. 420.

MITCHELL SCHWARZER

University of Illinois at Chicago

The forms and spaces of theater buildings—the division of the interior into stage and auditorium, the arrangement of seating, and the external design and appearance—constitute an architectural forum for reflection on the structure of society. Like theatrical performance, theater design embodies the rhetoric of cultural values, challenging architects to connect their designs with either accepted notions of social order or new visions of social reform. Theater architecture participates as much as drama or music in the creation of illusory worlds, stimulating architectural reflection on the physical structure of the real world.[1] Karl Friedrich Schinkel's opera set designs and his building for the Schauspielhaus (Theater; 1818–21; *fig. 1*) in Berlin exemplify these representational possibilities. As was the case with many of his fellow architects who designed cultural buildings, Schinkel envisioned the public theater as a vehicle for cultural ennoblement and epistemological exploration. The question addressed by Schinkel was central to his age: how can theater as both performance and architecture depict the freedom, variety, and potential of human existence within a unifying framework of nature and history?

This question leads us beyond Schinkel's designs. The growth of the public theater building during the eighteenth and early nineteenth centuries presented a challenging arena for his vision of theater. In fact, Schinkel's theater designs express the greater struggle of an increasingly bourgeois society to create a theatrical analogue of itself. For the middle classes of the eighteenth and early nineteenth centuries, theater was something they generally associated with the aristocratic court. Court theater had long been a dramatic incarnation of aristocratic mentality, a private display of luxury, diversion, and splendor, as much as it was a manifestation of absolute social hierarchies extending far beyond the palace compound. The emergence of public theater challenged the politics of inequality in aristocratic theater. Designed to mirror bourgeois society, the public theater stood for qualities of functional utility and perceptual realism.

Theaters were transformed from their earlier identification with social hierarchy and princely ceremony into a new public forum for the rationalization of middle-class life. In an architectural sense, the theater as a bourgeois public institution comprised a challenge to social distinctions in the seating organization of the auditorium; and a challenge to create a type of theater design that would be recognizable and prominent within the cityscape.

Integral to the reconfiguration of the court theater into public theater, however, was a discernible anxiety on the part of architects as to whether they should favor innovation or tradition in their designs. The architecture of the public theater demonstrates the problem of fashioning bourgeois society from aristocratic models. In the German-speaking lands, the transition from aristocratic to bourgeois control of society occurred over a long period, compromised by the incomplete ascension of the middle classes to political power during the nineteenth century. The development of the public theater illustrates a complex dialectic between aristocratic and bourgeois intentions. In the period under consideration here—roughly spanned by the construction of the first large public theater in Germany, the Königliches Opernhaus (Royal Opera House; now the Deutsche Staatsoper, 1741–42) in Berlin by Georg Wenzeslaus von Knobelsdorff (see *figs. 2–4*) and by Otto Brückwald's Festspielhaus (1872–76) in Bayreuth for Richard Wagner (see *figs. 18–20*)—the architecture of the public theater expressed significantly different aims. These included an external form that was reminiscent of the monarchial court; a rational and artistic analogue of the new middle-class society; and, finally, the birth of pre-modern organic culture. Public theaters represented programs both of egalitarian participation and hierarchical procession, of private perception and social advancement.

SPECTACLE AT THE COURT THEATER

Court theater of the Baroque age was an eloquent valorization of monarchial rule, a set of enticing yet demanding rituals and conventions that fostered a hierarchical society that emanated from an absolute center. Evolving from performances in dining halls and courtyards, the court theater was a setting for the consolidation of feudal power into monarchy. In this sense, the dynamics of court theater contributed to the construction of the centralized nation-state. Whereas, earlier, theater had been an affair of cities and towns, occurring in the public spaces of cathedrals or town squares and funded or organized by the church or guilds, court theater was private, removed into the palatial realm of the monarch. Even within palaces, theaters were not easily accessible. Mimicking the medieval armature of city gate, street passageways, and the cathedral square, complex processional pathways of elaborate hallways and stairways led to the court theater, deeply embedded within palace wings.

The leading actors of the court theater were the recently civilized nobility, and their star was the newly empowered prince, king, or emperor. As the theater historian Margarete Baur-Heinhold has written: "The theater was necessary to the prince to embody his vision of himself, to give life to his dreams of power, influence, and immortality."[2] Like triumphal processions, carnivals, banquets, tournaments, and races, theater was an ingredient in the transformation of feudal warrior society into the civilized and controlled spectacle of the court. Court society was bound by a tension between two sharply contrasting impulses. On the one hand, monarchs exacted the conformity of previously unregulated nobles to codes of conduct. This refinement of manners, achieved through the demand for their constant attention to details of every sort, pacified and subordinated the great nobility into vassals of the new absolutist lord.[3] On the other hand, the court's performances, which enacted the type of dramatic and heroic stories that had once been associated with the nobility, provided a distraction from their true loss of power.

For most of the eighteenth century, the formal innovations of Italian court theater, especially the models established by the theaters of the Farnese (1618) in Parma, and SS. Giovanni e Paolo (1654) in Venice, dominated designs for German theater. Following the revival of antique theater principles by Palladio, Italian architects developed the characteristic form of court theater design: the proscenium theater. Unlike its medieval and Elizabethan prototypes, in which the stage was often surrounded by the auditorium, the proscenium arch divided actors from audience, creating two distinct spaces. The width of the arch contributed to the distinctive, horseshoe-shaped plan of the court auditorium: its side walls gradually widened from the narrow proscenium arch only to culminate in a grand arc at the rear of the thea-

FIGURE I

Schauspielhaus, Berlin, 1818–21.

ter.[4] At this penultimate location, the princely patron typically sat in an elevated royal box. His courtiers were arranged in a semicircle of small elevated boxes to his right and left. The rest of the audience was seated either in the pit (orchestra) or in tiers of boxes and galleries above the level of the royal box.[5] Seating favored strict class hierarchies, a social stratification based on distance from the royal patron, not on distance from the stage. In Germany, the most important exemplars of court theater were the Residenztheater (1744–48) at Bayreuth by Giuseppe and Carlo Galli Bibiena, and the Residenztheater (1750–52) in Munich by François Cuvilliés.

While the auditorium was rigidly hierarchical, the stage of the court theater was the scene of wondrous illusion. Mechanized during the seventeenth century, scenic backdrops were opened, shut, raised, and lowered by a system of wheels, levers, pulleys, and counterweights.[6] Theatrical art, with the help of technology, provided spectacles that went far beyond day to day experience. The performance on stage was an illusionistic depiction of the magnificence of royal power, and, in conjunction with the architectural plan of the auditorium, exerted a civilizing influence on those present. The plays of Jean Racine, for example, as performed in the court theater of Louis XIV, exemplify the ceremonial significance of rules of appearance and conduct, reaching down from stage to audience. French theater, whether for Racine or his eighteenth-century follower Voltaire, aimed at elegance, harmony, and style. As Voltaire wrote in 1731: "Often the unusual way of saying ordinary things, and the art of embellishing by literary style what all men think and feel—these are what make great poets."[7] Thus, the rules of French theater were not crafted from example and custom, but from universal reason as embodied in the rigid decorum of the court.

The royal boxes, however, offered their own guide to civilized behavior. Seating boxes were lit throughout the performance, positing the display of the aristocratic spectator as equal to any activity on stage. Members of the audience were to learn rules, conventions, and taste as much from their observance of their fellow's conduct as from the performance on stage. Inasmuch as Baroque life made a priority of appearance, the necessity to look privileged and to behave according to a certain conduct led to the further submission and indebtedness of the court nobility to the royal patron.[8]

REASON AND THE EARLY PUBLIC THEATER

The elements that conspired to establish absolutist court society—the centralization of monarchial power through alliance with the ascendant bourgeois class—eventually contributed to its decline. Over time, the development of commercial interests shifted the spotlight of power from

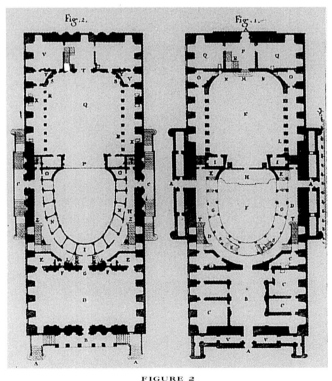

FIGURE 2

Georg Wenzeslaus von Knobelsdorff, Plans for ground and first floors of the Königliches Opernhaus (Royal Opera House), Berlin, 1742. SSG Potsdam-Sanssouci. Photo: Hans Lange, *Vom Tribunal zum Tempel* (Marburg, n.d.).

royal palaces to the growing cities. With this change, the court theater, born amidst a challenge to decentralized feudal authority, expired.

The public theater was born during the second half of the eighteenth century. While seating was at first reserved for the nobility, access for the bourgeoisie was gradually provided in the upper balconies. After the revolution in France in 1789, German public theaters opened their doors to the entire middle class. But differences in social rank were not forgotten, and the public theater reflected these hierarchies. Utilitarian planning for sight lines, structural daring to accommodate seating galleries, and external expressiveness all catered to new bourgeois values, but at the same time the use of classical ornamentation and courtly procession proclaimed the allegiance of bourgeois taste to aristocratic models. The close association of the public theater with palace prototypes—its external markings such as pediments and its internal stratification of classes—was very much the subject of intense debate by architects.

The first public theater in Germany was the Königliches Opernhaus (1741–42; *fig. 3*) in Berlin by Georg von Knobelsdorff (1699–1753). Constructed at the behest of the Emperor Frederick the Great, the opera house was envisioned as a landmark of the monarch's new rational state.[9] Facing the Zeughaus (Arsenal), the theater identified the rebuilding of the capital with artistic and not merely military symbolism. Frederick's Berlin was to be a cultural center of great vistas, gates, squares, and public buildings.[10] Knobelsdorff's theater was an orthogonal, free-standing edifice: two giant, colonnaded porticoes atop staircases articulated its entrance and auditorium. It also stood out for its harmonious assembly of complex needs into a regular rectangular volume (*figs. 2* and *4*).[11] Liberated from the confines of palaces, the theater proclaimed itself as a palatial establishment in its own right, constructed for the entertainment and edification of the citizens of the city. Its location at the center of the city along a major avenue presaged the role that public theaters would take in shaping the processional axes and points of emphasis within the nineteenth-century city. Still, the new public order, especially at this early point, derived much of its inspiration and vocabulary from the hierarchies of courtly architecture. The ample grand entrance hall of the Königliches Opernhaus, for example, was on an axis with the auditorium, imitating the forecourt and formal passages of a palace. To this extent, procession and showcase space would be important elements of the new public theater. Other aristocratic features also found their way into the interior space

FIGURE 3

Perspective view of the Königliches Opernhaus
(Royal Opera House), Berlin, designed
by Georg Wenzeslaus von Knobelsdorff, and
St. Hedwig's Church, Berlin, 1800
(cat. no. 47).

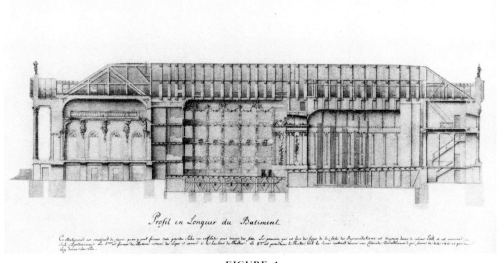

FIGURE 4

Georg Wenzeslaus von Knobelsdorff, Cross-section of the
Königliches Opernhaus (Royal Opera House), Berlin, 1742.
SSG Potsdam-Sanssouci. Photo: A. Streichhan, *Knobelsdorff
und das friderizianische Rokoko* (Burg, 1932), fig. 13.

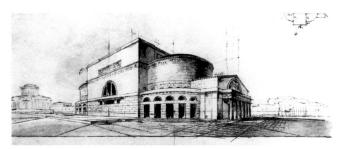

FIGURE 5

Friedrich Gilly, Perspective view of the exterior of the proposed National Theater, Berlin, 1797–98. Photo: Alste Oncken, *Friedrich Gilly, 1772–1800* (Berlin, 1935).

FIGURE 6

Friedrich Gilly, Perspective view of the interior of the proposed National Theater, Berlin, 1797–98. Photo: Alste Oncken, *Friedrich Gilly, 1772–1800* (Berlin, 1935).

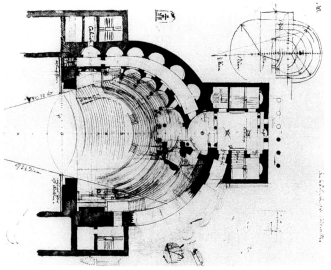

FIGURE 7

Friedrich Gilly, Ground plan of the proposed National Theater, Berlin, 1797–98. Photo: Alste Oncken, *Friedrich Gilly, 1772–1800* (Berlin, 1935).

of Knobelsdorff's auditorium, namely, a horseshoe plan, tiered box-seating, and a narrow proscenium opening.

But, in contrast to the court theater, which constructed social order through the interactive performance of actors and spectators, the public theater increasingly proclaimed the importance of the stage, and the perception of stage activity on the part of a democratized yet isolated mass of spectators. If the courtly theater stressed entertainment, appearance, and lively social interaction, the new public theater stood for education, naturalism, and private perception. If court theater was preoccupied with the adoption of conventions through regulated social interaction, the new public theater placed critical value on the spectator's private contemplation of the enormity of human life as depicted on stage. Public theater design was less absorbed with the active conduct of its spectators, who, in fact, were increasingly isolated from one another even though they shared progressively communal spaces. In this manner, the rigid community of the auditorium boxes was gradually sacrificed to the democracy of the orchestra and gallery seating.

The great theorist of theater in the late eighteenth century, Gotthold Ephraim Lessing (1729–1781), argued for naturalism, attacking the rule-bound artificiality of Baroque drama. According to Lessing, taste is governed not by abstract rule, but by a human genius that works in perfect harmony with nature.[12] He believed in the importance of musical (and especially dramatic) continuity in order to transform the audience from the stage. Foreshadowing Schinkel, Lessing stated that the spectator internalizes the art and morals on stage. Thus, in shaping a theatrical work, artists should avoid anything that prevents the full engagement of the spectator's imagination. The hall, too, should be dark and quiet so as to promote the spectator's subjective discovery.

The growing preference for Neoclassical design during the second half of the eighteenth century encouraged a simplification of buildings, sets, and themes.[13] Although many elements of the court theater relating to acoustics and stage mechanics were carried over into the public theater, great effort was made to reject Baroque extravagance in both plan and decoration. Architects avidly studied the possibility of a return to the simple, semicircular theater plans of the classical world, eliminating the complex Baroque forms of ellipses, horseshoes, and egg-shaped halls found in court theaters. Especially important for the nineteenth-century public theater in Germany were French developments. For example, Victor Louis's use of a truncated circle at the Grand

FIGURE 8

Friedrich Gilly, Night view of the proposed National
Theater, Berlin, 1797–98. Photo: Alste Oncken,
Friedrich Gilly, 1772–1800 (Berlin, 1935).

Théâtre (1777–80) at Bordeaux found later adherents in the designs of Friedrich Gilly (see *figs. 5–8*), Schinkel, and Gottfried Semper (see *figs. 15–17*).[14] In Claude Nicolas Ledoux's Besançon Théâtre (1778), banks of seating arranged in semicircular tiers recall the classical amphitheater.[15]

For building exteriors, Louis and Ledoux encouraged a massing that expressively demonstrated function. In Germany, the articulation of interior volumes in external massing was taken up by Friedrich Gilly (1772–1800) in his unrealized design for a new National Theater (1797–98) on the Gendarmenmarkt in Berlin. Gilly proposed sharp, undecorated geometric units each expressing internal function (see *fig. 5*). His bold shapes for the auditorium and projecting mass of the stage offered a new theatrical model (see *figs. 6 and 7*).[16] Borrowing from Knobelsdorff, Gilly also stressed the importance of public entrance and movement through the design of large foyers, staircases, and salons. In contrast to the court theater, the public auditorium now provided specific spaces for conversation and refreshment. Removed from the performance space, these social activities no longer competed with the drama on stage for the attention of the viewer.

Finally, the interior spaces and exterior forms of public theater also went hand in hand with a new aesthetic conception of theater architecture as a fine and autonomous art. Unlike the Baroque artist, whose artworks principally served his royal patron or the church, the bourgeois artist served above all else the idea of art. The rationalization of art into a process of subjective (yet universal) validity was crucial to the emergence of theater buildings as unique artistic objects (see *fig. 8*). In describing this phenomenon, Harald Zielske has written that "the theater building became an art object in its own right (sui generis)."[17] Artistic reality became the determinate factor for social reality.[18]

SCHINKEL AND THE PRIVATE PERCEPTION OF THE UNIVERSAL

Schinkel broadened the bourgeois reassessment of theater's representational dimensions. He also left us with a grandiose set of paintings, dioramas, set designs, and, of course, the completed building for the new Schauspielhaus (1818–21). His immersion into so many different aspects of theater is evidence of a deep interest in the construction of artistic reality through active relationships and not static forms. Schinkel's correction of sight lines and development of perspectival viewing embody his concept of theater, in which artistic creativity emerges from the relationship between performance and reception. The spatial relationship between the stage and the auditorium was, for Schinkel, a crucial component of successful theater. In his eyes, theater has the potential to function as a multileveled amplification of existence.

Already by 1805, Schinkel conceived of architecture as the combination of diverse materials and intentions into a complete whole.[19] Architecture, he later described, is a representation of nature's diverse appearances into a more perfect form: it makes ideal life visible in material forms.[20] Schinkel looked beyond classical theories of architectural

imitation. Like Friedrich Schiller's sentimental poet, he sought to restore to architecture that unity of expression that had been disrupted by the rise of abstract reason and scientific specialization during the Enlightenment. Equally, following Goethe's recommendations in the essay "Architecture" (1795), Schinkel saw the task of the architect as endowing architectural function with artistic harmony. His architectural theory epitomizes the Romantic quest to achieve an original art, where an idea springs from the soul of the architect, independent of classical traditions and the existing world.[21]

Romanticism, which had taken hold of Germany during the architect's youth, exerted enormous influence on his ideas for the theater. Theater offered the possibility to engage architectural design with representation on a variety of fronts. From the activity on stage, to the formation of the stage events in the minds of viewers, and, finally, to the direction of both these activities to the outer world, theater exemplified the possibilities of Romantic synthesis through artistic symbolism. Schinkel was well aware of the Romantic complaint that contemporary art lacked a focal point. His goal for art to express the dynamic variety of the world within the unitary setting of the theater recalls Friedrich Schlegel's suggestions for a new poetic mythology, one in which: "Everything interpenetrates everything else, and everywhere there is one and the same spirit, only expressed differently."[22] Through its oppositions between spectator and actor, music/dramatic development and architectural form, escape and immersion in real life, theater provided a setting for Schinkel to create a composite system of the arts conditioned by the unifying representations of the human consciousness.

Like Knobelsdorff and Gilly, Schinkel was engaged in the design for a new theater and concert hall in Berlin. Between 1800 and 1802, Carl Gotthard Langhans had constructed the National Theater on the Gendarmenmarkt, the commission that had been denied to Gilly's more creative design. Consisting of a palace façade with entrance portico, Langhans's design *(fig. 9)* was an undistinguished building repeating many of Knobelsdorff's earlier innovations. Schinkel's first major attempt at theater reform was his plan to reorganize Langhans's stage (see Forster, *fig. 10*). In a letter describing his intentions in 1813, Schinkel wrote of removing "the always deep labyrinth of weights and barriers" on the stage.[23] Although nothing came of this project, when the theater burned down in 1817, Schinkel received the commission for a new Schauspielhaus (see *fig. 11–14* and Forster, *fig. 14*).

In his design, Schinkel attempted to realize his intentions for a flat stage background recalling antique prototypes.[24] Schinkel's motivations were directly related to his ambition to establish a new mythology for modern society, one that would be based on perspectival naturalism and historicism. In large part, Schinkel's innovation was conditioned by his long career as a painter and designer of dioramas and theatrical sets.

Between 1807 and 1816, Schinkel had designed a series of dioramas and panoramas that depicted natural and man-made spectacles and even historical events (see essay by Birgit Verwiebe in this volume). After 1815, he began a career as a designer of opera sets. In these sets, most importantly, Schinkel developed a conception of illusionist space that

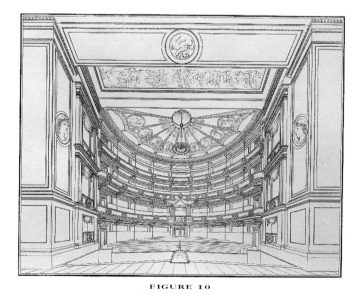

FIGURE 11

Elevation of the main façade of the Schauspielhaus,
Berlin, 1821 (cat. no. 52).

would be crucial to his architecture for the Schauspielhaus. As Rebecca Hilliker has explained, Schinkel, critical of the traditional organization of the stage, "replaced the deep-scaled, multiple-wing, and drop scenery with a painted linen backdrop, a central motif, and a uniform framing foreground. The result was clarity, simplification, and symmetrical balancing."[25] For one thing, the stress on a single scenic backdrop encouraged the audience to perceive nature as reaching beyond the stage. It established greater continuity not only between spectator and actor, but also between the entire theatrical performance and the external world; the background brought forth the idea of a binding perspective, in which an urban or natural landscape provides a unifying contrast to the dramatic variety of the stage. Like Schlegel's notion that a new and infinite realism could spring from a transcendent idealism, Schinkel's stage designs pushed musical and dramatic performance toward unifying symbolic archetypes. For example, as the first backdrop to be used in the newly completed Schauspielhaus, Schinkel provided a perspectival setting of the Gendarmenmarkt transformed by the addition of his building, an expansion of the illusion of the theater space to the horizon of the city as shaped by the master architect (see frontispiece).[26]

Another aspect of Schinkel's set designs was his Romantic desire to merge the artistic drive toward originality within the unity of history. He perceived history as an ironic unitary backdrop to human actions very much like nature. The concept of history tells us that humanity's desires for meaning and purpose occur within a changing world. For Schinkel, the dilemma presented by both history and nature—i.e., their ceaseless change and potential for chaos—is resolved by their aestheticization into an allegorical framework for the theatrical event. Like nature, which can be artistically manipulated to represent totality, historical images were used by Schinkel to project theatrical fiction onto a wider reflective plane. Schinkel's art of historical and natural integration through perspectival expansion relates to notions of enhanced representation in the paintings of Caspar David Friedrich (1774–1840). What may have been especially important for Schinkel's idea of the backdrop was Friedrich's use of images of wilderness peaks and ocean expanses, towering churches and crumbling ruins, to embrace a foreground scene within an incomparably large natural and cultural totality. Schinkel's creation of theatrical unity through sublime perspectivalism was indebted to these aspects of Romantic aesthetics.

FIGURE 12

Three plans
of the
Schauspielhaus,
Berlin, 1821
(cat. no. 57).

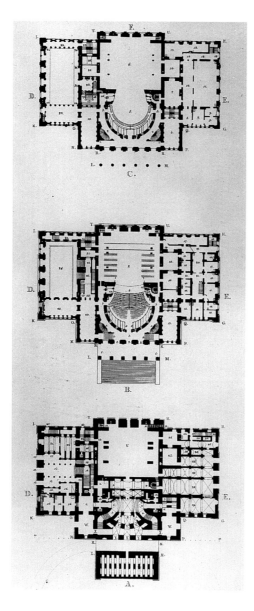

This line of thinking is immediately apparent in the design for the Schauspielhaus. Here, Schinkel was preoccupied with the possibility of creating the appearance of a more spacious interior—and hence a merger of interior and exterior space—through an expansion of the performance space into monumental scenes of nature and history.[27] In harmony with these aims to remove optical distortions for the audience, Schinkel eliminated the complexities of the Baroque stage with its mechanical apparatuses and multiple perspectives.[28] And in order to unite the viewer with the theatrical and architectural performance, he argued for a wider stage and less distracting decoration (see *figs. 10* and *12*).[29] Helmut Börsch-Supan has described Schinkel's idea of perspectival distance: "A basic motif in Schinkel's thinking is architecture that is not merely a housing that shuts off interior space from

exterior space, but something that opens outwards as a loggia, terrace or vestibule, and so links buildings and surroundings. The building not only has to fulfill a practical purpose, it has to occupy the eye and then the mind, and show it something of the world."[30]

What is more, Schinkel not only argued for a simplification of the theater space from the point of view of integrating internal and external space. For Schinkel, the traditional Baroque stage expressed a hierarchical orientation to the royal box, limiting clear perspectival views to this single point. He thus proposed a widening of the proscenium arch and a transformation of the auditorium seating from a squinched oval to a truncated circle. In proposing these simplifications and regularization of the stage and auditorium, Börsch-Supan tells us that: "Schinkel was fighting an absolutist principle that only allowed one privileged spectator access to the complete illusion."[31] Integral to Schinkel's program to ennoble reality through artistry and through multiple perspectives was the full visual participation of all spectators.

For the Schauspielhaus exterior *(fig. 11)*, Schinkel was obviously influenced by the profound Hellenism of eighteenth- and early nineteenth-century Germany, and particularly the expressive forms of Gilly's theater design. Still, Schinkel was drawn to a more literal Greek antiquity than Gilly, seeking a harmony between individual subjectivity and natural and historical reality. In his cubic massing and stark window detailing, Schinkel tried to reconcile the ancient feeling for finitude, simplicity of form, and corporeality with the modern spirit for function and variety. Built atop the foundation of Langhans's theater, the Schauspielhaus is divided into two predominant masses (see *fig. 13*). The dominant mass, consisting of the auditorium and stage, represents for architecture the unity that Schinkel sought to create for the perception of theatrical performance. Set atop a great foundation, and reachable only via a set of grand stairs, the theater building also projects monumental form into the cityscape. It dominates its plaza, and represents for the progressive urban vision of the bourgeoisie a new sort of temple, a place that offered the continual representation and examination of life through art.

With his set designs and Schauspielhaus, Schinkel sought to guide hierarchical court society into a rational modern world. In this regard, he looked less to so-called organic and folk traditions than to modern needs and the imperial past of both Prussia and its great European and Mediterranean progenitors. Regarding Prussia (and by ex-

FIGURE 13

Schauspielhaus, Berlin, 1818–21. (Photo 1909.)

tension Germany) as neither a natural, unchangeable, nor isolated culture, Schinkel's vision of theater as art forged intimate ties between Prussian/German identity and Western civilization. Schinkel, like the playwright Christoph Martin Wieland, regarded the theater as the stage where humankind could be taught the moral values inherent in the continuous traditions of Western civilization. Looking to the fragmentation between architecture and engineering, machine and handcrafts, urban and rural life, Schinkel saw the theater as a forum for healing modern society. It is partly from Schinkel that the architect Peter Behrens (who regarded theater as the highest symbol of culture) accepted the idea that theater architecture brings together art and life as a festive celebration of higher expression.

RICHARD WAGNER'S TOTAL THEATRICAL EXPERIENCE

Despite Schinkel's achievements, the unification of dramatic or musical theater within an architecturally created perspective was frequently forgotten. The bourgeois reform of theater in the service of reason and art was undermined by the actual conditions of industrial society. More than many other building types, the public theater exemplified the difficulties of a commodity society. While envisioned as a participatory arena that might become a temple to higher knowledge through art, the theater too easily became only a shrine to profits.

While the movement of the theater from the world of the palace into the modern city was initially viewed with great promise, by the middle of the nineteenth century it was apparent that the city lacked the order of the aristocratic

palace. Even in the case of Gottfried Semper's first Opera House in Dresden (1837–41), whose magisterial curving façade rationally expressed the geometry of the auditorium *(fig. 15)*, the theater had become merely one bourgeois institution amidst a multitude of competing centers: government buildings, stock exchanges, libraries, museums, and universities and arts academies. Indeed, Semper's theater, which realized Gilly's ambition of a cylinder motif as the embodiment of clear functional expression (see *figs. 16* and *17*),[32] was unable to counter the effects of the increasingly loose assembly of different edifices in Dresden's cultural center. A competitor for the artistic soul of bourgeois civilization, the theater became a symbol of its fragmentation. According to historian Rémy Saisselin, the bourgeoisie imitated the lifestyle of the old court as a commercial endeavor: "only then could the image of the sweetness of life pursued by the old court society come to be marketable in the form of tourism, palatial hotels, furniture styles imitating those of the past, eclectic millionaire architecture, and the dream world of romanticism."[33] The rationalization of architecture and performance had not led to the representational unification of culture.

Richard Wagner was well aware of these contradictions. His nationalistic challenge to bourgeois culture argued that the actual essence of modern art was its promotion of industry, the aesthetics of making a fortune. Wagner's idea for theater reform contrasted sharply with the bourgeois project to develop a monumental urban landscape comprised of theaters and other public buildings. Because of his anti-cosmopolitanism, Wagner removed his festival theater from the confusion of Germany's cities to the small town of Bayreuth.

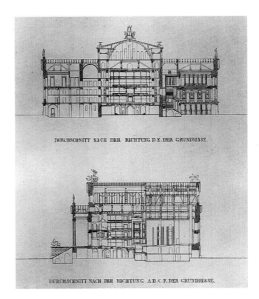

FIGURE 14

Two sections of the Schauspielhaus, Berlin, 1821, showing the concert hall and theater (cat. no. 56).

DURCHSCHNITT NACH DER RICHTUNG D.E. DER GRUNDRISSE.

DURCHSCHNITT NACH DER RICHTUNG A.B.C.F. DER GRUNDRISSE.

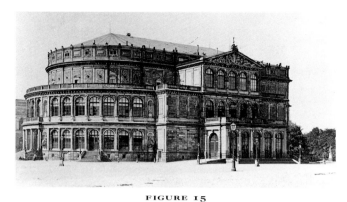

FIGURE 15

Gottfried Semper, First Opera House, Dresden,
1837–41.

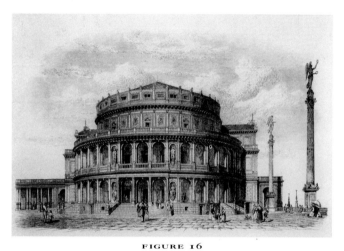

FIGURE 16

Gottfried Semper, First Opera House, Dresden,
1837–41.

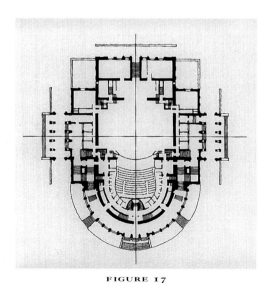

FIGURE 17

Gottfried Semper, Ground plan of the first Opera House,
Dresden, 1837–41.

Here, the theater had no institutional competitors. It could become a unitary shrine to artistic/cultural rejuvenation. In the words of historian Marvin Carlson, "Instead of a major urban landmark or the organizing node of an urban district, at Bayreuth the theater became the central element of an entire community."[34]

Wagner wanted to re-affiliate theater with its heritage in Greek antiquity. Alongside Nietzsche, Wagner felt that the bourgeois rational investigation into the art of theater had not led to greater insights of human existence, but merely to an elucidation of the distance that separated the bourgeois subject from those truths. In his essay "Die Kunst und die Revolution" (1849), Wagner inveighed strongly against artistic specialization and irrelevance. Contrasting ancient Greek and modern theater, Wagner found a great impoverishment of spirit in the latter. Greek art, he believed, expressed the deepest and most profound consciousness of a collective people; it merged culture and nature.[35] Modern art smelled only of property and power.

Theater must then renew industrial society. In Wagner's words: "Tragedy will become the celebration of humanity: in it, released from every convention and etiquette, the free, strong, and beautiful man will celebrate the delights and pains of his loves."[36] The aim of Wagner's opera and theater proposals was to recapture an organic world in which artistic purposiveness, theatrical performance, and overall culture were united: to found a new community upon a fusion of art and spirit in the creation of a *Gesamtkunstwerk*.[37] Opera became a new religion; it was the modern form of Greek tragic drama. And following Friedrich Schopenhauer's theory of the musical sublime, Wagner foresaw the theatrical experience as an artistic release from worldly cares and the domination of humanity by ceaseless desires. In his vision of theatrical architecture and performance, Wagner sought to bolster neither the hierarchical world of the aristocratic court nor the rational perceptions of order in democratic bourgeois society. Instead, within the all-embracing confines of the operatic performance, the audience would lose sense of itself and its divisions from the rest of reality.

The culmination of Wagner's vision of the theater was the Bayreuth Festspielhaus (Festival Theater; 1872–76), designed by Otto Brückwald (1841–1904).[38] For the interior, Brückwald followed the precedent of Semper's first Opera House and designed a fan-shaped auditorium with a steeply raked incline in order that all seats would afford clear sight lines of the picture stage (see *figs. 19* and *20*). Although the rear wall still contained royal boxes, other tiered boxes and galleries were eliminated to correspond to Wagner's vision of an egalitarian social community.[39] The darkened auditorium re-established the priority of the primordial mytho-poetic act on the Wagnerian stage. Unlike Schinkel's obsession with representation and Romantic extension of theatrical experience into wider realms of life, Wagner sought to create a complete world within the theater. His realistic interior sets required frequent scene changes.

For the exterior, the Festspielhaus followed the advances of Gilly's and Semper's theater physiognomy in part—the external form clearly communicated the volumes of the interior space. But, due to the building's bulky orthogonal massing—except for its elliptical curve at the rear of the auditorium—it achieved these results in decidedly ungraceful fashion (see *fig. 18*). To complement this disharmony, the façade ornamentation utilized motifs from both classicism and medieval heavy-timber stucco. Conflicts between the Greek image of the theater as an elevated platform for artistic creation and the medieval sources of the Germanic tales in Wagnerian opera are apparent. Wagner's new artistic assemblage drew its inspiration from mythical images of artistic and social conditions whose harmony is understandable only through their supposed distance from modern bourgeois ideology.

CONCLUSION

Throughout its history in nineteenth-century Germany, the public theater was subject to bourgeois aspirations, which were torn between hostility and affiliation to aristocratic culture. These divergent aspirations led to mixed architectural solutions that go a long way to explaining the historicist identity of bourgeois architecture. In some cases, architects sought to maintain and mimic the order of the court theater through the manipulation of conventional forms representing aristocratic values and spatial organization. In others, they allied themselves with the spirit of the bourgeois revolution by assuming scientific empiricism and Neoclassical ideology, transforming the public theater into a version of a new rational order.

In all cases, the public theater expressed distinct ambitions from its predecessor, the court theater. In the Baroque age, power and artistic representation were intentionally removed from public view, imperceivable through the thick, plastic walls and highly ornamented exteriors of palace façades. As Gilles Deleuze has written: "Baroque architecture can be defined as the severing of the façade from the inside,

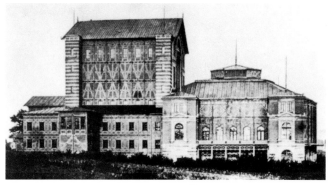

FIGURE 18

Otto Brückwald, Festspielhaus, Bayreuth, 1872–76. Photo: Detta and Michael Petzt, *Die Richard-Wagner-Bühne König Ludwigs II.* (Munich, 1970), fig. 747.

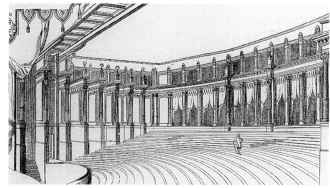

FIGURE 19

Otto Brückwald, Perspective view of the interior of the Festspielhaus, Bayreuth, 1872–76. Photo: Otto Brückwald, "Das Bühnenfestspielhaus zu Bayreuth," *Deutsche Bauzeitung*, 9 (1875), p. 5.

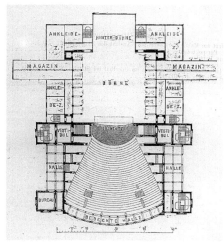

FIGURE 20

Otto Brückwald, Ground plan of the Festspielhaus, Bayreuth, 1872–76. Photo: Otto Brückwald, "Das Bühnenfestspielhaus zu Bayreuth," *Deutsche Bauzeitung*, 9 (1875), p. 1.

of the interior from exterior…in such conditions that each of the two terms thrusts the other forward."[40] Likewise, for the court society, artistic representation severed the public and private realms, and in the process made them dependent upon each other to a degree greater than ever before. The hermetic spectacles of the court contained evolving notions of national unity that would gradually envelop world culture.

The public theater, in its incarnation as the exteriorization of artistic representation and nation-making, left the court model behind. Replacing the rhetorical emblem of monarchial character with the new universal values of art and reason, the public theater strove toward an emancipation of humanity through performance architecture. Unlike court theater, where representation never pointed beyond its own paths of inflection, the public theater endowed artistic representation with the momentous qualities of connecting interior to exterior, private to public, and contemporary society to nature and history. Utilizing the theater as an artistic mirror, the rising bourgeois class attempted to create more meaningful worlds than that which they experienced in the fragmented reality of everyday life. Theater design offered a renewed status for architecture as the center of the arts, and for the architect as the master builder of modern culture.

Nonetheless, the history of theater design during this era expresses the difficulties inherent in the bourgeois attempt at creating an isomorphism of their thoughts and artistic institutions. Theater design led to a quest for self-realization on the part of the bourgeoisie in both the culture of everyday life and the heroic simplicity of history and nature. All levels of theatrical representation witnessed a conflict between Romantic notions of the imagination and originality and Neoclassical ideas of rule and imitation. In this sense, the emergence of the public theater was a result of the nineteenth century's attempt to dissolve barriers between the new notions of individuality and nature. Designs for public theater stand out as bourgeois visions of new unified landscapes of reality. From seating, to stage, to a building's external design and appearance, to urban scheme, the theater insinuated a duplication (though in more perfect form) of existence. In Schinkel's set designs, a multiplicity of representational realms were created as analogue of natural and historical unity. Here, art (as architecture) represents art (as performance) represents art (as life).

Yet, for Schinkel as for other theater designers, the aesthetic universal was an investigatory system, and not a metaphysical foundation. Theatrical art was incapable of merging or dissolving the different layers of reality it disclosed. For the bourgeois public theater, aesthetic realism was shackled to its instinct for perpetual representation.

This sentiment for privatized artistic perception contributed to a state of artistic isolation that mirrored the social isolation endemic to the emerging industrial city. In the theaters of Gilly, Schinkel, and Semper, the audience was in many ways more separated from the stage than in the court theater, and, at the same time, also separated from each other. Thrust by drama or music into a demanding and almost hypnotic realm of art, spectators were subject to a hegemonic regime as imperial as that of the most powerful royal patron. Presumably, theater spectators were to experience a release from sensuous desire and everyday distractions. More truthfully, they became enslaved to the idea of art itself, and to the power of its representations to make poetry out of their everyday lives. Art became a pedigree of bourgeois society, profitable for material as well as social advancement, and thus a barrier to the harmonious and egalitarian image of nature and history it promoted.

Between the time of Knobelsdorff and Wagner, design for the public theater expresses one of the central dilemmas of modern culture: the further fragmentation of culture at the hands of artistic representation which, then, stimulates calls for a rejection of reason and an organic rebirth of society. For Wagner, as his many successors would realize, the bourgeois project of a society governed by art was unable to nurture satisfactory community. As its many critics during the second half of the century were quick to point out, the artistic universal created increasingly egocentric portraits of reality, independent of the hierarchical undertones of the court stage, but unable to attain a cohesive culture comparable to that of the aristocracy. Wagner's *Gesamtkunstwerk* was a compromise: a removal of public theater from middle-class society to a newly isolated domain; and the enshrinement of a collective artistic experience. But, seen from its anti-cosmopolitan standpoint, Wagner's theater enshrinement of art as a collective religion was overtly antagonistic to everyday reality. Art assumed a reclusive and exclusive nature at Bayreuth. If Wagner had sought to replicate in some way both aristocratic isolation and Greek naturalism, his self-centered form of artistic representation left the theater bereft of either monarchial order or bourgeois measure and tolerance.

NOTES

1. For a detailed discussion of these philosophical issues in theater design from ancient Greece to the twentieth century, see Dagobert Frey, "Zuschauer und Bühne: Eine Untersuchung über das Realitätsproblem des Schauspiels," in *Kunstwissenschaftliche Grundfragen* (Vienna: Rudolf M. Rohrer, 1946).

2. Margarete Baur-Heinhold, *The Baroque Theater: A Cultural History of the 17th and 18th Centuries* (New York: McGraw-Hill, 1967), p. 14.

3. Norbert Elias, *Power and Civility*, trans. Edmund Jephcott (New York: Pantheon, 1982), pp. 258–70.

4. Jo Mielziner, *The Shapes of Our Theater* (New York: Charles N. Potter, 1970), pp. 42–43.

5. Ibid., p. 48.

6. Donald C. Mullin, *The Development of the Playhouse* (Berkeley and Los Angeles: University of California Press, 1970), p. 44.

7. Voltaire, "A Discourse on Tragedy," in Barrett Clark, ed., *European Theories of the Drama* (New York: Crown, 1945), p. 236.

8. Rémy Saisselin, *The Enlightenment against the Baroque: Economics and Aesthetics in the Eighteenth Century* (Berkeley and Los Angeles: University of California Press, 1992), p. 37.

9. For a history of this cultural institution, see Erich Meffert, *Das Haus der Staatsoper und seine Baumeister* (Leipzig: Max Beck Verlag, 1942).

10. Marvin Carlson, *Places of Performance: The Semiotics of Theater Architecture* (Ithaca: Cornell University Press, 1989), p. 73.

11. Hans-Joachim Kadatz, *Georg Wenzeslaus von Knobelsdorff, Baumeister Friedrichs II* (Munich: C. H. Beck, 1983), p. 131.

12. Gotthold Ephraim Lessing, *Hamburgische Dramaturgie* (Halle: Buchhandlung des Waisenhauses, 1878), p. 40.

13. Similarly, the modeling of theatrical representation on Greek dramatic tragedy is well illustrated by the ancient themes in Gluck's operas and Goethe's plays, even if ancient tragedies themselves were not performed in most German theaters. On the predominance of French classical dramas and antique themes by German authors, see Lothar Schirmer, "Theater im 19. und 20. Jahrhundert," in Willmuth Arenhövel and Christa Schreiver, eds. *Berlin und die Antike: Aufsätze* (Berlin: Wasmuth, 1979), pp. 303–17.

14. Franz Benedikt Biermann, "Karl Friedrich Schinkel und Gottfried Semper als Reformatoren des Theaterbaues," *Wasmuths Monatshefte für Baukunst*, 13 (1929), pp. 251–58.

15. Mullin (note 6), p. 103.

16. Alfred Rietdorf, *Gilly: Wiedergeburt der Architektur* (Berlin: Hans von Hugo Verlag, 1940), p. 120.

17. Harald Zielske, *Deutsche Theaterbauten bis zum zweiten Weltkrieg* (Berlin: Selbstverlag der Gesellschaft für Theatergeschichte, 1971), p. 28.

18. Frey (note 1), p. 197.

19. Karl Friedrich Schinkel, "Das Prinzip der Kunst in der Architektur," in Goerd Peschken, ed., *Das architektonische Lehrbuch* in *Karl Friedrich Schinkel: Lebenswerk* (Berlin: Deutscher Kunstverlag, 1979), pp. 21–22.

20. Ibid., p. 32.

21. Karl Friedrich Schinkel, *Aus Tagebüchern und Briefen* (Berlin: Henschelverlag, 1967), p. 149.

22. Friedrich Schlegel, *Dialogue on Poetry* (1800), trans. and ed. Ernst Behler and Roman Struc (University Park: Pennsylvania State University, 1968), p. 82.

23. Paul Ortwin Rave, ed., *Berlin, Erster Teil, Bauten für die Kunst, Kirchen, Denkmalpflege* in *Karl Friedrich Schinkel: Lebenswerk* (Berlin: Deutscher Kunstverlag, 1941), p. 80.

24. Ibid., p. 87.

25. Rebecca Hilliker, "Karl Friedrich Schinkel's Scenic Designs for *Die Zauberflöte*: The Definitive Expression of Illusion and Symbol," *Nineteenth Century Theater*, 17 (Summer-Winter 1989), p. 15.

26. Hermann G. Pundt, *Schinkel's Berlin: A Study in Environmental Planning* (Cambridge, Mass.: Harvard University Press, 1972), p. 137.

27. Schinkel was by no means the only architect to seize upon the possibility for realizing a pure realm of artistic representation in theater. In the *Vorschlagen zur Verbesserung der Schauspielhäuser* (1802), Louis Catel proposed a rationalization of the stage, including the removal of fixed backdrops and a wider proscenium.

28. Eberhard Werner, *Theatergebäude: Geschichtliche Entwicklung* (Berlin: VEB, 1954), p. 102.

29. On the details of Schinkel's interior transformation, see Klaus Wever, "Karl Friedrich Schinkels Position und Beitrag zur Reform des Theaterraums," in *Karl Friedrich Schinkel: Werke und Wirkungen*, ed. Jan Fiebelkorn (Berlin: Der Senat von Berlin, 1981), pp. 196–97.

30. Helmut Börsch-Supan, *Karl Friedrich Schinkel: Bühnenentwürfe. Stage Designs* (Berlin: Ernst & Sohn, 1990), vol. 1, p. 21.

31. Ibid., p. 35.

32. Wolfgang Hänsch, *Die Semperoper: Geschichte und Wiederaufbau der Dresdner Staatsoper* (Stuttgart: Deutsche Verlags-Anstalt, 1986), p. 32.

33. Saisselin (note 8), p. 66.

34. Carlson (note 10), p. 88.

35. Richard Wagner, *Dichtungen und Schriften*, ed. Dieter Borchmeyer, 10 vols. (Frankfurt: Insel, 1983), p. 290.

36. Ibid., pp. 302–03.

37. Heinrich Habel, *Festspielhaus und Wahnfried: Geplante und ausgeführte Bauten Richard Wagners* (Munich: Prestel, 1985), p. 15.

38. See Otto Brückwald, "Das Bühnenfestspielhaus zu Bayreuth," *Deutsche Bauzeitung* 9 (1875), pp. 1–5.

39. Richard Leacroft and Helen Leacroft, *Theatre and Playhouse: An Illustrated Survey of Theatre Building from Ancient Greece to the Present Day* (London and New York: Methuen, 1984), pp. 113–14.

40. Gilles Deleuze, *The Fold: Leibniz and the Baroque*, trans. Tom Conley (Minneapolis: University of Minnesota Press, 1993), p. 28.

CHRISTOPH MARTIN VOGTHERR

Freie Universität, Berlin

Even a brief glance at Schinkel's own publication of his architectural works shows how much importance he attached to the environment of his buildings. In his *Sammlung architektonischer Entwürfe (Collection of Architectural Designs)*, Schinkel not only used standard ground plans, elevations, and cross-sections, but also presented many of his projects in perspective drawings, with the aim of indicating their natural or built surroundings.[1] On a few occasions, he added area maps to give an exact sense of a building's location.

Two of his projects, the Charlottenhof villa and the Römische Bäder (Roman Baths), are situated in the royal

FIGURE 1

Peter Joseph Lenné, Project for the Charlottenhof
gardens, Potsdam, 1825. Pen, wash,
and pencil on paper, 61 x 56.8 cm.
SSG Potsdam-Sanssouci, Plansammlung,
no. 3695.

gardens at Potsdam, southwest of Berlin. Schinkel used several perspective views and an area map for both of these buildings in the *Sammlung*—a strong indication of how much he considered them to be part of their environment.[2] More than with other buildings, he seemed to think that only a sequence of views could convey their spatial arrangement and interdependence. In Potsdam, it is still possible to experience Schinkel's buildings as intended: Charlottenhof and the Römische Bäder have been well preserved. The gardens around them are among the most carefully restored landscape gardens in Europe.

That Schinkel's connection with landscape design has received little attention is due to the underestimation of the artistic importance of landscape gardens.[3] Even today, gardens are too often considered mere appendages to buildings. In the eighteenth and nineteenth centuries, however, the design of landscape gardens was recognized as a major art form, one that had reached an advanced degree of theoretical development and sophistication. In the words of the English landscape designer Humphry Repton, landscape gardening was an "appeal…to the understanding," because the contribution of the designer would be largely hidden to the uneducated.[4] Landscape design "must studiously conceal every interference of art, however expensive, by which the scenery is improved, making the whole appear the production of nature only."[5]

Schinkel applied the full palate of possibilities that landscape gardening offered in order to intensify the experience of all of his buildings. Not only did he seek to make each building part of a natural environment, but he also used gardening to control the way each would be perceived. Thus, all of Schinkel's country houses and villas can be fully appreciated only if they are seen in the context of their surrounding gardens. The first part of this essay will investigate this interaction through a close analysis of the Charlottenhof site. Furthermore, many methods and techniques of landscape garden design actually influenced Schinkel's output as an architect and as a city planner; the second part of this essay will explore this by example of the Berlin city center.

FIGURE 2

Perspective view of Charlottenhof, Potsdam, from the
northwest and from the northeast, with a small elevation of
the building prior to remodeling, 1831.
Photo: *Sammlung architektonischer Entwürfe* (Berlin, 1866).

FIGURE 3

Site plan and perspective view of Charlottenhof,
Potsdam, 1831 (cat. no. 40).

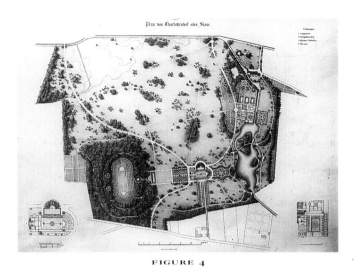

In 1825, Crown Prince Friedrich Wilhelm of Prussia received a small estate with an eighteenth-century house called Charlottenhof, immediately south of the royal gardens in Potsdam, as a present from his father, King Friedrich Wilhelm III. This modest site was to become one of the major nineteenth-century extensions to the vast expanse of Rococo gardens that Friedrich II had laid out around Schloß Sanssouci beginning in 1744. Over a span of several decades starting in the mid-1820s, various buildings and gardens were added to Charlottenhof, most notably the Römische Bäder.[6] (As is customary, in this essay "Charlottenhof" will be used to designate this whole area.) Charlottenhof was the work of three men: the architect Karl Friedrich Schinkel, the garden designer Peter Joseph Lenné, and Crown Prince Friedrich Wilhelm (later King Friedrich Wilhelm IV).[7] The Crown Prince was a gifted dilettante in architecture and actively influenced the design of his villa. Since the individual contributions of Schinkel, Lenné, and Friedrich Wilhelm remain unclear, given the often informal working relationships and the long and continous development of the Charlottenhof grounds, it is sensible to consider Charlottenhof a collective project.[8]

At the time that Friedrich Wilhelm received the estate, the court gardener Lenné presented three drawings, with options for transforming the area into a landscape garden. Lenné's designs were altered many times before they were executed. While I shall not reexamine the long and complicated planning history of Charlottenhof in this essay, it is illuminating to look at Lenné's first project of 1825 (fig. 1), which was apparently designed before Schinkel and Friedrich Wilhelm joined the project.[9] From the beginning, Lenné planned to demolish all minor buildings of the former estate, such as stables and sheds. His general layout of the paths was already close to what was later executed. But in this early state he still expected to maintain the shape of the villa, as is shown on one of the plates of Schinkel's *Sammlung architektonischer Entwürfe (fig. 2)*. Given the limited funds for remodeling the existing house, this assumption was certainly realistic. Consequently, Lenné at first treated the house as a plain rectangle. Only on its south side did he plan to extend the former main avenue into a small grove.

By contrast, Friedrich Wilhelm and Schinkel pushed for fundamental alterations. Though Schinkel kept the walls of the eighteenth-century house—its original simple shape can still be traced both on the exterior and in the basic rectangle of its ground plan *(fig. 3)*—around this core the building was transformed in several significant respects. Far more than simply in the Doric detailing, which was applied to the surface of the building, these changes dramatically altered the way in which Charlottenhof related to its environment.[10] Several additions to the house opened up its ground plan, most notably the large terrace on the east side of the building. Here, a large, rectangular area was raised to the level of the villa's upper floor. A pergola defined the southern edge of the terrace, which sloped down to the level of the park on its north side. The eastern end was marked by an exedra, an elaborate, half-circular stone bench, offering principal views of the east façade and of the garden grounds (see *fig. 3*). These changes of the building's outline were later marked on Lenné's first garden plan, possibly by the Crown Prince himself (see *fig. 1*). In the end, the executed garden design responded to these changes by the insertion of an entire group of small, formal areas between the building and the park *(fig. 4)*. These alterations accorded with the opinion of Humphry Repton, who advised in favor of regular elements near the house.[11]

Paths and drives are the basis of every landscape garden. The visitor is required to stay on them in order to have the appropriate garden experience. Surface relief, plants, and architecture are arranged to create vistas that can be seen at certain moments from the paths. Like a script for a film, the paths of a garden determine the sequence of images that a visitor should see—when buildings, lakes, and other scenic features become visible, how often, from which perspective, and in what combination. Although the paths are fundamental for the experience of the landscape garden, they are not meant to be visual features themselves: "Paths are the silent guides of the walking person and they must serve to have them find each delight that the area can offer without constraint."[12] Due to the paramount importance of paths, their layout was the first stage of work done at Charlottenhof.[13] As the house was situated close to the southern border of the newly acquired estate, a large lawn stretched north of it. Two major new approaches were planned in order to link the Charlottenhof estate with the existing grounds: one from the northwest, leading from Friedrich II's gigantic Neues Palais (New Palace) of 1763 to 69; the other from the northeast, connecting it with Sanssouci and the Rococo Chinese Teahouse. The existing approach from the south, a straight avenue, was kept, although as the least important one. Visitors were expected to approach the villa from either the Neues Palais or Sanssouci (see *fig. 4*).

One should therefore imagine Charlottenhof as perceived by a visitor while walking. Coming from the Neues Palais, one gets a first, brief glimpse of the villa from a great distance. It then disappears, and only much later reemerges. Through a grove, one sees the villa frontally, as the rather austere west façade comes into view: on a wide socle, a narrow, pedimented building now seems to rise in its center, very much like a temple in a holy grove *(fig. 5)*.[14] Only upon further approaching the building does one realize that this shape of the façade is a deception: the trees of the quincunx grove blend out the lateral parts of the villa's upper story.[15] The trees are cut in such a way that the socle is fully visible, while the upper stories are hidden on both sides. This illusion only works from straight ahead, and, accordingly, the garden design forces the viewer to approach the building from that direction. Schinkel's area map from the *Sammlung (fig. 3)* outlines two greenhouses that were originally planned to frame the grove on both sides, but were never executed; two arbors now fulfill a similar function. The protruding central bay of the west façade, which appears to be the temple, has a very flat surface relief, simply because it is only visible from straight ahead.[16] It marks the main entrance to the villa, where a vestibule with a double flight of stairs leads to the living quarters on the upper level of the building. Two fountains, one at the center of the grove and the other within the vestibule, visually link inside and outside.

Approaching Charlottenhof from the northeast, one gathers an impression of the building that seems incompatible with the temple one sees on the other side. Over long

FIGURE 5

West façade of Charlottenhof, Potsdam, 1826–28.

FIGURE 6

South side of the pergola at Charlottenhof, Potsdam, 1826–28.

intervals of time, the villa remains visible from the main path. Yet again, the visitor is deceived. Because of the sloping lawn on the north side of the terrace, the lower story of the villa is largely hidden. The building appears to be a one-story structure, even smaller than it actually is. This impression can also be sensed on one of Schinkel's engravings *(fig. 2*, bottom). The same illusion works in the view from the exedra on the terrace *(fig. 3)*.

Only when approaching the building from the south does the visitor get a less composed view *(fig. 6)*. The old avenue leads straight towards the south side of the terrace, where the substructure and the pergola on top can be seen. This view is much less official in character. Entering the garden from this side, one first expects a truly rural complex, consisting of plantings and Italian vernacular architecture.

Only gradually is one led around the building to experience its main façades and its connection with Sanssouci park.

Schinkel and Lenné had to deal with a flat and unattractive site, a virtual *tabula rasa*. When the artificial lake east of the villa was dug out, the soil was used to create several slight surface modulations in the park. But the major feature employed to overcome the dullness of the area was the terrace, for it offers a view like that from a balcony while at the same time varying the appearance of the villa. The exedra on the eastern end of the terrace offers the most extensive garden experience from any point around the building.[17] Schinkel's engraving demonstrates how carefully this perspective was staged *(fig. 3)*. An awning over the exedra frames the field of vision.[18] The east façade is seen frontally, with the three fountains on the terrace in front. In fact, the combination of the half-circular exedra and the east façade is like an abbreviation of an antique theater.[19] To the left, the view is closed off by the pergola, which gives the picture a strong perspectival force, making the villa appear more distant. This is clearly the main façade of the building. It can be seen both from the terrace, offering a straight view of the building, and from the garden, where the whole complex appears from different oblique angles. Accordingly, the pedimented central bay of the east façade is much more sculptural than the flatter west façade, which is meant to be seen from straight ahead only.

From the terrace, the view stretches far into the park. In the background, one can see the large dome of the Neues Palais, as well as the two smaller domes of the so-called Communs (the service buildings of the palace) and the Antikentempel (Temple of Antiquities), all four buildings

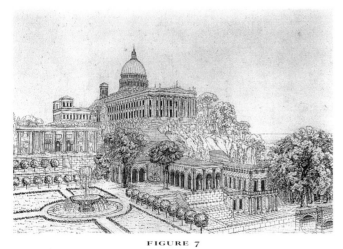

FIGURE 7

Perspective view of a domed cathedral or palace on a hill, overlooking a garden, c. 1803–30 (cat. no. 26).

erected under Friedrich II. A change of planning served to cover more of the buildings by trees; only the dome and the upper part of the Neues Palais can still be seen today. This view offers the perspective of a mature landscape with a seemingly long history, a *Kulturlandschaft*. More specifically, the Neues Palais evokes Friedrich II, the period of Prussian history that was considered most glorious by Crown Prince Friedrich Wilhelm and many of his contemporaries, and thus, it could not be screened out, even though its architectural style was hardly appreciated at Schinkel's time. The dome of the Neues Palais also served to rouse memories of the dome of St. Peter's in Rome, adding to the strongly Italian flavor of the Charlottenhof area. Later, St. Peter's was more literally quoted by Schinkel in his Potsdam Nikolaikirche (1826–49), the classical dome of which served as a backdrop for most of the royal residences in and around Potsdam, such as Schloß Glienicke and Schloß Babelsberg, further strengthening the illusion of a southern Arcadia.[20]

The Charlottenhof terrace was adapted from Italian villas that Schinkel had visited on his first Italian journey (1803–04). Schinkel and Friedrich Wilhelm also knew them through Percier and Fontaine's *Choix des plus célèbres maisons de plaisance de Rome et de ses environs*, which contained ground plans and views of many villas.[21] The general layout of the terrace closely resembles the plan for the much larger Villa Albani, as published by Percier and Fontaine. The shape and position of the central fountain, for example, were directly taken from these Italian models. More importantly, several villa gardens from the *Choix* were laid out on different levels, offering views onto the countryside, and one of Percier and Fontaine's plates of the Villa Medici even featured the dome of St. Peter's just where Neues Palais appears in Schinkel's view of Charlottenhof.[22] Schinkel singled out similar elements in his description of Italian villas: "Majestic hedges, terraces, stairs, pine-tree groves, fountains, flower *parterres*, situated in a way that the major part of Rome and all the distant areas around can be seen in between."[23] These comparisons show how concretely the allusions to Italian design were meant. But at the same time they demonstrate how ingeniously these devices were applied to a radically different situation. For while the Italian villas could make full use of their spectacular settings, their features were used in Potsdam to create marvels out of an originally unremarkable place, one which lacked the rich views, differences in elevation, and lush vegetation of its Italian models.

FIGURE 8

Perspective elevation of a landscaped garden arranged
as a hippodrome at Charlottenhof, Potsdam, c. 1830
(cat. no. 39).

The combination of a terraced garden with a fountain in its center and a large, domed building recurs several times in Schinkel's œuvre, e.g., in his painting *Landscape with a Pilgrim*[24] and in his depiction of a domed cathedral or palace on a hill *(fig. 7)*. In both cases, the viewer is situated far above the terrace, although his location is unclear. But the painting, the drawing, and the actual garden all use the same vocabulary, alluding to the same ideal of a classical, southern, cultivated landscape.

From inside, the villa presents two main views of the grounds: one, looking east across the terrace, a view actually included in Schinkel's *Sammlung*;[25] and the other looking north across the wide lawn in the center of the Charlottenhof gardens. Three windows on the north side offer a wide-angled panorama. Departing once again from the shape of the original building, Schinkel added a small half-circular protruding bay, following Repton's advice that "it is not sufficient to have a cross light or windows in two sides of the room at right angles with each other; but there must be one in an oblique direction, which can only be obtained by a bow-window: and although there may be some advantage in making the different views from a house distinct landscapes, yet as the villa requires a more extensive prospect than a constant residence, so the bow-window is peculiarly applicable to the villa."[26] Thus, while the design of the two main façades mainly served the outside appearance of the building, the alteration of the north side focused on the perception of the garden from the inside.

The same combination of views in different directions is also the topic of a pair of watercolors that Schinkel made for a Prussian noblewoman. Schinkel produced both a view of a villa through an arbor and a view out of a loggia onto a wide landscape. He used the entire vocabulary of the Italian villa for these scenes. One of these drawings *(pl. 7)* features a round-arched loggia, terraces, and a large arbor over a wide flight of stairs. The characteristic shape of the fence in the foreground, composed of semicircular terracotta elements, is used at the Römische Bäder in Charlottenhof. Schinkel took this feature directly from the Villa Albani.[27] As a play with German words, he named the drawing shown here an *Einsicht* (insight), its counterpart *Aussicht* (perspective). Both terms are meant to be understood as complementary states of mind. It is particularly telling that Schinkel chose the garden of an Italian villa to represent this literal and symbolic dichotomy.

After the villa at Charlottenhof had been finished, work did not stop on the site. Continuously, smaller and larger changes were introduced, buildings and sculptures were added, and grounds modified. Just west of the villa, Friedrich Wilhelm intended to erect an antique country-house, a free adaptation of Pliny's villas. A hippodrome, a large plantation in the shape of a racecourse, features prominently in Pliny's description of his villa Tuscum. Erected from 1836 onwards, the hippodrome is the only part of Friedrich Wilhelm's large scheme that was ever carried out.[28]

Schinkel's cross-section of the hippodrome *(fig. 8)* was included in the last group of drawings that constitute the *Sammlung*.[29] The arrangement of several stepped rows of trees, surrounding the central area, goes back to Friedrich Wilhelm. According to the Crown Prince's wishes, Schinkel put these rows closer together, in order to intensify the impact of the resulting open-air space. Of the two projected structures inside the hippodrome, only the *stibadium*—a raised and covered viewing platform (visible on the left in the drawing)—was built. Friedrich Wilhelm wanted the hippodrome to be accessible only through a labyrinth of small, winding paths in the surrounding wooded area. He hoped thereby to heighten the impression of an enclosed space, in contrast to Pliny's stress on the visual links between his villa and the hippodrome. As a feature of the Charlottenhof garden grounds, the hippodrome does not have much to do with Schinkel's very careful efforts to have architecture and surrounding gardens interlink, though Schinkel did try to increase its architectural character in his contribution to the planning process.[30] The Potsdam hippodrome should rather be seen as a enclosed, thematic garden, as described by Repton.

Most important among the additions to Charlottenhof, however, are the so-called Römische Bäder (Roman Baths), a group of buildings northeast of the villa. Work on them

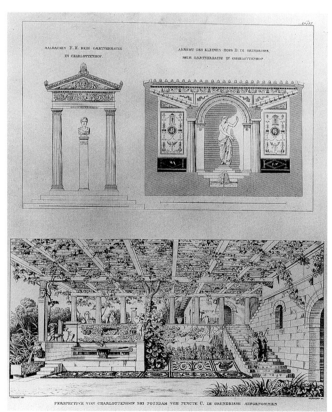

started in 1829 and continued until 1836.[31] They number among the most sophisticated of Schinkel's works, and only a few of their features can be pointed out in this essay. In contrast to the Charlottenhof villa, the Römische Bäder are a fundamentally picturesque grouping of buildings in different styles, mixing Italian vernacular and classical architecture. Once again, buildings and gardens are intimately linked. The Römische Bäder added a new, important view from Charlottenhof. Italian rural architecture could now be seen from the villa, increasing the power of the southern allusion.[32] When the trees were still smaller, this view even blended with Friedrich II's artificial antique ruins on the Ruinenberg (a hill near Schloß Sanssouci) in the far distance beyond the Römische Bäder, as if offering a glimpse of classical antiquity.[33]

The house of the court gardener, a large, asymmetrical structure with a tower, forms the core of the Römische Bäder. While the gardens and terraces of Charlottenhof refer to Italian villas, Schinkel here very directly quoted rural architecture. Similar to many Italian vernacular houses that he had drawn on his trips to Italy, it is surrounded by pergolas linking it with other units of the complex. The largest one of them, just north of the house, covers the entrance to the courtyard *(fig. 9)*.[34] In the shadow of a vine, a raised seat and a fountain invite the visitor to rest. The view of the park from under the pergola is visually structured by the geometric grid of the wooden beams above, which functions like a coordinate system for the perception of the surrounding spaces. As a transitional room, this pergola leads into the park, into the courtyard, and onto the roof. Its geometric grid prepares for all these impressions. In Schinkel's view of the Traunsee of 1811 (see Forster, *fig. 9*), a grid of wooden beams is suspended between an Austrian village house and a large tree, framing and defining the view of the Traunsee in the distance in a similar way. Some benches and a table on the left and a fountain on the right furnish the arbor. The pergola at the Römische Bäder translates the same situation into Italian vernacular, but all the basic elements stay the same. Here we have two versions of a universal vocabulary of architectural vernacular.[35]

The Römische Bäder offered new views on Charlottenhof, most importantly from the roof of the arcaded hall, a perspective Schinkel used for his *Sammlung architektonischer Entwürfe (fig.10)*. Charlottenhof appears in the background, again as a seemingly one-story building. Because of its small size, it looks more distant than it actually is. The Dampfmaschinenhaus (Steam Engine House),

FIGURE 10

Perspective view of the courtyard of the Römische Bäder
(Roman Baths), Potsdam, from above and northeast, with
Charlottenhof in the background, 1835. Photo: *Sammlung
architektonischer Entwürfe* (Berlin, 1866).

containing the engines and pumps for the fountains, features quite prominently on the left, the smoke rising from its chimney fusing with the water of the fountain within the courtyard. Thus, with the growing importance of this addition, Charlottenhof was also transformed into a background vista, completing the southern landscape created around the Römische Bäder.

One of the pavilions of the Römische Bäder actually housed a copy of one of Schinkel's chief works as a painter: *Blick in Griechenlands Blüte (A View of Greece in Its Prime;* see Van Zanten, *fig. 1).*[36] This painting depicts a Greek city in a wide landscape, complete with a whole range of public buildings, monuments, and a major temple under construction in the foreground. It is Schinkel's vision of a perfect community, defining itself through culture, through the high importance of public affairs, and through the personal commitment of its citizens. Not by chance, this ideal place is set in Greece, the major historical reference for early nineteenth-century Berlin. From inside the Tea Pavilion, Schinkel's painted vision fused with the landscape garden around it, giving the latter an additional layer of meaning.

Not incidentally, neither the painting nor the Charlottenhof grounds feature ruins, which were otherwise so typical of landscape gardens.[37] On the contrary, the painting depicts the process of construction. Schinkel's vision of antiquity and of the South is not melancholic, but emphatically forward-looking and in many respects utopian. Schinkel's painting is like a hidden clue to his understanding of landscape, both in Potsdam and, as we shall see, in his designs for the Berlin city center. For the landscape garden was, like many of Schinkel's buildings, a social space. In fact, the engravings of Schinkel's *Sammlung* are often enlivened with groups of people looking at the buildings and landscapes; they converse in small groups while walking or enjoying the views, reasoning about their observations. The intention was to move the viewer as an emotional and as a rational being, as a citizen.[38] Not by chance, Schinkel usually depicted men in his engravings, inasmuch as women were still denied the status of citizens. Schinkel's painting in the Tea Pavilion of the Römische Bäder shows how the Charlottenhof grounds can be interpreted as a political landscape.

At Charlottenhof, then, Schinkel used the full range of techniques of landscape gardening to enhance his buildings. The relatively small villa is staged in different views, effectively combining different building types and styles in one building—the stern classical temple, the small antique villa, the Italian rural building. Charlottenhof can only be experienced fully while moving—and reasoning. Fundamental to Schinkel's landscape approach is the fact that he (and Lenné) cared not only for the view *of* but also *from* the building. The terrace of Charlottenhof presents a panorama of Potsdam, while the windows on the protruding bay on the north side of the villa provide a sequence of framed pictures. These techniques reappear to different degrees in Schinkel's work as an architect and a city planner. The reasons for this are two-fold: first, that landscape gardening was one of the central art forms of Schinkel's time, and, second, that Schinkel consistently sought to emphasize the interaction between a building and its environment.

Schinkel also designed the Potsdam residences for two of Friedrich Wilhelm's brothers: Schloß Glienicke for Prince Karl, Schloß Babelsberg for Prince Wilhelm, the future Prussian king and German emperor, Wilhelm I. The three princes also employed Schinkel for new designs or the rebuilding of their Berlin palaces. For Wilhelm in particular, Schinkel designed several projects on different locations, none of which were executed. Yet, three of them were published in the *Sammlung* and gardens play an important role throughout.[39]

Schinkel's design of 1832 for a palace for Prince Wilhelm on the site of the Royal Library *(fig. 11)* was a major attempt to improve the Opernplatz (Opera Square), one of Berlin's major plazas.[40] The library building had been erected by Friedrich II in the forms of the Viennese Baroque; it remains today a stylistic alien in the Neoclassical heart of Berlin. Schinkel wanted to substitute for the library and an adjacent building a massive, rectangular block along the main avenue, Unter den Linden, though this structure would be complemented by a terraced, sloping part along the Opernplatz. The façades exposed to Unter den Linden were to stay in keeping with the regular character of the boulevard. The back part of the proposed palace along the Opernplatz, however, was to become an architectural garden similar to the hanging gardens of Semiramis, which Schinkel had once illustrated in one of his dioramas.[41]

Schinkel himself described this layout in his *Sammlung:* "The arrangement of the garden in this form in the center of the city gives the impression that the main story of the palace is located on a mountain. The height of the garden grants peace and quiet from the hustle and bustle in the streets and allows one to enjoy the garden completely undisturbed. The installation of this amphitheater-like garden would significantly improve the entire Opernplatz. The present somber appearance, caused by the high library building, would be changed to a lovely and serene view. The crowning glory of the whole complex would be the arcades, which would conceal from view both the city behind and the unpleasant rear buildings and gables."[42]

The terraces of this "amphitheater-like garden" were to offer a view of the Berlin city center—an urban version of the Charlottenhof terrace.[43] The plants on the terraces would screen and frame the buildings of Berlin, including the Opera House, Schinkel's own Neue Wache (New Guardhouse), and the eastern end of Unter den Linden, creating the impression, once again, of a *Kulturlandschaft.*

As Schinkel pointed out in his text, the shape of the design was also determined by the way it would be looked at, improving the shape of the Opernplatz considerably. Schinkel's drawing for the *Sammlung* features the palace in an oblique view from the northeast, exactly the perspective from which the curved baroque façade of the library looked most awkward. Schinkel's drawing tries to make a strong point for its replacement.

The design of the Lustgarten (Pleasure Garden) in central Berlin is a prime example of how Schinkel applied landscaping techniques to city planning.[44] In 1817, Schinkel developed his first master plan for the restructuring of the Berlin city center. With the Neue Wache and the Schauspielhaus (Theater), Schinkel had already altered the shape of central Berlin, and now he was given the opportunity to restructure the very heart of the political capital, the Lustgarten north of the Königliches Schloß (Royal Palace). The combination of the palace, the cathedral on the east side, and the Zeughaus (Arsenal) on the west side, just across the Kupfergraben branch of the River Spree, made this site into the political center of Berlin, where king, church, and army were represented.

The Lustgarten had originally been laid out as the Baroque garden of the Königliches Schloß, but by the 1820s, it had lain neglected for a century.[45] This area was the starting point of Unter den Linden, Berlin's major boulevard, but only a provisional wooden bridge connected it with this avenue. The view that it offered from the palace was bleak: an unsystematically developed industrial area

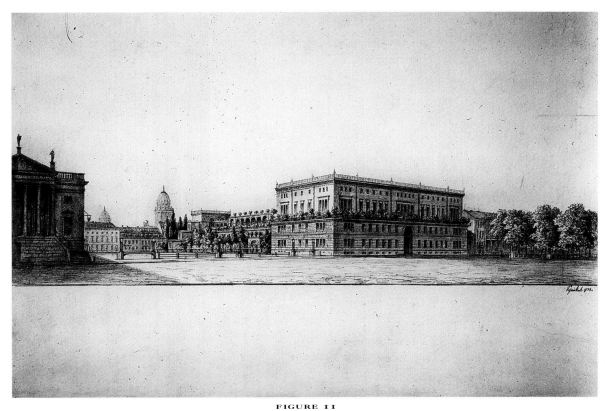

FIGURE 11

Perspective view of a proposed palace for Prince Wilhelm
on Unter den Linden, Berlin, 1832 (cat. no. 33).

FIGURE 12

Perspective rendering of the Schloßbrücke, Berlin, 1819
(cat. no. 32).

FIGURE 13

Rendered elevation of the Altes Museum (1822–30), Berlin,
with the fountain in the foreground, c. 1826 (cat. no. 34).

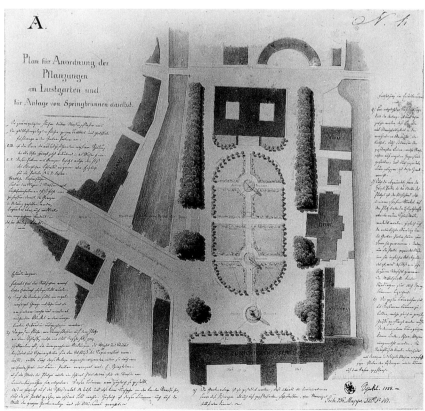

FIGURE 14

Site plan for the redesign of the Lustgarten, Berlin,
adjacent to the Altes Museum, 1828 (cat. no. 36).

stretched to the north and an industrial canal cut across what had once been a refined garden.

Schinkel first had the opportunity to tackle the problems of the Lustgarten area in 1819, when he designed a new bridge, the Schloßbrücke, linking the Lustgarten and Unter den Linden *(fig. 12)*.[46] Instead of the narrow wooden bridge, a wide and lavishly adorned stone bridge now continued in the same width of the avenue, visually linking it with the square. Schinkel planned sculptures of warriors and winged victories on eight socles along the bridge to commemorate the Prussian victory against Napoleon.[47] A few years earlier, in connection with the construction of Neue Wache, Schinkel had already eliminated another narrowing of the avenue. Running from the Brandenburger Tor (Brandenburg Gate) via the Schloßbrücke to the Royal Palace, Unter den Linden now formed a triumphal avenue. As Schinkel's drawing of the Schloßbrücke shows, at this time he imagined the Lustgarten (visible on the right) to be rather densely planted with trees.[48]

The situation changed entirely in 1822, for in that year it was decided that a new museum (now called the Altes [Old] Museum) would be erected on the north side of Lustgarten. Together with the king, the army, and the church, art was now symbolically promoted to be one of the central powers of the new Prussia. The choice of this site was Schinkel's idea, for he had been involved with an earlier scheme for the conversion of the building of the Königliche Preußische Akademie der Künste und Mechanischen Wissenschaften (Royal Prussian Academy of Arts and Mechanical Sciences) as an art museum. With his design for a new and independent museum building on a new site on the Lustgarten, Schinkel sought to resolve two problems that occupied him at that time: the construction difficulties at the Academy building and the unsatisfying situation at the Lustgarten. Schinkel proposed to create a large urban square, closing off the Lustgarten to the north with the museum building *(fig. 13)*. The culmination of Unter den Linden would thus become a true public forum.

When the exterior of the museum was finished in 1828, the future design of the Lustgarten remained to be decided upon. Schinkel's first plan from that year *(fig. 14)* shows how he intended park and museum to form an urban landscape together.[49] (The executed design is fundamentally different, because the king objected to Schinkel's plan.) In the center of the new square, Schinkel designed a large, ornate scheme of lawns, flower beds, and fountains. On both the east and west sides of the Lustgarten, rows of trees were to frame the central area. On the east side they covered all the irregularities of the adjacent buildings: the existing smaller buildings north of the cathedral, among them the Börse (Exchange), and the old and irregular pre-Baroque part of the palace. Even large parts of the cathedral would become invisible. Only its central protruding bays, which Schinkel had rebuilt into a classical portico in 1820-21, were intended to be seen. The classical colonnade of the museum and the north façade of the Königliches Schloß, would combine with it to form a group of regular classical buildings. The half-circular ends of the central lawn were also to help hide the fact that the angles formed by the main buildings were not at all regular. Schinkel's design has a very conscious character of camouflage.

Having formulated this regularization of the Lustgarten, Schinkel also staged the experience of it in a manner reminiscent of landscape gardens.[50] As one approached the square from Unter den Linden, the palace was to remain visible the whole time as a *point de vue* for the avenue. Right before the Schloßbrücke, a view onto the portico of the cathedral was to open up. Schinkel had left a gap in the western row of trees along the Lustgarten to make this view possible. Visually, the cathedral was to be linked with the Kronprinzenpalais (Crown Prince's Palace), a smaller palace on Unter den Linden where the king was living.[51] Schinkel was careful, however, not to "give away" the whole square at that point: walking towards the Schloßbrücke, one would see the cathedral portico, but not the museum, which was still covered by trees. In front of the city palace, Schinkel planned a large fountain, right on axis with Unter den Linden, which would increase the directedness of both the avenue and the Schloßbrücke towards the palace. One would next see the half-circular south end of the lawn, gently bending one's route to walk along the north façade of the palace. At that point, the museum building would become suddenly visible in its entirety. Two more fountains in the center of the square were to link the museum building to the palace. The large fountain in front of the palace was situated so that it linked several main axes: that of Unter den Linden, that of one of the portals of the palace façade (this fountain could even be seen through the palace courtyard from south of the palace), and that of the museum. As Schinkel's view of the rotunda in the center of the museum proves, the fountain also provided a *point de vue* from inside the museum, linking inside and outside in a fashion similar to the fountains in the vestibule and in front of the west façade of Charlottenhof.

The visitor first entered the museum through its grand colonnade, which was still more a part of the Lustgarten than of the museum proper—an antique stoa, dedicated by Schinkel to the memory of great Prussians whose busts were to be erected here. As at Charlottenhof, a balcony was intended to offer a view onto the Lustgarten and the city center. The staircase of the museum was situated behind the colonnade. In a unique way, it combined inside and outside, being outside the entrance doors of the museum, but already under its roof. As Schinkel's perspective view of the staircase proves, he wanted this space to be perceived in a fashion similar to his garden buildings (fig. 15).[52] Groups of men appear, marvelling at the view from the upper podium, reflecting on the message of Schinkel's frescoes on the upper floor of the staircase. This space was transitional: it led into the rooms of the picture gallery on the upper floor of the building, while at the same time it presented the spectacle of the museum colonnade, the Lustgarten, and the Berlin city center.[53] Walking upstairs, the visitor had to cross the dark lower area of the stairs to come back into the light on the second flight of stairs.[54] Upstairs one would be startled by the light, the great height one had reached, and the wide view onto the center of Berlin. The lower part of the columns would have disappeared from view, making their upper halves appear as dark, treelike objects, heightening the view onto the wide and bright space of the Lustgarten. Many years earlier, Schinkel had used a similar screen of columns in front of a distant landscape in his study of a columned hall overlooking the sea (fig. 16). In the Altes Museum, Schinkel developed this idea into a much more daring constellation. Once again, one is reminded of Schinkel's contemporary *Blick in Griechenlands Blüte* (see Van Zanten, fig. 1), where the viewer, as in the museum, is situated on the same level as the upper halves of the columns and enjoys a wide view onto a flowering community and its public buildings. Berlin has become, in the phrase of the time, *Spree-Athen*, Athens-on-the-Spree, the center of a New Greece.

Thus, the approach to the Lustgarten and the museum applies the main technique of the landscape garden, namely controlled approach, disguise, surprise, contrasts, and the staging of scenic features (in this case the civic and royal monuments of the Prussian capital). Schinkel's projects in the city center aimed to create a city landscape. Along the Kupfergraben, a side channel of the River Spree, Schinkel had the opportunity to develop this landscape to the point of perfection: with his warehouse buildings, the Altes Museum, the Schloßbrücke, and the Bauakademie (Architectural Academy), a whole sequence of geometric units stretched along the water, forming one complete river panorama.[55]

Very early in his career, Schinkel had already drawn garden scenes and had put his architectural projects in a garden context.[56] While these first attempts applied a very conventional language, his perception of landscape as a phenomenon changed fundamentally on his first trip to Italy in 1803–04. Schinkel summarized his experience in a letter to the architect David Gilly: "For the most part, the monuments of antiquity do not offer anything new for an architect, because one has been acquainted with them since one's youth. But the sight of these works in their natural setting holds a surprise which comes not only from their size, but also from their picturesque grouping."[57] His new insight into the impact of the environment and grouping of buildings became a major inspiration for his work.

Schinkel was never interested in the traditional furnishing of landscape gardens with follies and pavilions. But parallel to contemporary developments in landscape gardening, Schinkel saw many of his buildings as dynamic and consciously three-dimensional, and he carefully staged their perception by a visitor in motion. He applied these techniques not only when working in an actual garden setting, but also in the completely different environment of the Berlin city center and in his landscape paintings.

In contrast to Caspar David Friedrich and others, Schinkel was exclusively interested in the inhabited, tamed, civilized landscape. First experienced by him in Italy, this landscape showing "traces of human life" became his ideal of aesthetic harmony and of political well-being in a community.[58] It is the basis for Schinkel's work in gardens and urban spaces. It provided his vision for the transformation of the Berlin city center into a city landscape, wherein he expressed his conception of the utopia of a free, rational, and humane people.

FIGURE 15

Perspective view of the upper vestibule, main staircase, and
colonnade of the Altes Museum, with a view of the
Lustgarten, 1831.
Photo: *Sammlung architektonischer Entwürfe* (Berlin, 1866).

FIGURE 16

Perspective study of a columned hall overlooking the sea,
1802 (cat. no. 8).

The author wishes to dedicate this essay to Prof. Dr. Martin Sperlich on the occasion of his 75th birthday.

1. Karl Friedrich Schinkel, *Sammlung architektonischer Entwürfe* (28 parts; Berlin, 1819–40). Of the numerous reprints, see that of the 1866 edition, *Collection of Architectural Designs*, trans. Karin Cramer (New York: Princeton Architectural Press, 1989).

2. For Charlottenhof, see *Sammlung* (note 1), pls. 109–12, first published in 1831 in part 18; for the Römische Bäder, *Sammlung* (note 1), pls. 145–48, first published in 1835 in part 24.

3. Martin Sperlich, "Schinkel als Gärtner," in Julius Posener, ed., *Schinkel zu Ehren. Festreden 1846–1980* (Berlin, n.d.), pp. 363–92; Eva Börsch-Supan, "Architektur und Landschaft," in Jan Fiebelkorn, ed., *Karl Friedrich Schinkel: Werke und Wirkungen*, exh. cat., Senat von Berlin, Martin Gropius Bau (Berlin, 1981), pp. 47–77; Klaus von Krosigk, "Schinkel als Gartenkünstler: Aspekte und Hinweise im Zusammenhang mit den gartendenkmalpflegerischen Maßnahmen in Glienicke," *Das Gartenamt*, 31 (1982), pp. 357–65.

4. Humphry Repton, *Observations on the Theory and Practice of Landscape Gardening* (London, 1805), p. 6.

5. See Humphry Repton, *Sketches and Hints on Landscape Gardening* (1795), reprinted in Humphry Repton, *The Art of Landscape Gardening* (Boston and New York, 1907), p. 43.

6. August Kopisch, *Die königlichen Schlösser und Gärten zu Potsdam* (Berlin, 1854), pp. 174–87; Kurt Kuhlow, *Das Königliche Schloß Charlottenhof bei Potsdam baugeschichtlich und kunstgeschichtlich dargestellt unter besonderer Berücksichtigung der Handzeichnungen König Friedrich Wilhelms IV.* (Berlin, 1912); Hermann Schmitz, "Schloß Charlottenhof," *Hohenzollern-Jahrbuch 20* (1916), pp. 1–21; *Schinkel in Potsdam*, exh. cat., SSG Potsdam-Sanssouci: Ausstellung zum 200. Geburtstag, 1781–1941 (Potsdam, 1981), pp. 66–111; *Karl Friedrich Schinkel: Eine Ausstellung aus der Deutschen Demokratischen Republik*, exh. cat., Hamburg Architektenkammer und Kunsthalle (Berlin, 1982), pp. 231–50; Hans Hoffmann, *Schloß Charlottenhof und die Römischen Bäder*, 2nd ed. (Potsdam-Sanssouci, 1985). In several articles, Heinz Schönemann has proposed an elaborate iconographic interpretation of the Charlottenhof complex. See his most recent essays, "For the Enjoyment of Rural Life: Schinkel's 'Roman Baths' in Sanssouci Park," *Daidalos*, 46 (Dec. 1992), pp. 92–103; and, "Charlottenhof: Schinkel, Lenné und der Kronprinz," in *Potsdamer Schlösser und Gärten: Bau- und Gartenkunst vom 17. bis 20. Jahrhundert*, exh. cat. (Potsdam, 1993), pp. 173–181.

7. These men first collaborated on the Casino at Schloß Glienicke; see Schönemann, "Charlottenhof" (note 6), pp. 173–74.

8. On the importance of Friedrich Wilhelm's share, see Kuhlow (note 6), and Ludwig Dehio, *Friedrich Wilhelm IV. von Preußen. Ein Baukünstler der Romantik* (Munich and Berlin, 1961), pp. 45–46. The judgement of Friedrich Wilhelm's artistic output is still heavily disputed and highly influenced by ideological positions. A new account of his architectural work is urgently needed for the literature on the period. In this essay, these questions of attribution are not tackled. It is assumed that the final result reflects Schinkel's conception.

Clemens Alexander Wimmer has argued convincingly that Lenné actually opposed regular elements introduced into Friedrich Wilhelm's gardens. If he is correct, these facts would further support the argument of this essay, linking these elements with Schinkel; "Äußerungen Lennés zur Gartentheorie," in Florian von Buttlar, ed., *Peter Joseph Lenné: Volkspark und Arkadien*, exh. cat. (Berlin, 1989), pp. 60–68. Krosigk (note 3), p. 360, describes a similar contrast between Schinkel and Lenné at Glienicke; see also Sperlich (note 3), p. 369.

9. In addition to the drawing included here, see two additional ones from 1825, Potsdam-Sanssouci, Stiftung Schlösser und Gärten, Plansammlung, nos. 3696 and 3697. See Harri Günther and Sibylle Harksen, *Peter Joseph Lenné: Katalog der Zeichnungen* (Berlin and Tübingen, 1993), pp. 60–61, cat. nos. 116–18. On Lenné's activity at Charlottenhof, see Gerhard Hinz, *Peter Joseph Lenné: Das Gesamtwerk des Gartenarchitekten und Städteplaners* (Hildesheim, Zurich, and New York, 1989), pp. 55–71; and Harri Günther, *Peter Joseph Lenné: Gärten, Parke, Landschaften* (Berlin, 1985), pp. 31–80. Most recently, see Gerd Schurig, "Die Anlage Charlottenhof, Potsdam," in Harri Günther, ed., *Gärten der Goethezeit* (Leipzig, 1993), pp. 272–81.

10. Hartmann Manfred Schärf, *Die klassizistischen Landschloßumbauten Karl Friedrich Schinkels* (Berlin, 1986), pp. 193, 205. On Schinkel and landscape gardening, see pp. 227–28. The present article cannot deal with the more complex question of the extent to which Charlottenhof can be regarded as a reconstruction of Pliny's villas.

11. Repton (note 4), pp. 126–33. Repton's attempts to reintroduce regular elements around the house also cast light on Schinkel's planning; Nikolaus Pevsner, "Humphry Repton," *Studies in Art, Architecture and Design*, vol. 1 (London, 1968), pp. 138–55. Schinkel stressed the mediating function of formal garden elements near buildings in a conversation with the Danzig painter Johann Karl Schultz; Max Neumann, *Menschen um Schinkel* (Berlin, 1942), pp. 116–17.

Contemporary garden theory distinguished between garden, pleasureground, and park. In Schinkel's immediate circle, this standard distinction could be found in Count Pückler's writings; see Hermann Fürst von Pückler-Muskau, *Andeutungen über Landschaftsgärtnerei verbunden mit der Beschreibung ihrer praktischen Anwendung in Muskau* (Frankfurt, 1988), pp. 46–51. Pückler's *Andeutungen* first appeared in 1834. While the Potsdam garden of Glienicke contains all three zones, there is no pleasureground at Charlottenhof: Kuhlow (note 6), p. 59. On German adaptations of this typology and Charlottenhof, see Dieter Hennebo, "Vom 'klassischen Landschaftsgarten' zum 'gemischten Styl': Zeittypische Gestaltungstendenzen bei Peter Joseph Lenné," in *Peter Joseph Lenné* (note 8), pp. 49–59.

12. Pückler (note 11), p. 106; on Pückler's definition of paths and their function in the landscape garden, see pp. 84, 106–09. See also Martin Sperlich, "Vorgefundener und gestalteter Raum: Der Weg bei Lenné," *Peter Joseph Lenné und die europäische Landschafts-und Gartenkunst im 19. Jahrhundert, 6. Greifswalder Romantikkonferenz* (Greifswald, 1992), pp. 47–53. First published as "Über das Gehen im Garten," in Heinz-W. Hallmann and Jürgen Wenzel, ed., *Peter Joseph Lenné: Die Entwicklung des Auges. Dokumentation des Fachbereichstages 1989. Fachbereich 14, Landschaftsentwicklung, TU Berlin* (Berlin, 1990), pp. 62–67. The function of paths is fundamentally different in French gardens, where they form the actual structure of the garden.

13. Kuhlow (note 6), p. 10; Hoffmann (note 6), p. 6.

14. Many elements of the grove were inspired by Percier and Fontaine; see Charles Percier and Pierre François Fontaine, *Choix des plus célèbres maisons de plaisance de Rome et de ses environs*, 2nd ed. (Paris, 1824), pl. 5.

15. The entire west façade can be seen in *Sammlung* (note 1), pl. 112, center.

16. Apparently, Friedrich Wilhelm wanted a portico, which Schinkel changed into the present flat façade; Kuhlow (note 6), p. 11.

17. On exedrae in the Potsdam gardens, see Klaus von Krosigk, "Die Exedra bei Schinkel und Lenné. Anmerkungen zu ihrer Verwendung in der Zeit des landschaftlichen Gartens," in *Peter Joseph Lenné* (note 8), pp. 112–24. According to Krosigk, the frequent application of exedrae around Potsdam is due to Schinkel (p. 113). In contrast to other types of garden benches, the exedra offers a focussed view.

18. A few years later, the awning was replaced by a vine trellis; Kuhlow (note 6), p. 19. The combination of a pergola and a seat with an awning first appears in Schinkel's project of an architectural textbook of 1804; see Goerd Peschken, ed., *Das architektonische Lehrbuch*, in *Karl Friedrich Schinkel: Lebenswerk* (Munich and Berlin, 1979), pp. 11–21, in particular, p. 16, pls. 1 and 7.

19. Heinz Schönemann, "Theaterelemente in Karl Friedrich Schinkels Entwürfen für Charlottenhof," *Mitteilungen der Pückler-Gesellschaft*, n.f. 6 (1989), pp. 63–78, esp. p. 65.

20. *Peter Joseph Lenné* (note 8), pp. 139, 244, cat. nos. 240–41. The importance of St. Peter's for the experience of Rome and the Campagna is apparent in Schinkel's diary of his first Italian journey, 1803–05: "But suddenly the view of the first temple of the world, the cathedral of St. Peter's, appearing first behind the hills strikes like lightning into one's heart. Then, gradually wide Rome on the seven hills with all its treasures unfolds below the marvelling into the most rich plain." ("… aber plötzlich fährt wie ein Blitzstrahl der Anblick des ersten Tempels der Welt, des Doms von St. Peter, der hinter den Hügeln zuerst sich zeigt, in das Herz, und dann breitet sich in der reichsten Ebene nach und nach auf den sieben Hügeln das weite Rom mit seinen unzähligen Schätzen unter dem Staunenden aus"); see Alfred Freiherr von Wolzogen, *Aus Schinkels Nachlass*, vol. 1 (Berlin, 1862), p. 35. On Friedrich Wilhelm's influence on the Potsdam skyline, see Dehio (note 8), pp. 85–86.

21. Percier and Fontaine (note 14). Both Schinkel and Friedrich Wilhelm had met the architects in person and highly appreciated their work. On the relationship of Charlottenhof to Percier's and Fontaine's work, see Kuhlow (note 6), pp. 62–64; *Schinkel in Potsdam* (note 6), pp. 72–73. Schönemann has related Charlottenhof to the work of Durand. Even if this is correct, Durand does not play an important role in building the close relationship between buildings and their environment described in this article: Heinz Schönemann, "Die Lektionen des Jean-Nicholas-Louis Durand und ihr Einfluss auf Schinkel," in Hannelore Gärtner, ed., *Schinkel-Studien* (Leipzig: Seemann, 1984), pp. 77–90.

22. Percier and Fontaine (note 14), pl. 10. Also closely comparable is the view out of the loggia, pl. 11, which is similar to *Sammlung* (note 1), pl. 110, in its general arrangement. Schinkel tried a similar view onto an ideal Italian city with a large domed church: see Helmut Börsch-Supan and Lucius Grisebach, eds., *Karl Friedrich Schinkel: Architektur, Malerei, Kunstgewerbe*, exh. cat. (Berlin: Verwaltung der Staatlichen Schlösser und Garten und Nationalgalerie, 1981), cat. no. 145, p. 229.

23. "Majestätische Hecken, Terrassen, Treppen, Pinienhaine, Wasserkünste, Blumenparterres, so gelegen, daß der größte Theil Roms und alle Fernen ringsumher dazwischen gesehen werden können"; Wolzogen (note 20), vol. 2, p. 10 (on the Villa Pamphili).

24. Private collection; see Börsch-Supan and Grisebach (note 22), cat. no. 174, p. 242–44.

25. Sammlung (note 1), pl. 110.

26. Repton (note 4), p. 24. On his British journey, Schinkel often commented on views out of windows, e.g. in Eaton Hall; see Reinhard Wegner, ed., Die Reise nach Frankreich und England im Jahre 1826, in Karl Friedrich Schinkel: Lebenswerk (Munich and Berlin, 1990), pp. 163–64; or see Karl Friedrich Schinkel, The English Journey: Journal of a Visit to France and Britain in 1826, ed. David Bindman and Gottfried Riemann, trans. F. Gayna Walls (New Haven and London, 1993), pp. 183–84.

27. Kuhlow (note 6), p. 66. The fence at the Roman Baths was called the "Albani fence."

28. On the hippodrome and Friedrich Wilhelm's project for an antique country-house, see Kuhlow (note 6), pp. 23–32; Eva Börsch-Supan, "Friedrich Wilhelm IV. und das antike Landhaus," in Willmuth Arenhövel and Christa Schreiber, eds., Berlin und die Antike, vol. 2, Aufsätze (Berlin, 1979), pp. 491–94; Schinkel in Potsdam (note 6), pp. 106–11; Karl Friedrich Schinkel (note 6), pp. 313–15.

29. Sammlung (note 1), p. 54, pls. 173–74. Schönemann unconvincingly relates the hippodrome to Durand; Schönemann (note 21), p. 86.

30. Schinkel himself had, of course, included a hippodrome in his own earlier reconstruction of Pliny's villas; see Börsch-Supan and Grisebach (note 22), pp. 205–06. His first design of a hippodrome, part of an unexecuted project for a city palace of Prince Wilhelm of 1829, shows a much closer link between architecture and gardens. Here, the hippodrome is right on axis with the main entrance to the palace and offers a view onto the house. Even more importantly, this structure can fulfill its function as Schinkel himself called this hippodrome a facility for horse-racing. Accordingly, the stables frame it on its western side. In contrast, the Potsdam hippodrome is a mere symbol, created entirely through natural means, unlike the highly architectural hippodrome at Wilhelm's palace; Sammlung (note 1), p. 50, pls. 131–32. On the city palaces for Wilhelm, see below in this article.

31. The term Römische Bäder originally only referred to the northern part of the complex, while it is now generally used for the whole group of buildings.

32. Schinkel's descriptions of Italian venacular architecture strongly resemble the Römische Bäder; see letters to Valentin Rose, May 3rd, 1804, and to David Gilly, December 1804, in Wolzogen (note 20), vol. 1, pp. 85–88 and 160–70.

33. Schönemann, "Enjoyment of Rural Life" (note 6), p. 95.

34. Sammlung (note 1), pl. 171.

35. A similar arbor appears on a painting in the Berlin Nationalgalerie; see Börsch-Supan and Grisebach (note 22), pp. 237–38, 246, cat. no. 165, 178. The closest parallel among Schinkel's many depictions of Italian vernacular houses with a pergola is probably his drawing of a farm in Sicily; see Peschken, Lehrbuch (note 18), p. 17, pl. 12.

36. The Tea Pavilion housed this painting from 1836 on: Kuhlow (note 6), p. 38, n. 1. On the painting, see Adolf Max Vogt, Karl Friedrich Schinkel, Blick in Griechenlands Blüte. Ein Hoffnungsbild für 'Spree-Athen'(Frankfurt, 1985). On the different versions of the painting, see Börsch-Supan and Grisebach (note 22), pp. 261–62. There are also painted views of the Villa d'Este at Tivoli and of the Alhambra. The latter offers a parallel for the shape of the little canals on the terrace of Charlottenhof; see Kuhlow (note 6), p. 65.

37. The ruins on Ruinenberg, only visible in the far distance, were built by Friedrich II in 1748.

38. Schinkel could draw on a long tradition in the landscape garden; Börsch-Supan (note 3), pp. 48–50.

39. Sammlung (note 1), pls. 131–35. Pl. 136 features Wilhelm's Potsdam country house Schloß Babelsberg. On Schinkel's projects for Wilhelm; see Johannes Sievers, ed., Die Arbeiten von K.F. Schinkel für Prinz Wilhelm späteren König von Preussen, in Karl Friedrich Schinkel: Lebenswerk (Berlin, 1955). On the projects for a city palace, see pp. 61–156.

40. Sievers (note 39), pp. 79–85.

41. Schinkel followed a seventeenth-century reconstruction of the Babylonian gardens in the four levels of terraces he employed; Sperlich (note 3), p. 386.

42. "Das Hauptgeschoß des Palastes gewinnt durch diese in der Höhe angeordnete Gartenanlage mitten in der Stadt den Charakter einer Anlage an einem Bergabhange, und diese Höhe gewährt zugleich eine gewisse Abgeschiedenheit vom Getümmel der Strassen, welche den Genuss ungestörter macht. Der Opernplatz würde einen bedeutenden Gewinn durch diesen amphitheatralischen Garten erhalten. Das düstere Ansehen, durch das hohe

Bibliothek-Gebäude veranlaßt, würde sich in ein freundliches, heiteres umwandeln, und die Krönung des Ganzen durch die leichte Arcadenhalle auf der Höhe würde Alles von der dahinterliegenden Stadt bedecken und nichts von unangenehmen Hinterhäusern und Giebeln sichtbar werden lassen"; translation from Sammlung (note 1), p. 50.

43. Several drawings by Friedrich Wilhelm feature similar sequences of terraces. As a brother of Wilhelm, he was involved in the planning of Wilhelm's palace. Friedrich Wilhelm pursued plans for restructuring the Opernplatz. Sievers has even claimed that both the idea of the hanging gardens and the intended demolition of the library do not fit into Schinkel's work, but should rather be attributed to Friedrich Wilhelm directly. This article, however, tries to make the point that Schinkel's design is actually very well in keeping with general tendencies in his work; Sievers (note 39), pp. 79–85.

44. Hermann G. Pundt, "K. F. Schinkel's Environmental Planning of Central Berlin," Journal of the Society of Architectural Historians, 26 (1967), pp. 114–30; Hermann G. Pundt, Schinkel's Berlin: A Study in Environmental Planning (Cambridge, Mass.: Harvard University Press, 1972), pp. 138–58. On the Lustgarten and on the granite bowl, see Paul Ortwin Rave, Berlin: Stadtbaupläne, Brücken, Straßen, Tore, Plätze, in Karl Friedrich Schinkel: Lebenswerk (Berlin 1948; rpt: Munich and Berlin, 1981), pp. 106–28.

45. On the history of the Lustgarten, see Folkwin Wendland, Berlins Gärten und Parke von der Gründung der Stadt bis zum ausgehenden neunzehnten Jahrhundert. Das klassische Berlin (Frankfurt, Berlin, and Vienna, 1979), pp. 15–53.

46. Rave (note 44), pp. 63–79, 139.

47. They were only executed after Schinkel's death.

48. On Schinkel's drawing for the Lustgarten area of 1819, designed in connection with Schloßbrücke, a double row of trees framed a free, central lawn, see Rave (note 44), p. 107, pl. 78.

49. For Schinkel's intentions, see his remarks on the drawing in Karl Friedrich Schinkel (note 6), p. 84.

50. The composition of Schinkel's city as a sequence of views similar to a landscape garden has already been noted; see Börsch-Supan (note 3), pp. 50–51.

51. The Royal Palace was not used by Friedrich Wilhelm III; see Goerd Peschken and Hans-Werner Klünner, Das Berliner Schloß. Das klassische Berlin (Frankfurt, Vienna, and Berlin, 1982), p. 100.

52. Kurt W. Forster, "Schinkel's Panoramic Planning of Central Berlin," Modulus, 16 (Charlottesville: The University of Virginia School of Architecture, 1983), pp. 63–77.

53. Kurt W. Forster, " 'Vento preistorico dalle montagne gelate …' Vorzeitiges und Zukünftiges im Werk Karl Friedrich Schinkels," in Beat Wyss, ed., Bildfälle: Die Moderne im Zwielicht (Zurich and Munich, 1990), pp. 61–72.

54. Schinkel introduced this feature after the publication of the designs in the Sammlung. Originally, the lower flight of stairs would not have been situated in this tunnel-like interval; see Wolfgang Illert, Das Treppenhaus im Deutschen Klassizismus (Worms, 1988), pp. 5–12. The first design resembles the flight of stairs in the pergola of the Römische Bäder; see Sammlung (note 1), pl. 171.

55. Goerd Peschken, "[Eine Stadtplanung Schinkels]," Archäologischer Anzeiger (1962), columns 861–75.

56. Börsch-Supan and Grisebach (note 22), pp. 210–23; Helmut Börsch-Supan, Karl Friedrich Schinkel: Bühnenentwürfe. Stage Designs, 2 vols. (Berlin: Ernst & Sohn, 1990), vol. 1, pp. 17–21.

57. "Der grösste Theil der Denkmäler alter Baukunst bietet nichts Neues für einen Architekten, weil man von Jugend auf mit ihnen bekannt wird. Allein der Anblick dieser Werke in der Natur hat etwas Ueberraschendes, was nicht sowohl von ihrer Grösse, als von der malerischen Zusammenstellung herkommt." Schinkel to David Gilly, December 1804; in Wolzogen (note 20), p. 166. Translation from David Watkin and Tilman Mellinghoff, German Architecture and the Classical Ideal (Cambridge, Mass., 1987), p. 86.

58. "Spuren menschlichen Daseins"; Schinkel's remarks on A View of Greece in Its Prime are quoted in Börsch-Supan and Grisebach (note 22), pp. 262.

The Harmony of Landscape, Architecture, and Community: Schinkel's Encounter with Huyot, 1826

DAVID VAN ZANTEN

Northwestern University

In May 1825 Karl Friedrich Schinkel completed a large, broad canvas that he entitled *Blick in Griechenlands Blüte (A View of Greece in its Prime)*, intended as a gift from the City of Berlin to Princess Luise of Prussia upon her marriage to Crown Prince Frederik of the Netherlands.[1] This painting was immediately recognized as a central statement of Schinkel's ideal, and it was copied three times, in 1826 and 1836 by Wilhelm Ahlborn, and in 1826 by Carl Bechmann, this last for Crown Prince Friedrich Wilhelm (1795–1861) to hang in his villa Charlottenhof at Potsdam, just completed for him by Schinkel. Unfortunately, only the Ahlborn copy of 1836 survives; it is presently in the Nationalgalerie, Berlin *(fig. 1)*. In 1846 the painting was reproduced in a steel engraving for the Verein der Kunstfreunde im preußischen Staate (Association of Friends of Art in the Prussian State).

Our concern here is the ideal Greek city that Schinkel depicted in the middleground of his painting. Well-informed contemporaries have enumerated its contents. At the moment of its completion, Bettina von Arnim (1785 to 1859) wrote in a letter of May 24, 1825: "In the middle ground a Greek city is depicted on the basis of descriptions and ruins with temples, monuments, a market, a circus, palaces, and fortifications, a forested acropolis in the middle with a temple of Jupiter. There is no lack of comfortable, pleasant retreats, spring-fountains, and gardens, etc. This is all surrounded by a river with islands, which sometimes bear fertile green meadows, sometimes their hot sands stretch out under the sun. A range of mountains stretches around across the horizon from left to right, the majesty (I almost want to say holiness) of whose forms—so beautifully touched by the fire of the sun and the veils of atmosphere, their upper parts half in sunlight, half in cloud—loose themselves at the extremity of the landscape in the sea. Those who have seen this landscape are astounded, and I almost wish to say it will bring him [Schinkel] more fame than his buildings."[2]

Later, in 1844, Schinkel's friend the art historian Gustav Friedrich Waagen (1800–1873) described the painting again, cataloguing the middle ground similarly: "[A] Greek

FIGURE 1

Wilhelm Ahlborn after Karl Friedrich Schinkel, *Blick in Griechenlands Blüte (A View of Greece in its Prime)*, 1824–25 (copy 1836). Oil on canvas, SMB-PK, Nationalgalerie.

FIGURE 2

Perspective view of the landscape from the garden of a
proposed residence for a prince, 1835 (cat. no. 42).

city of regular lay-out. Among its beautiful buildings a gymnasium, a mausoleum; the market with temples and colonnaded halls rises very picturesquely in the middle interweaving their architectural lines; the great temple of the city on the acropolis above. Further back, the port with its buildings and the protecting wall."[3]

In Ahlborn's copy, the walled theater and circus are evident at the left and right, flanking a complex of colonnades and temples that are interpreted as the markets, with a mausoleum (modeled on that at Halicarnassus as it had been restored by Schinkel in 1812)[4] and a temple of Jupiter on the hill beyond. The complex on the hillside next to the mausoleum must be what is identified as a gymnasium or academy. We should note that no palaces seem identifiable in the actual canvas (although there is a jumble of private houses) and that an impressive storehouse or arsenal is overlooked in these texts.[5] The city thus resembles Halicarnassus as it was depicted in Vitruvius's famous description (book II, chapter 8), port below, templed citadel above—commemorative mausoleum between them—but lacking the palace.

Beside the richness and power of this particular image there lies, for us, its suggestion of a bridge between the most fascinating but puzzling parts of Schinkel's extraordinarily varied œuvre: on one hand, that mass of images of elaborate monuments in dramatic landscapes that he executed for

paintings, dioramas, and theater decorations, or simply in their own right, roughly between 1800 and 1820 (see *figs. 2 and 3*); and, on the other, from the last decade of Schinkel's career in the 1830s, that series of elaborate architectural compositions of various degrees of practicability: his reconstruction of Pliny's Laurentian Villa of 1833; his 1834 project for a palace erected on the Athenian Acropolis *(pl. 10);* his fantasy of 1835 inscribed "Die Residenz eines Herrschers der überall auf der Höhe der Bildung steht und sich demgemäß umgiebt" (The residence of a ruler who in all respects stands at the pinnacle of culture and arranges his surroundings accordingly);[6] and finally his 1838 project for a summer residence near Orianda on the Crimean coast for Crown Prince Friedrich Wilhelm's sister, Czarina of Russia *(pls. 11, 12).*[7] This link to his architectural work is underlined by Schinkel's use of several of his own designs in the city—the mausoleum, the markets, and perhaps the warehouse. The implication is that these two bodies of work manifest an important and continuous undercurrent of elaborate spatial composition in Schinkel's work—one distinct from his focused study of expressive construction displayed in his *Lehrbuch* manuscripts and in his designs for the Altes Museum and the Bauakademie (Architectural Academy).[8] Furthermore, the implication is that *Blick in Griechenlands Blüte* is the link and encapsulation.

FIGURE 3

Perspective view of a palace complex with a bridge,
c. 1803–30 (cat. no. 25).

FIGURE 4

Jean-Nicolas Huyot, Reconstruction of the Temple of
Fortune, Praeneste, 1811. Ecole Nationale Supérieure des
Beaux-Arts, Paris. Photo: Arthur Drexler, ed.,
The Architecture of the Ecole des Beaux-Arts (New York, 1977),
p. 145.

FIGURE 5

Jean-Nicolas Huyot, Panorama of Thebes.
Ecole Nationale Supérieure des Beaux-Arts, Paris.
Photo: Werner Szambien, *Schinkel* (Paris, 1989), pp. 126–27.

II

Schinkel's painting was executed between a pair of important and lengthy trips. From June 29 to December 4, 1824, he toured Italy, from Venice to Naples, with Waagen and two other friends, Henri-François Brandt and August Krell. Then, from April 17 to August 22, 1826, he visited Paris, London, and the British Midlands in the company of Peter Christian Wilhelm Beuth (1781–1853).[9] These were the only trips outside of Germany he took aside from a student trip to Italy in 1803–04. He was at the height of his career in 1824 to 26 with entrée to the most sophisticated architectural, engineering, and archeological circles.

Schinkel's letters and especially his diary of his 1826 trip have long been recognized as remarkably observed, especially in their record of British industrial construction. They have usually been examined from the perspective of Schinkel's effort to formulate a "modern" structural vocabulary, but they record indications of other interests as well. In Paris, Schinkel was taken in hand by his friend Alexander von Humboldt (1769–1859) and the Franco-German architect Jakob Ignaz Hittorff (1792–1867), and he was introduced most particularly to Jean-Nicolas Huyot (1780–1840). Although Huyot died prematurely in 1840 and is largely forgotten today, he was one of the most considerable personalities of Paris during the Restoration: the master of the most innovative and respected teaching atelier of the time, as well as the architect of several of the city's most impressive construction projects—the Arc de Triomphe, the calvary and church at Mont-Valérien, the church projected at Bellechasse (later built as Sainte-Clothilde), and the reorganization of the construction at the Colline de Chaillot (begun in 1810 by Percier and Fontaine as the Palais du Roi de Rome). In the 1830s Huyot was charged with the rebuilding of the Palais de Justice astride the Ile de la Cité.[10] In addition, Huyot was Professor of History at the Ecole des Beaux-Arts, a post he had earned by his exemplary reconstruction of the city and temple complex at Praeneste of 1811 (*fig. 4*, executed while he was a student at the French Academy at Rome) and by a study trip to Egypt, Greece, Asia Minor, and Italy of 1817–23, made in part with the Count de Forbin and the architect Pierre-Anne Dedreux (1788–1849).

Huyot was Schinkel's precise contemporary, and critics compared the two.[11] Most of Schinkel's Paris notes are very brief. When on May 5 he first visited Hittorff's studio and examined his celebrated reconstructions of Greek painted architectural decoration, all we read is, "Besuch bei Hittorff. Sizilianische Tempel, farbig" (Visit to Hittorff. Sicilian tem-

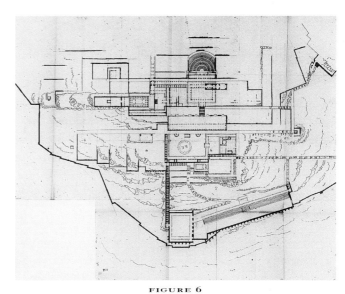

FIGURE 6

Jean-Nicolas Huyot, Reconstructed plan of the city of Priene, 1817/21. Cabinet des Manuscrits, Bibliothèque Nationale, Paris.

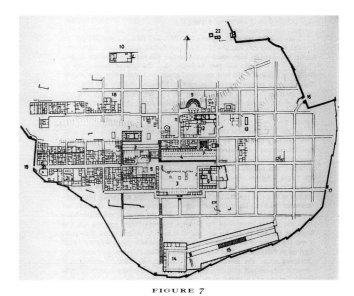

FIGURE 7

Archeological plan of Priene. Photo: Ekrem Akurgal, *Ancient Civilisations and Ruins of Turkey* (Istanbul, 1969), p. 186.

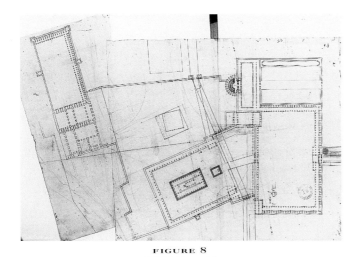

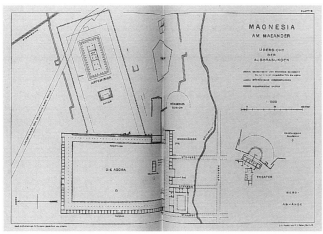

ple, colored). But, when he visited Huyot's dramatic (and
now destroyed) Mont-Valérien complex on May 16, he responded with considerable (and flattering) detail.[12] Earlier,
on May 6, when he had seen Huyot's archeological work in
his studio, he had also reacted with excitement: "Saw his
enormous work of views of the buildings and of whole cities
in Egypt, Syria, Turkey, Halicarnassus, and Ephesus, beautiful sites, all sorts of terrace forms, substructures, stadia with
seats on only one side to leave the other open to the view out
to sea; Greek vaults of the earliest period, city walls, gates,
old cities. His large drawings of the cities of Athens, Rome,
Thebes, the pyramids (orthographic, done with surveying
instruments). Large bundles of drawings which I still
haven't seen."[13]

III

Huyot's library and papers had to be sold after his death,[14]
but large masses of material survive: the series of panoramic
watercolor reconstructions of Thebes, the pyramids, Athens,
and Rome (i.e., those mentioned by Schinkel; see *fig. 5*), together with his Praeneste reconstruction, and some Egyptian studies at the Ecole des Beaux-Arts; his history course
lectures at the Bibliothèque Doucet of the Institut d'Art et
Archéologie; and his travel notes and rough sketch of
1817–23 in the Cabinet des Manuscrits of the Bibliothèque
Nationale (see *figs. 6, 8*, and *10*).[15]

Huyot's project was not to focus on the decorative and
structural system of single ancient buildings, but instead to
discover and restore the whole monumental layout of cities
in terms of their public institutions. We read in his introduction to his history course from one of his years at the Ecole:

"I begin this course by telling you its end and objective, and how the study of history is inseparable from the
rules, principles and precepts of all good architecture.

I next explain what are the causes that give birth to
works of architecture and, after having refuted different sys-
tems based on caves, tents and cabins, I examine the *physical*
and *moral* causes to which all peoples owe the emergence of
the arts.

I demonstrate that the principles that gave birth to the
first societies are the same as those of architecture; a principle that emanates from the social instinct innate in all men,
to which must be attributed the first religious and political
institutions from which architecture was born. It is to this social affection [amour social] that we owe the erection of the
temples and buildings of Egypt. One owes to it further the
origin of the three inseparable arts, architecture, sculpture

and painting, who have as their essential function the transmission to posterity of the memory of the gods, the heroes, the victories and the conquests of races.

Nothing imitates huts less than the immense structures raised in Asia, Greece and Italy by the Pélasages to protect their struggling society.

The temples, stadia, theaters of ancient Greece are again structures erected to serve social needs.

Finally, Rome, itself containing all the buildings of the religious and political institutions of the Roman people."[16]

This was an important and fundamental change in the way architectural archeology had been practiced up to Huyot's return from his travels in 1823. A representation of the first "excavation" of the temple at Bassae by the respectable team of architects C. R. Cockerell (1788–1863) and Haller von Hallerstein (1774–1817) accompanied by the scholars Peter Oluf Brönsted (1780–1842) and Otto Magnus von Stackelberg (1787–1834) in 1811 and 1812 was used as the frontispiece of Stackelberg's publication of the sculpted frieze discovered there, *Der Apollotempel zu Bassae in Arcadien* of 1826 *(fig. 13)*.[17] I use excavation in quotation marks because what is shown transpiring is the wrenching of architectural and sculptural pieces out of the earth by unsupervised Greek workmen and the transportation of these remains to a shelter where the "archaeologists" examine and draw them.[18] It is assumed that what is of value is the temple physiognomy alone, as a sculptural entity, and that what should be documented are details of shape, ornament, and arrangement—although these were to be studied with great care. Hittorff's letters from his trip a decade later (1822–24) document the Greek temples of Sicily and show him rapidly recording the details of temple orders—and discovering traces of painted decoration—but not studying sites as a whole.[19] The history of architecture that these men sought to discover was that of proportioning and decoration, a history still confined to the conceptions of the Abbé Laugier's and Quatremère de Quincy's metaphysical hut.[20]

Huyot's approach was different, as his attacks on the theory of the hut in his lectures make clear. Among his sketches, for example, is a triangulation of the monuments of Athens and a map of the ruins at Magnesia in Asia Minor with survey lines and distances recorded *(fig. 8)*. He was trying to establish the precise relationships in the whole architectural complex. In doing so, he established the exact size of the gaps between the known monuments and these monuments' precise orientation so that they themselves might suggest what was buried and missing between them. In

FIGURE 10

Jean-Nicolas Huyot, Reconstructed view of the city of Heracleia, 1817/23. Cabinet des Manuscrits, Bibliothèque Nationale, Paris.

FIGURE 11

Georg Tippel, Birds-eye view of the archeological reconstruction of Heracleia. Photo: Fritz Krischen, *Die Befestigungen von Herakleia am Latmos* (Berlin and Leipzig, 1922).

FIGURE 12

Giovanni
Battista
Piranesi,
Campus
Martius,
1761–62. Photo:
*Il Campo Marsio
dell'antica Roma*
(Rome, 1762),
frontispiece.

Huyot's reconstruction of Stratoniceia, as well, one can see how this might work. There had been an archeology of ensembles—most evidently in the most familiar site, Rome, and most dramatically in the engraved vision of the Campus Martius by Piranesi of 1761–62 *(fig. 12)*—but this had largely been an excuse for megalomaniac projection.[21] Huyot's work implied that there was as much value to the truth of the layout of an ancient city as there was to the details of ancient ornamental construction.

During the last three decades of the nineteenth century there came a celebrated series of studies of ancient Greek city sites as social and architectural wholes: by the Germans Ernst Curtius, Adolf Furtwängler, Carl Humann, and Theodor Wiegand with their architect assistants Friedrich Adler and his student Wilhelm Dörpfeld; and by the French architect *pensionnaires* Emmanuel Pontremoli, Jean Hulot, and, especially, Tony Garnier with his simultaneous reconstruction of Tusculum and projection of his utopian "Cité industriel" (1901–04).[22] This work had been preceded by an intensive study of the Athenian Acropolis by the scholars and architects of the Ecole française d'Athènes after its founding in 1846, culminating in Ernest Beulé's *Acropole d'Athènes* (1853–54) and Fustel de Coulanges's *Cité antique* (1864). Synthesizing English and German discoveries, the French reconceived Greek architecture as subtly curved,

painted, and integrated into its natural setting to produce an ineffable harmony of the works of nature and man.[23] Most of these "Athenians" had been students in Huyot's atelier[24] (and all had attended his course as Professor of History), but between this generation and that of their master lay another group of younger admirers studying in the 1820s—that of Henri Labrouste (1801–1875) and Marie-Antoine Delannoy (1800–1860) as well as the Paris-trained Gottfried Semper (1803–1879)—who were inspired by Huyot's Praeneste reconstruction but who put a particular Romantic tilt to it *(figs. 14 and 15)*.[25] Where Huyot at Praeneste *(fig. 4)* restored a complicated formal ensemble (in Italy but supposedly of Greek foundation) terracing down a dramatic hillside, but omitted any trace of the city houses crowded between it and the city wall, Labrouste and his friends included the hodgepodge of houses and even folded that incidental aesthetics back on the monumental ensembles to depict them cluttered with ex-votos and graffiti. The Académie in the 1820s protested that this obstructed the study of the details and proportions of the orders, but this was just the point—the Romantics saw the marble remains of Greek architecture as only the dry skeleton of a rich communal life and imagery that had once filled it and was the real accomplishment of the Greeks.

IV

The descriptions of Schinkel's *Blick in Griechenlands Blüte* quoted from von Arnim and Waagen at the beginning of this essay would imply that Schinkel might have seen the Greek city as Huyot and his admirers did, not as an array of beautifully sculpted architectural artifacts, but rather as a manifes-

FIGURE 13

Otto Magnus von Stackelberg, Excavation of the temple of Bassae, 1811–12. Photo: Otto Magnus von Stackelberg, *Der Apollotempel zu Bassae in Arcadien* (1826), frontispiece.

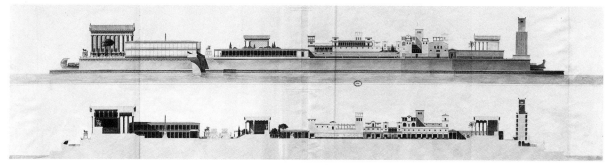

FIGURE 14

Marie-Antoine Delannoy, Reconstruction of the Tiber
Island, Rome, 1832. Ecole Nationale Supérieure des
Beaux-Arts, Paris.

FIGURE 15

Gottfried Semper, Reconstruction of the Parthenon and the
Acropolis in Athens, c.1832. Semperarchiv, Eidgenössische
Technische Hochschule, Zürich.

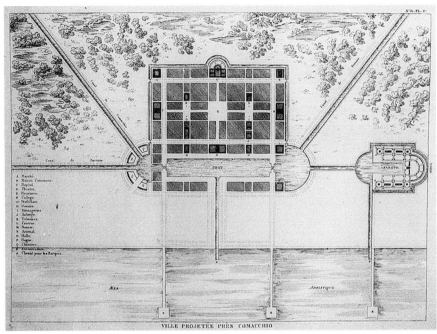

Louis Bruyère, Plan for a town to be built near Comacchio,
Italy, 1805. Photo: Louis Bruyère, *Etudes relatives à l'art des
constructions* (1823–28).

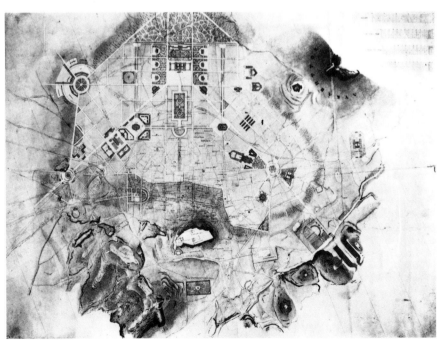

Eduard Schaubert and Stamatios Kleanthes, Plan for
Athens, 1834. Photo: Willmuth Arenhövel and Christa
Schreiber, eds., *Berlin und die Antike*, vol. 2 (Berlin, 1979),
p. 511.

tation of a community made concrete in its built institutions (although without the Romantics' insistent decoration). This interpretation suggests a second parallel, one in practical architecture, with the Neoclassical new towns of the early nineteenth century with their arrays of institutional buildings, with Louis Bruyère's Napoleonic plan for a town near Comacchio in North Italy (1805; *fig. 16*) or that of Napéonville (Pontivy) in the Vendée or even Claude-Nicolas Ledoux's imaginary town of Chaux (1804), as well as— most appropriately at least geographically—the plan for Athens as the capital of the new Greek state first sketched in 1834 by Eduard Schaubert and Stamatios Kleanthes, both of whom had been students of Schinkel's at the Berlin Bauakademie *(fig. 17)*.[26] Citing these familiar examples, however, immediately points up a difference: all were working on flat sites (except Schaubert and Kleanthes, who restricted themselves to what they could find that was flat beyond the Acropolis). Their institutions are inserted in a grid. Schinkel's city is integrated into a gorgeous piece of topography with a temple-topped acropolis and a villa-dotted estuary beyond, as well as the foreground temple and tombs fixed to enjoy the panorama above the town. These Neoclassical city plans are as different from Schinkel's painting as they are from his project for a palace of the Acropolis *(pl. 10)*.

This integration of building and landscape, again, would seem to have been Huyot's project: to restore the ruins of the Greek cities in such a manner as to relate to and valorize their site. Schinkel understood this when he visited Huyot, noting the stadium (at Priene?; *fig. 7*) restored with the seats towards the view (of the Meander mouth and the Aegean sea?) omitted to permit enjoyment of the panorama.

I have described Huyot's surveyed and measured city plans as uniquely accurate for the period of 1817–23. Glancing at his reconstruction of Priene and Magnesia *(figs. 6 and 8)*, or that of Stratoniceia, one realizes that Huyot nonetheless set his imagination free in filling in the spaces between the preserved monuments with courtyards and colonnades that bind the pieces together and link them with the site. He imagined a continuous, interlocking series of monumental axes at Priene that were mostly contradicted in Wiegand's formal excavations of 1895–98, when private houses were found to cover most of the site *(fig. 7)*.[27] Such monumental linking was, in fact, not a principle of Periclean Greek planning.[28] But it is this space that Huyot found for his own projections a symphonic interweaving of built and natural space. Huyot's reconstruction sketch of Stratoniceia shows

FIGURE 18

Gottfried Semper, Project for city hall and surrounding buildings in Hamburg, 1843. Stadtarchiv, Hamburg. Photo: Fritz Schumacher, *Wie das Kunstwerk Hamburg nach dem großen Brande entstand* (Hamburg, 1969), pl. 13b.

organizing axes that he seems to impose on the (quite slight) surviving evidence to elaborate it into impressive spatial compositions. In his fascinating reconstruction of Heracleia *(fig. 10)*, Huyot opens the city to the rocky masses defining the hillside site with a concatenation and an urbanistic generosity that Wiegand and Krischen later found quite wishful (see *fig. 11*).[29] Landscape was nature's architecture; Adalbert Behr cited Schinkel's *Lehrbuch*: "Die Architektur ist die Fortsetzung der Natur in ihrer konstruktiven Tätigkeit" (Architecture is the extension of nature in her constructive function).

V

This was a painter's as much as an architect's conceptualization of the Greek city, with building and nature blending together as in the less architecturally systematic, Claude-like canvases of Schinkel's early career or those of the Austrian painter Josef Anton Koch, and we should note that Huyot had begun his own career as a painter in the studio of Jacques-Louis David.[30]

Schinkel's vision is tableau-like in more than its debt to Claudian composition. Helmut Börsch-Supan has observed that many of Schinkel's graphic works divide into a forward "acting" space and a "characterizing" vista beyond.[31]

The landscape is enframed to give it a meaning. In the case of *Blick in Griechenlands Blüte*, the middle-ground townscape that we have focused upon is enframed by a scene of the construction of an Ionic temple in the foreground, especially the emplacement of a relief depicting Nike with Zeus and Hera, while part of a pediment group of a genius over a fallen warrior is set behind.[32] A Greek inscription (thought to be from Aristotle) is painted on the cella wall to the right, praising Virtue (Nike) as the object of the Greek warrior's quest and the bestower of sweetest joy in death.[33] Börsch-Supan proposes that the tombs beyond the temple to the left memorialize such heroic deaths; the city in the middle ground symbolizes the harmonious life.

One might take Börsch-Supan's observation one step further with French contributions in mind. Huyot's impetus culminated in his student (and assistant on the Palais de Justice) Jean-Arnould Leveil's reconstruction of Augustan Rome for the second edition of Dezorby's *Rome au siècle d'Auguste* of 1846–47. That, in turn, was the culmination of a literary genre depicting the barbarian's discovery of ancient culture manifested in the monuments of antiquity's cities, one established in Abbé Jean-Jacques Barthelémy's monumental *Anacharsis* of 1757–88 and reworked in the architect François Mazois's *Palais de Scaure* of 1822. The genre is structured as a Bildungsroman, the slow assumption of classical culture by the barbarian through the exploration of its sites, geographical, physical, and social. Should we, then, see Schinkel's *Blick* as a "Bildungsbild," an encapsulation of such a site which, by contemplation, Greek elevation might be furthered—in Crown Princes Frederik and Friedrich Wilhelm? More specifically, are the signs of the strength of the state in Schinkel's painting—the public institutions but also the storehouse/arsenal, the lack of emphasis upon a dominating palace, and the mausoleum raised by a grateful posterity—the terms of an exemplum? And also, to fold this back on the French parallels, were Mazois's, Huyot's, and Leveil's archeological enterprises informed by such a moralizing objective?

Schinkel's seems not, then, just a picture of a group of buildings in a landscape; nor is it even a portrait of an ideally provided community: rather it is a symbol of the Greek culture. As such it touches on a final aspect of contemporaneous archeological conceptualization, the depiction of the Greek polis as an ideal community, unified socially within and topographically without. We have cited Fustel de Coulanges's famous *Cité antique* of 1864, as proceeding from the work at the Ecole française d'Athènes. There had been a broader

tradition earlier in Germany, inspired eventually by Schiller, but that had become antiquarian and precise in the work and the teaching at the University of Berlin of August Boeckh (1785–1867), in that at Goettingen of his student Karl Otfried Müller (1797–1840), and in Berlin and Athens of Müller's student Ernst Curtius.[34] Otfried Müller also had in the 1820s another student who had broader impact, but as an architect and theorist, Gottfried Semper, who created his own vision of the Greek city in brilliantly colored and decorated architecture *(fig. 15)*.[35]

Here we arrive back at the whole undercurrent, as I have described it, that might run through Schinkel's work from the 1810–20 fantasies to the 1830s projects. Both his early sketches and his later palatial designs for Athens or Orianda *(pls. 10–12)* are not just combinations of architectural forms, but compositions of clearly distinguished building types set on terraces in a landscape. What is the message?

Here seems to lie a disappointment: in their purely palatial subject matter, these late works do not raise the question of community that informs Huyot's reconstructions or Schinkel's own *Blick in Griechenlands Blüte*. There is no market, no hodge-podge of private dwellings, no storehouse/arsenal as in the 1825 canvas. The late drawings play at the Greek ideal. By the 1830s the young Romantic architects had even rendered them out of date. Instead, Schinkel's late projects seem in the fantastic mode of the Havel landscape around Potsdam that he and Crown Prince Friedrich Wilhelm had been refining since the mid–1820s, in the project for the villa "Belriguardo" and the realized villa Charlottenhof. A similar criticism might be made of Schaubert and Kleanthes's Athens project *(fig. 17)*: it is a royal city only—everything is subordinate to the palatial axis, north-south from the Acropolis. It is not Boeckh's or Müller's polis recreated.

In a peculiar way, the implications of Huyot's reconstructions and Schinkel's *Blick in Griechenlands Blüte* were realized by others, by Labrouste and his friends and, most pointedly, by Semper and his contemporaries when in 1842 a fire destroyed the center of Germany's great free commercial port, Hamburg, and projects were formulated to create a new city linked to its northern topography, its spaces, and materials (brick). Private houses, arcades, and warehouses become the elements of composition around the city hall, bourse, and churches *(fig. 18)*.[36] Here Semper and his contemporaries broke out of the formal imagery of royal architecture to create the institutions of German community, simply and with the materials at hand.[37]

NOTES

1. See the catalogue entry by Helmut Börsch-Supan in Helmut Börsch-Supan and Lucius Grisebach, eds., *Karl Friedrich Schinkel: Architektur, Malerei, Kunstgewerbe* (Berlin: Verwaltung der Staatlichen Schlösser und Gärten und Nationalgalerie, 1981), pp. 261–63; Adalbert Behr, "'Griechenlands Blüte' und die 'Fortsetzung der Geschichte': Zur Kunsttheorie Karl Friedrich Schinkels" in Hannelore Gärtner, ed., *Schinkel-Studien* (Leipzig: Seemann, 1984), pp. 14–24; Willmuth Arenhövel and Christa Schreiber, eds., *Berlin und die Antike* (Berlin: Deutsches Archäologisches Institut, 1979), vol. 1, pp. 127–29; Adolf Max Vogt, *Karl Friedrich Schinkel: Blick in Griechenlands Blüte* (Frankfurt: Fischer, 1985); P. O. Rave, *Blick in Griechenlands Blüte* (Berlin: Mann, 1946). See also Kurt W. Forster, "Schinkel's Panoramic Planning of Central Berlin," *Modulus*, 16 (Charlottesville: University of Virginia School of Architecture, 1983), pp. 63–77; Alex Potts, "Schinkel's Architectural Theory" in Michael Snodin, ed., *Karl Friedrich Schinkel: A Universal Man* (New Haven and London: Yale University Press, 1991), pp. 47–55; as well as the catalogues *Berlin und die Antike: Architektur, Kunstgewerbe, Malerei, Skulptur, Theater und Wissenschaft vom 16. Jahrhundert bis Heute*, 2 vols. (Berlin: Deutsches Archäologisches Institut, 1979); Norbert Lieb and Florian Hufnagel, eds., *Leo von Klenze: Gemälde und Zeichnungen* (Munich: Callwey, 1979); and *Ein griechischer Traum: Leo von Klenze der Archäologe* (Munich: Glyptothek, 1985).

2. "Der Mittelgrund ist eine griechische Stadt nach Beschreibung und Ruinen gebildet, mit Tempeln, Denkmälern, Markt, Zirkus, Pälasten, und Festungswerken, in der Mitte eine umbuschte Anhöhe mit Jupiters Tempel; es fehlt nicht an heimlichen, lieblichen Plätzchen, Springbrunnen, Gärten, p. p. Dies alles ist umkreist von einem Fluss mit Inseln, die zum Teil fruchtreiche grüne Auen, zum Teil ihre heissen Sandsteppen der Sonne entgegenbreiten; am Horizont geht eine Gebirgskette von der Linken zur Rechten, von den majestätischsten, ja ich möchte beinah sagen heiligen Formen, so schön umduftet von Brand der Sonne und von ihren Dünsten umlagert, die Häupter halb in der Sonne, halb in Wolken gehüllt, die sich am Ende der Landschaft ins Meer verlieren. Wer diese Landschaft gesehen, war erstaunt, und ich möchte beinahe sagen, das sie ihm mehr Ruhm einbringen wird als seine Gebäude." Börsch-Supan and Grisebach (note 1), p. 262.

The entry by Gottfried Riemann in the 1991 exhibition catalogue reproduces in addition a letter from von Arnim to Goethe of June 6, 1825, which is more evocative but less accurate in its enumeration of details: "[A] new Athens devised with all the sense of place of one imbued with the customs and spirit of Greece. The Temple of Jupiter rises at the very center between its forecourts on an eminence, surrounded by palm trees, which absorb into themselves the gift of the sun. Colossi, academies and a circus surround it, then come the markets, suburbs arising on all sides." Snodin (note 1), p. 207. Reproduced in its entirety in Walter Schmitz and Sibylle von Steinsdorff, *Bettine von Arnim: Goethe's Briefwechsel mit einem Kinde* (Berlin: Deutscher Klassiker Verlag, 1922), pp. 736–38. Rave (note 1) transcribes this and other descriptions.

3. "[E]ine griechische Stadt von planmässiger Anlage. Aus den schönen Gebäuden, dem Gymnasium, einem Mausoleum, dem Markt mit Tempeln, Theatern und Säulenhallen ragt, höchst malerisch im Mittelgrunde die Linien durchschneidend, einer von Haupttempeln der Stadt auf einer Anhöhe empor. Mehr ruckwärts der Hafen mit seinen Gebäuden und die Ringmauern." See Gustav Friedrich Waagen, "Karl Friedrich Schinkel als Mensch und als Künstler," *Berliner Kalender* (Berlin: Königliche Preußische Kalender Deputation, 1844), pp. 377–78.

4. Börsch-Supan and Grisebach (note 1), p. 19.

5. In style it is also like Schinkel's contemporaneous customs house complex behind the Altes Museum, the Packhof Gebäude, of 1819–32. But if it is an arsenal, one would compare it to descriptions of Athens's port, Piraeus, especially the shiphouse there described in an ancient inscription. (Quatremère de Quincy, "Architecture," *Encyclopédique méthodique* [Pancouke], III (1825) p. 174.

6. To use Alex Potts's translation in Snodin (note 1), p. 53.

7. For Pliny's villa, see *Architektonisches Album*, fasicle 7 (Helen Tanzer, *The Villas of Pliny the Younger* [New York: Columbia University Press, 1924], pp. 90–91); on the Acropolis palace and Orianda, see *Werke der höheren Baukunst* (Potsdam, 1840–42); Rand Carter, "Karl Friedrich Schinkel's Project for a Royal Palace on the Acropolis," *Journal of the Society of Architectural Historians*, 38, no. 1 (March 1979), pp. 34–46; and Margarete Kühn, "Entwurf für den Palast des Königs Otto von Griechenland auf der Akropolis,"in *Ausland: Bauten und Entwürfe*, in *Karl Friedrich Schinkel: Lebenswerk*, ed. Margarete Kühn (Munich: Deutscher Kunstverlag, 1989); on the "Residenz," see Goerd Peschken, ed., *Das architektonische Lehrbuch*, in *Karl Friedrich Schinkel: Lebenswerk*, ed. Margarete Kühn (Munich: Deutscher Kunstverlag, 1979).

An interesting project in a similar "bridge" position in Schinkel's œuvre is that for the villa "Belriguardo" for Crown Prince Friedrich Wilhelm executed contemporaneously with the *Blick in Griechenlands Blüte* in 1824, an extravagant composition of colonnades and terraces confronting Sans Souci across the Havel; see Ludwig Dehio, *Friedrich Wilhelm IV von Preußen: Ein Baukünstler der Romantik* (Munich: Deutscher Kunstverlag, 1961), pp. 23–33.

8. On this interpretation, see August Grisebach, *Carl Friedrich Schinkel: Architekt, Städtbauer, Maler* (Leipzig: Insel-Verlag, 1924; republished Munich: Piper, 1981).

9. See Karl Friedrich Schinkel, *Reise nach England, Schottland und Paris im Jahre 1826*, ed. Gottfried Riemann (Berlin: Henschelverlag, 1986), or Reinhard Wegner, ed., *Die Reise nach Frankreich und England im Jahre 1826*, in *Karl Friedrich Schinkel: Lebenswerk*, ed. Margarete Kühn (Munich: Deutscher Kunstverlag, 1990); or see the recent English translation, Karl Friedrich Schinkel, *The English Journey: Journal of a Visit to France and Britain in 1826*, ed. David Bindman and Gottfried Riemann, trans. F. Gayna Walls (New Haven and London: Yale University Press, 1993).

10. Desiré Raoul-Rochette, "Funérailles de M. Huyot" (Paris: Didot, 1840); Charles Lenormant, "Huyot," *Biographie universelle ancienne et moderne* 20 (1858), pp. 231–33; Adolphe Lance, "Notice sur Huyot," *Annuaire de l'architecte*, 1 (1864), pp. 89–110; Hector Lefuel, "Notice sur Huyot," *Bulletin de la société de l'histoire de l'art français* (1920), pp. 19–21. Werner Szambien focuses on Schinkel's visit to Huyot in *Schinkel* (Paris: Hazan, 1989), pp. 126–27.

11. Hippolyte Fortoul wrote in 1842: "M. Schinkel peut être considéré comme le représentant de la génération et des idées qui se sont élevées en Allemagne immédiatement après celles dont M. de Klenze a été l'interprète à Munich. C'est à peu près ainsi que chez nous, à côté de l'école de M. Percier, qui se condamnait, avec une austérité trop peu appréciée, à une imitation étroite de l'antique, M. Huyot est apparu tout-à-coup avec des études plus larges et plus savantes, avec un esprit tourmenté par le besoin de l'invention, avec l'instinct de la richesse, du grandiose, de l'extraordinaire." *De l'art en Allemagne* (Paris: Labitte, 1842), vol. 1, p. 531.

12. Wegner (note 9) illustrates the complex before it was destroyed in 1840 to build the fortress on the site today.

13. "… sahn dessen enorme Arbeiten über die Aufnahmen der Gebäuden und ganzer Städte in Agypten, Syrien, Kleinasien, Halicarnassus und Ephesus, herrliche Lage, Motive aller Art für Terrassen, Unterbaue, Stadien auf einer Seite nur mit Stufen umgeben, die andere für die Aussicht ins Meer offen gelassen; griechische Gewölbe der frühsten Zeit, Stadtmauern, Tore, alte Städte. Seine grossen Zeichnungen der Städte Athen, Rome, Thebes, Pyramiden (geometrisch und auf ein Niveau gebracht). Grosse Pakete von Zeichnungen, die ich noch nicht sah."

14. *Catalogue des livres sur l'architecture et les antiquités du cabinet du feu M. Huyot, architecte* (Paris: Merlin, 1841).

15. Institut d'Art et Archéologie, Bibliothèque Doucet, MS 15; Bibliothèque Nationale, Cabinet des Manuscrits, NAF 664, 691, 5080, 5081.

16. "Je commence ce cours par faire connaître quel en est l'objet et le but et comment l'étude de l'histoire est inséparable, des principes, des règles et des prèceptes de toute bonne architecture.

J'explique ensuite quelles sont les causes qui donnèrent naissance aux ouvrages d'architecture, et après avoir refuté les différents systèmes basés sur les grottes, sur les tentes, et sur les cabanes, j'examine les causes *physiques* et *morales* auxquelles chez tous les peuples on doit l'origine des arts.

Je démontre le principe qui donne naissance aux premières sociétés, est le même que celui de l'architecture; principe qui émane de cet instinct social inné chez les hommes, auquel il faut attribuer les premières institutions réligieuses et politiques, d'où naquît l'architecture. C'est à cet amour social qu'on doit l'érection des temples et des édifices de l'Egypte; on lui doit encore l'origine des ces trois arts inséparables de l'architecture, la sculpture et la peinture, qui ont pour objet essentiel de transmettre à la postérité le souvenir des dieux, des héros, des victoires et des conquêtes des peuples.

Rien n'imite moins les cabanes, que ses immenses constructions élevées en Asie, en Grèce, et en Italie, par les Pélasages, pour la défense de leur société naissante.

Les temples, les stades, les théâtres de l'ancienne Grèce, sont encore des édifices élevés pour les besoins sociaux.

Enfin Rome seule renfermait tous les édifices des institutions réligieuses et politiques du peuple Romain."

Institut d'Art et Archéologie, Bibliothèque Doucet, MS 15. Huyot's emphasis. It is interesting to note here the next two paragraphs of Huyot's introduction:

"Mais, si cette cause première de la civilisation porte les arts à leurs plus haut degré de perfection, ce fut l'intérêt personnel qui, agissant en sens inverse sur le but que se propose les arts, amène la décadence de l'architecture; et ces palais somptueux construits pour que de simples particuliers dans les derniers temps des Grands Empires, attestent assez que les arts, en prostituant, pour ainsi dire, leurs œuvres à la mode et aux caprices de la fortune, périrent eux mêmes avec les institutions auxquelles ils devaient leur origine.

"Ainsi, l'amour social et l'amour individuel sont donc les deux principales causes morales, auxquelles nous assignerons à l'une l'origine de l'architecture, à l'autre sa décadence."

17. Pieter B. F. J. Broucke, *The Archeology of Architecture: Charles Robert Cockerell in Southern Europe and the Levant, 1810–1817* (New Haven: Yale Center for British Art, 1993).

18. This excavation technique is documented in Martinus Rørby's *Greeks Working in the Ruins of the Acropolis*, 1855, in the Statens, Museum for Kunst, Copenhagen.

19. Nachlass Hittorff, Stadtarchiv, Cologne. Using the example of Cockerell is not entirely fair. Although not systematic, he did sketch site reconstructions in his notes (now in the Royal Institute of British Architects, London).

20. Joseph Rykwert, *On Adam's House in Paradise* (New York: Museum of Modern Art, 1972); Anthony Vidler, *The Writing of the Walls* (Princeton: Princeton Architectural Press, 1987); Sylvia Lavin, *Quatremère de Quincy and the Invention of a Modern Language of Architecture* (Cambridge: MIT Press, 1992).

21. Compare William Gell's project to map the Roman Campagne, *The Topography of Roman and Vicinity with Map* (London: Saunders, 1834) and Ludwig Ross's work in the 1830s to survey monumental topography of Athens. At the time of his death, Huyot was working on an archeological topography of Rome, published posthumously: *Forum Romanum* (Paris: Rapilly, 1841): map with explanatory introduction. See also John Pinto, "Origins and Development of the Ichnographic City Plan," *Journal of the Society of Architectural Historians*, 35 (March 1976), pp. 35–50. Quatremère de Quincy, Huyot's mentor and *secrétaire perpetuel* of the Académie des Beaux-Arts, had already called for a systematic chronological-geographical elucidation of the great cities of antiquity in his entries "ruine" and "restitution" in the third volume of his contribution to the *Encyclopédie méthodique* (1825).

22. Wolfgang Schiering, "Zur Geschichte der Archäologie," in Ulrich Hausmann, *Allgemeine Grundlagen der Archäologie* (Munich: Beck, 1969), especially pp. 55ff., 99ff. On Adler, see Eva Börsch-Supan, *Berliner Baukunst nach Schinkel, 1840–1870* (Munich: Prestel, 1977), pp. 145–50. See also *Paris. Rome. Athènes* (Paris: Ecole des Beaux-Arts, 1982); Pierre Pinon and François-Xavier Amprimoz, *Les Envois de Rome, architecture et archéologie* (Rome: Ecole française de Rome, 1988).

23. See David Van Zanten, *Designing Paris: The Architecture of Duban, Labrouste, Duc and Vandoyer* (Cambridge: MIT Press, 1987), chap. 6. See also Ernst Curtius, *Die Peloponnesos, eine historisch-geographische Beschreibung der Halbinsel*, 2 vols. (Gotha: Perthes, 1851–52); F. C. Penrose, *An Investigation of the Principles of Athenian Architecture* (London: Society of the Dilettanti, 1851). See also the observations of J. J. Ampère, "Une course dans l'Asie mineur," *Revue des deux mondes*, 29 (January 15, 1842), pp. 161–85; "La poésie grecque en Grèce," *Revue des deux mondes*, 35 (June 15, 1844), pp. 982–1015, and 36 (July 1844), pp. 38–65.

24. Namely: Paccard, Chaudet, Louvet, André, Tétaz, Lebouteux.

25. Van Zanten (note 23), chap. 1; Gottfried Semper, *Vorläufige Bemerkungen über bemalte Architektur und Plastik bei den Alten* (Altona: Hammerich, 1834) and *Die Anwendung der Farben in der Architektur und Plastik. In einer Sammlung von Beispielen aus den Zeiten des Alterthums und Mittelalters* (Dresden, 1836). See Leopold Ettlinger, *Gottfried Semper und die Antike* (dissertation, Halle, 1937).

26. On Athens, see Margarete Kühn, "Schinkel und der Entwurf seiner Schüler Schaubert und Kleanthes für die Neustadt Athen," in Arenhövel (note 1), vol. 2, pp. 509–522; Alexander Papageorgiou-Venetas, *Hauptstadt Athen. Ein Stadtgedanke des Klassizismus* (Munich: Deutscher Kunstverlag, 1993). Schinkel's palace on the Acropolis was a contribution to this project to create a new Greek capital city. See also Schinkel's work in Oslo: Ulf Hamran and Truls Aslaksby, "Schinkels Begutachtung des Entwürfes von Christian Heinrich Grosch für die Universität in Oslo," in *Ausland* (note 7), pp. 185–87.

One should not forget that Schinkel's first architectural appointment was as the member in charge of esthetics of the Oberbaudeputation overseeing all public construction in Prussia. See Steven Moyano, "Karl Friedrich Schinkel and the Administration of Architectural Esthetics in Prussia, 1810–1840" (Ph.D. diss., Northwestern University, 1989). See also Helga Nora Franz-Duhme and Ursula Röper-Vogt, *Schinkels Vorstadt Kirchen: Kirchenbau und Gemeindegründung unter Friedrich Wilhelm III. in Berlin* (Berlin: Wichern-Verlag, 1985).

27. Theodor Wiegand and H. Schrader, *Priene, Ergebnisse der Ausgrabungen und Untersuchungen in den Jahren 1895–1898* (Berlin: Reimer, 1904). See also Joseph Coleman Carter, *The Sculpture of the Sanctuary of Athena Polias at Priene* (London: Society of Antiquaries, 1983).

28. See Roland Martin, *L'Urbanisme dans la Grèce antique* (Paris: Picard, 1956).

29. Theodor Wiegand, *Milet: Ergebnisse der Ausgrabungen und Untersuchungen seit dem Jahre 1899* (Berlin: Reimer, 1913); Fritz Krischen, *Die Befestigungen von Herakleia am Latmos* (Berlin and Leipzig: de Gruyter, 1922).

30. E.-J. Delécluze, *Louis David: son école et son temps* (Paris: Didier, 1855), pp. 88, 93. The archeologist Charles Lenormant wrote of Huyot's Praeneste: "Huyot y avait déployé un sentiment élevé d'architecture romaine, une imagination poétique et un talent d'exécution qui jusqu'à la était resté le privilège des peintres"; Lenormant (note 10), p. 232.

31. Helmut Börsch-Supan, *Karl Friedrich Schinkel: Bühnenentwürfe. Stage Designs*, 2 vols. (Berlin: Ernst & Sohn, 1990).

32. I take this reading from Börsch-Supan and Grisebach (note 1), pp. 261–63.

33. To translate Börsch-Supan's translation:
"Battle-daring Virtue,
The most noble longing of the human race!
For you, O' beautiful godly maiden
Greece's youths died a hero's death,
For you they suffered gladly the anguish of burning
wounds and the trial of labor.
You strew the seeds of immortal fruit, your love, in the
hearts of men!
These seeds grow and bloom and awaken better joys
than gold
and the ancestors' pride, sweeter than the pilgrim's
balm, a cool slumber."

34. See, for example, August Boeckh, *Die Stadthaushaltung der Athener*, 2 vols. (Berlin: Realbuchhandlung, 1817); Karl Otfried Müller, *Geschichte hellenischer Stämme und Städte: Orchomenos und die Minyer*, 3 vols. (Breslau: Max, 1820); and Curtius (note 23). Adalbert Behr, in his essay cited above (note 1), links Schinkel's vision in the *Blick in Griechenlands Blüte* to Schiller through Wilhelm von Humboldt. See also the work of Otto Magnus von Stackelberg cited above. Is it by chance that Schinkel's canvas was commissioned by the City of Berlin as a present of the Crown Prince of commercial Holland? Börsch-Supan surmised from von Arnim's first letter that the painting was already begun when the City of Berlin approached Schinkel.

35. Semper studied at Goettingen in 1823–25, being inspired by Müller, then he studied the Greek remains from 1830 to 1833, returning to produce the two works *Vorläufige Bemerkungen* (1834) and *Anwendung* (1836) cited above (note 25).

36. Fritz Schumacher, *Wie das Kunstwerk Hamburg nach dem großen Brande Entstand* (Hamburg: Hans Christians Verlag, 1969). On Schinkel's and Semper's relative social orientations, see Goerd Peschken, "L'Origine e la posizione sociale di Schinkel e Semper nella formazione del lavoro pensiero teorico," in Augusto Romano Burelli, ed., *Le Epifani di proteo: la saga nordica del classicismo in Schinkel e Semper* (Venice: Rebellato, 1983), pp. 45–56.

37. Schinkel himself adopted the modest, square, brick vocabulary when he projected a theater and opera house for Hamburg in 1825 (see cat. no. 61).

Plates

PLATE I

Panoramic perspective view
overlooking Prague, 1803
(cat. no. 11)

PLATE 2

Perspective view of Dresden
(as seen through a telescope?), 1803
(cat. no. 13)

PLATE 3

Bohemian mountains at sunset,
c. 1803-05
(cat. no. 14)

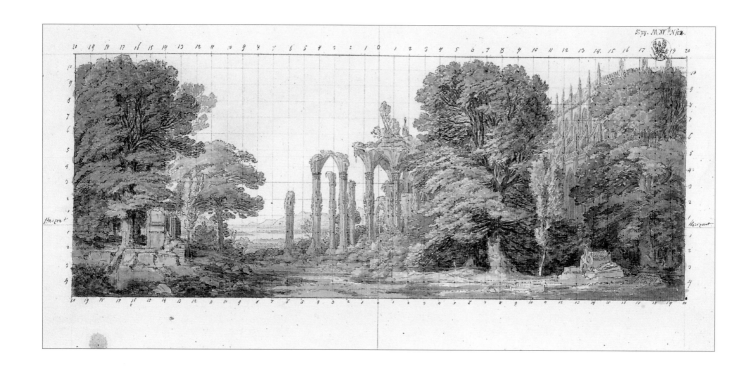

PLATE 4

Perspective view of the ruins of
a Gothic cloister and church
amidst trees, 1809
(cat. no. 15)

PLATE 5

Panoramic view of Rome,
with rooftops in the foreground,
c. 1803-04
(cat. no. 21)

PLATE 6

Gamblers with the Spanish steps
and Sma. Trinità dei Monti, Rome,
in the background, c. 1803-04
(cat. no. 22)

PLATE 7

View from a garden, through an
arbor, to a palace for a Prussian
noblewoman, c. 1830-31,
entitled *Einsicht (Insight)*
(cat. no. 30)

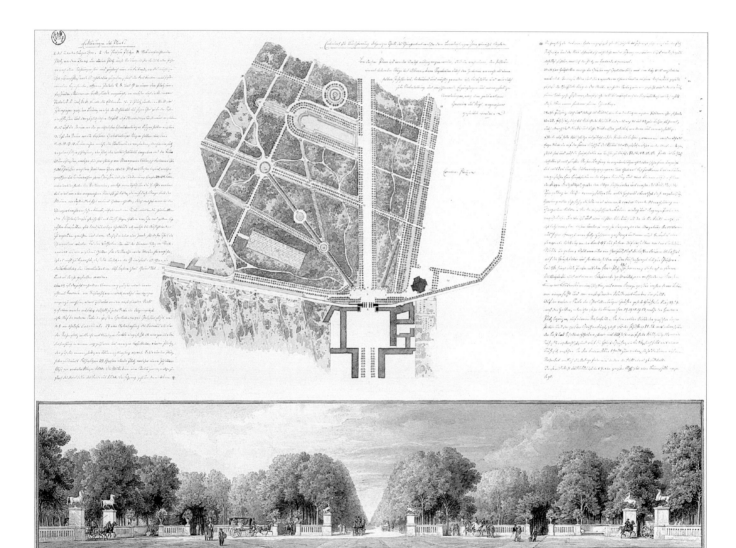

PLATE 9

The Mourning on the Tumulus,
a study for a wall-painting in the
staircase of the Altes Museum,
Berlin, signed and dated 1832
(cat. no. 35)

PLATE 10

Interior perspective view of
a proposed great hall for a palace
on the Acropolis,
signed and dated 1834
(cat. no. 41)

PLATE II

Perspective view of the terrace
of a proposed palace at Orianda
in the Crimea, 1838
(cat. no. 43)

Perspective view of the atrium
of a proposed palace at Orianda
in the Crimea, 1838
(cat. no. 44)

PLATE 13

Grove of the Temple of Isis,
a set design for *Die Zauberflöte*
(*The Magic Flute*), 1815
(cat. no. 72)

PLATE 14

Interior perspective view of
a forecourt or grotto, a set design
for *Die Zauberflöte*
(The Magic Flute), 1815
(cat. no. 73)

PLATE 15

Interior perspective view of the
testing place at the entrance to
the Temple of the Sun,
a set design for *Die Zauberflöte*
(The Magic Flute), 1815
(cat. no. 75)

Interior perspective view of
the Temple of the Sun with a
statue of Osiris, the final scene
in *Die Zauberflöte*
(The Magic Flute), 1815
(cat. no. 77)

PLATE 17

Perspective view of a
marketplace with a fountain,
a set design for *Undine*, 1816
(cat. no. 78)

PLATE 18

Interior perspective view of
Kühleborn's water palace,
a set design for *Undine*, 1816
(cat. no. 79)

116

PLATE 19

Evening view of Edgar's palace,
a set design for *Ariodant*, 1816
(cat. no. 80)

PLATE 20

Interior perspective view of the
Temple of Jerusalem (Temple of
Solomon), a set design for
Athalia, 1817
(cat. no. 82)

PLATE 21

Interior perspective view of the
Temple of Apollo, a set design
for *Alceste*, 1817
(cat. no. 83)

PLATE 22

Entry to the underworld, a set
design for *Alceste*, 1815
(cat. no. 84)

PLATE 23

Perspective view of the temple
square, a set design for *Die Vestalin
(The Vestal Virgin)*, 1818
(cat. no. 85)

PLATE 24

Interior perspective view of
the Temple of Vesta, a set
design for *Die Vestalin
(The Vestal Virgin)*, 1818
(cat. no. 86)

PLATE 25

Interior perspective view of
a hall, a set design for
Agnes von Hohenstaufen, c. 1827
(cat. no. 87)

PLATE 26

Interior perspective view of
a great hall, a set design for
Agnes von Hohenstaufen, c. 1827
(cat. no. 88)

124

PLATE 28

Panoramic perspective view of
Mexico and the Spaniards'
tented encampment, a set design
for *Fernando Cortez*, 1818
(cat. no. 91)

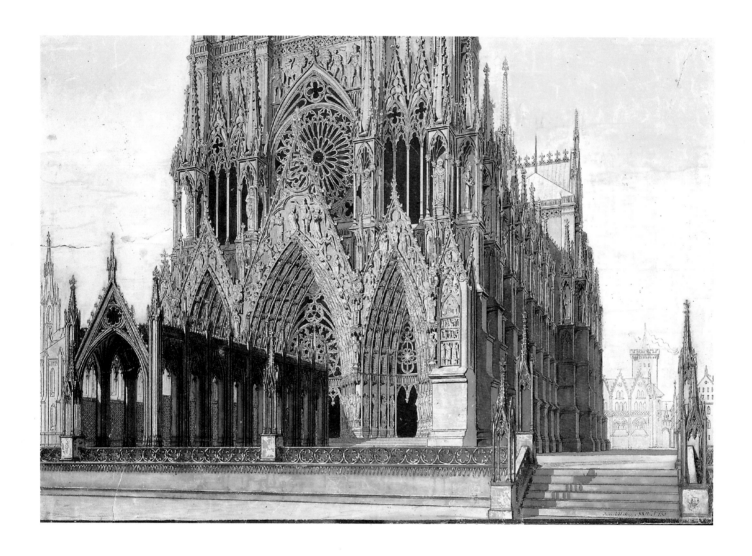

Perspective view of the entrance
to the Cathedral of Reims,
a set design for *Die Jungfrau
von Orléans (The Maid of
Orléans)*, 1818
(cat. no. 93)

PLATE 31

Perspective view of the city and
Cathedral of Reims, from a
Gothic balcony, a set design for
*Die Jungfrau von Orléans
(The Maid of Orléans)*, 1818
(cat. no. 92)

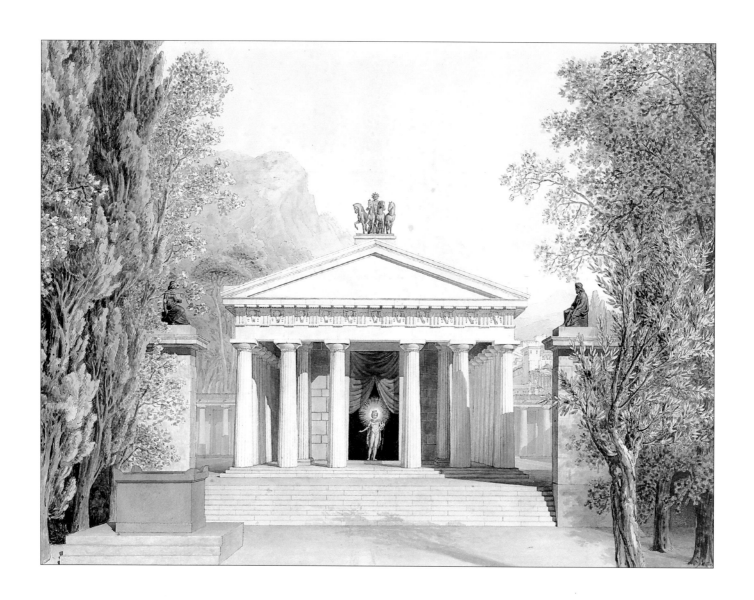

PLATE 32

Perspective view of a Doric
temple, possibly a set design for
Olympia, 1821
(cat. no. 95)

PLATE 33

Interior perspective view of the
Temple of Diana, a set design
for *Olympia*, 1821
(cat. no. 96)

PLATE 34

Perspective view of an
Indian scene, a set design
for *Nurmahal*, 1822
(cat. no. 98)

WOLFGANG PEHNT

The legacy of Karl Friedrich Schinkel is a remarkable success story. Few architects have received as much recognition—and from as many diverse parties—as the man who served in the Königliche Technische Oberbaudeputation (Royal Office of Works) for over thirty years, ending as Prussia's Oberlandesbaudirektor (Supreme Director of National Public Works). Schinkel's contemporaries praised his strict discipline and unusual versatility, his elegance and rationality, his historical knowledge and artistic certainty of taste. An "immensely rich and magnificent talent for all aspects of the creative arts, combined with the greatest modesty and the liveliest and quickest production," is how the great Romantic poet Clemens Brentano praised him. The "breath of this hero," wrote the poet Emanuel Geibel, rustles "in the souls of his disciples."[1]

To modernists, Schinkel seems to have anticipated the principles of modern construction in his adherence to objectivity, sensibility, and tectonics. The National Socialists claimed the Prussian state architect as the model of Hellenistic spirit, come to life on Germanic soil. Cultural politicians in the Socialist East cited him when it was necessary for them to oppose the International Modernism of the West with a national program. Finally, Postmodernism found itself confirmed in his liberal handling of historical material, in his appeal to both the historical and the poetic, and in the "endless diversity of the relationships unfolding in social life."[2] In German-speaking areas, at least, no architect has achieved a comparably large and correspondingly varied impact over a similarly lengthy period. Karl Friedrich Schinkel has meant and indeed still means for Central Europe during the last 180 years what Andrea Palladio has meant for the Western world for 450 years.

THE NEW STYLE

Whereas Palladio, however, understood himself as united with his patrons and admirers in his rediscovery of and high regard for the ancient world, and whereas he also hoped with them that architecture could be "brought to that pitch of perfection, which in all the arts is greatly desired,"[3] Schinkel was conscious of the uncertainty of his age and even of his own work. He lived in a time that was not a threshold to a Golden Age, and his era did not allow itself to be interpreted as such. It did not promise a rebirth, but rather announced

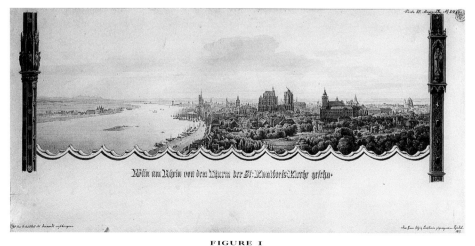

FIGURE I

Panoramic perspective view of Cologne, 1817
(cat. no. 16).

unforeseeable problems and tasks, which he at least recognized could not be overcome with the "piled treasure of often very heterogeneous objects." "It was life's task for me to gain clarity in this. But the deeper I worked into the object, the greater the difficulties appeared to me."[4] Even in industrially backward Prussia these problems could not be overlooked, although they first appeared to Schinkel in all their urgency during his trip to England in 1826. "In such a time education cannot, as it should, proceed from the public; instead, everything must be offered to enlighten the public and make it sensitive to the meaning of forms in architecture."[5] The architect and his public lived at a distance from each other, which Schinkel as pedagogue sought to overcome through aesthetic education, as was appropriate to his idealistic position. Moral quality remained a characteristic of his architecture.

Clearly, an increase in knowledge, expanded geographical horizons, and archeological studies had made the designing of new buildings a matter of selecting between simultaneously available stylistic alternatives—this was already widely acknowledged by Schinkel's generation.[6] The possibilities and dangers of historicism accompanied Schinkel throughout his life as a constant provocation. He was faced with the necessity of creating something new and—in the terminology of German Neoclassicism—something "naive." But Schinkel was not of the opinion that he could do so without the aid of history. The level of participation of the new and the familiar and the method of determining their relationship to each other was variously described by Schinkel at individual phases of his career.

In one of his famous remarks, which his biographer Alfred von Wolzogen published in 1863, Schinkel warned against exaggerated expectations from the novelty of the new, and he reiterated the obligation to keep artistic production, especially that of the architect, lucid and comprehensible; that is, to work with elements that were already known: "This new style will not therefore emerge from all that is available and older, like a phantom that would impose itself on everyone and become comprehensible; on the contrary, many would be barely able to perceive its innovation, whose greater merit would become [rather] the consistent application of a set of existing inventions over time, which earlier could not be united skillfully."[7]

Among the historical material that Schinkel and his students adapted, the architecture of the Greeks took the first place. The goal was to modify it and subject it to contemporary needs: "If one could take ancient Greek architec-

FIGURE 2

Interior perspective view of the proposed
Gertraudenkirche, Berlin, 1819 (cat. no. 38).

ture in its most spiritual principle and then could expand it to the conditions of our new era in which at the same time the harmonious blending of the best from all intervening periods lies, then perhaps one may have found the most appropriate principle for the task," Schinkel wrote in 1834 to the Crown Prince and future King Maximilian II of Bavaria, who made an effort to remain informed about new styles for the future through recommendations and competitions.[8] Gothic architecture, the "style of the fatherland," experienced a high point in its esteem during the period of national and Romantic enthusiasm that followed the Napoleonic wars, and thus it stood as one element in this desired synthesis, though it was also available as the appropriate form of expression for sacred buildings (see *figs. 1* and *2*). There it competed with the Romanesque style of the early Christian basilica, which was supported by the temporal proximity of its model to ancient heritage, and which was prized by Schinkel's most important patron, the Prussian Crown Prince Friedrich Wilhelm, later to become King Friedrich Wilhelm IV. Whether they were to be used for country homes or rural palaces, the memories of Italian villas offered themselves to master builders and architects returning home from trips to Florence, Rome, and Naples, supported by their reading of ancient authors, especially Pliny the Younger (see *fig. 3*).

Contact with historical stylistic epochs was selective in Schinkel's circle. Roman arch-building, the High Renaissance, and Baroque and Rococo styles played no part. Whatever history offered for inspiration had to be subjected to the

FIGURE 3

Perspective view of an Italian seacoast with an imaginary
villa for Peter Beuth, 1839 (cat. no. 45).

FIGURE 4

Friedrichswer-
dersche Kirche,
Berlin,
1824–30.
Photo: John
Zukowsky,
Chicago.

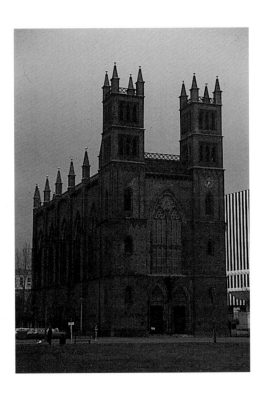

One could learn a lot from Schinkel. Only those who did not want to make the effort to think misunderstood his buildings and designs as promoting imitation. As a contemporary of G.W.F. Hegel, Schinkel, himself, did not believe he could withdraw from the dialectic of development. As the son of an historicist age, he saw himself as historical. In the preface to his planned textbook, he looked back at the early stages of his work, and criticized his own mistake: a "pure radical abstraction" which he had developed "from the nearest trivial purpose and from the construction." Two essential elements, namely the "historical" and the "poetic," had been excluded by this "dry," "stiff" type of formation, which one would call in present-day vocabulary a functionalism of purpose and construction.[11]

THE SCHINKEL SCHOOL

It is primarily in conjunction with the persuasiveness of Schinkel's work, as well as secondarily in the organization of the construction industry of the time, that one can speak of a Schinkel school in Prussia and Berlin until well into the 1870s, over three decades after his death. As the Prussian Oberbaudirektor and director of the Oberbaudeputation, Schinkel was the highest construction official of the Prussian state. All public building projects with expenditures over 500 Talers had to be presented to him. He made greater use of his rights of intervention than might have been popular with construction officials in the country. Schinkel's students, like Friedrich August Stüler (1800–1865), Johann Heinrich Strack (1805–1880), and Richard Lucae (1829 to 1877) taught at the Bauakademie (Architectural Academy), erected by Schinkel in 1831–36 *(fig. 5)*, and they passed on

aesthetic ideas of the master and his students, which functioned as a type of meta-style among all the historical citations and continually edited their use of them.[9] Tightly stretched surfaces were always desired, and these contrasted in representative assignments with large sculptural forms such as columned halls or gables, and underscored the geometry of the architectonic bodies. Slender relationships, preference for the horizontal conception of the building mass, and clear articulation of the parts predominated. On the other hand, these were tendencies that also defined the selection of historical models. Thus, Berlin Neo-Gothic is analogous to the comparatively flat, plain surfaces of the English Perpendicular style or to Italian Mendicant Gothic, not, however, to the plastic arrangement of parts in French cathedrals (see *fig. 4*).

Schinkel's life accomplishment was walking a fine line between reflection and spontaneity, between contact with what already existed and the search for originality. His attractiveness over many epochs lay not in offering an obligatory, even if variable formula, as Palladio had worked out for the villa, the palazzo, and the church, but rather in a position oscillating between the fascination with the possible and self-imposed limitation. His style did not know any finality, but nevertheless came to definable qualities. For Schinkel, the chance for artistic individuality, a moment of "exalted freedom in which all true art is recognizable," also lay in the uncertainties of his difficult times.[10]

FIGURE 5

Bauakademie (Architectural Academy), Berlin, 1831–36
(now demolished). Landesbildstelle Berlin.

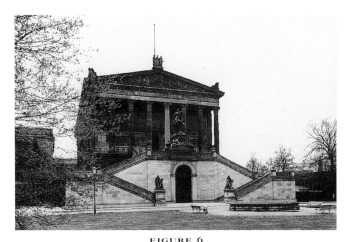

the teachings of their master to future construction officials (see *figs. 6–8*). "In the most surprising way, one recognizes the continuing beneficial influence of Schinkel in almost all provincial or local construction councillors in Prussia, even if only in their beautiful style of drawing."[12]

Schinkel's reputation was secured especially by the most prominent advocate whom he could have had in Prussia, Friedrich Wilhelm IV. During his time as Crown Prince, Friedrich Wilhelm, himself a lay architect of some stature, had helped Schinkel attain the most prominent commissions that the court and state could give. His familial relationships with the reigning houses of Europe also benefitted his architect. Schinkel's projects and those of his colleague in garden design, Peter Joseph Lenné (1789–1866), were welcome presents of the Prussian king for friends who were themselves monarchs. For his nephew by marriage, Otto I, the second son of the Bavarian King Ludwig I and the elected King of Greece, the design for a royal palace on the Acropolis was created (1834; *pl. 10*). The design of the pleasure palace Orianda on the Crimean peninsula (1838; *pls. 11* and *12*) was made for Tsarina Alexandra Feodorowna, Friedrich Wilhelm's sister. Both projects were apotheoses of German Neoclassicism in its most Romantic and fairy-tale form, removed from all possibilities of being realized.

Schinkel had students and disciples in more than his own country. The city planners of Athens, Eduard Schaubert (c. 1800 until after 1850) and Stamatios Kleanthes (1802 to 1862), were students of the Berlin Bauakademie and sought the advice of the master in crucial questions. Theophil Hansen (1813–1891), the architect of important public buildings in Athens and Vienna, had received his education in Copenhagen, but he was profoundly impressed by Schinkel's work and called the Altes Museum in the Lustgarten (Pleasure Garden) "the most beautiful architecture that he had seen."[13] It is significant for Schinkel's prestige that he even enjoyed the recognition of colleagues who were of similar age and rank. Thus for Carl Ludwig Engel (1778–1840), the creator of the Neoclassical style in Helsinki, Schinkel's work was a constant model, alongside that of St. Petersburg. Even if Engel condemned his colleague's inclination for Gothic, it was not only Schinkel's colonnaded state buildings that impressed him, but also his functional buildings in unplastered brick. Jakob Ignaz Hittorff (1792–1867), a Rhinelander by birth, and one of the most influential architects in Paris at that time, was in friendly contact with Schinkel. They visited each other and discussed Hittorff's theses on the coloration of the ancient temples—one of the many relationships that Schinkel especially nourished during his journeys to Paris and England in 1826 (see the essay by David Van Zanten in this volume).[14] In the Europe of open borders, Schinkel left tracks in the Hague and in Oslo, in Vienna and in Athens—in the north and the east more than in the west. He was a member of the Parisian Académie des Beaux-Arts, of the Royal Institute of British Architects, and of the academies in St. Petersburg and Stockholm.

In 1840, the year in which Schinkel's great patron ascended to the Prussian throne, Schinkel became extremely ill. After his death the following year, Friedrich Wilhelm IV appointed building masters for personal and state commissions who worked essentially in the style of their master, architects such as Ludwig Persius (1803–45) and, after Persius's death, Friedrich August Stüler. The Schinkel school in Berlin continued to have an effect long after the death of its leader. Even in distant Chicago, architects from Germany such as Frederick Baumann (1826–1921) and Edward Baumann (1838–1889), among others, continued Schinkel's tradition under very different conditions (see *figs. 9* and *10*). The rational components of his work and the appropriateness of his example entered into the development of the early Chicago School as it took from him the skeleton style and blocklike unity of his utilitarian buildings.[15] At the other end of the world, in Tokyo, Hermann Ende (1829–1907) and Wilhelm Böckmann (1832–1902)—a successful architectural firm from imperial Berlin—from 1886 on designed the parliament and governmental buildings in Prussian brick style (see *fig. 11*).[16]

The posthumous influence of Schinkel was also secured institutionally: in the Schinkel Museum, which for forty years, until 1884, was open to the public in the Bauakademie; in the publication of model collections, of which the most important were Schinkel's own *Sammlung architektonischer Entwürfe* and the *Werke der höheren Baukunst*; and in the monthly and annual competitions that the Berliner Architekten-Verein (Berlin Architectural Association) sponsored. These competitions still bear Schinkel's name. Even today, the tradition of the annual Schinkel Lecture is continued in Berlin, always on the architect's birthday.[17] The speakers do not confine themselves to aspects of Schinkel's work. Many of the lectures are dedicated to hydraulic engineering or transit studies; one was even on "construction tasks in the colonies with special reference to conditions in German East Africa." Nevertheless, these rhetorical efforts in their continuity represent a unique measuring stick for the popularity of and esteem for an individual architect.

FIGURE 9

Frederick and Edward Baumann, perspective view of the Ashland Block, Chicago, 1872. Photo: *Land Owner*, 4 (Aug. 1872).

FIGURE 10

Edward Baumann and Harris W. Huehl, Chamber of Commerce Building, Chicago, 1888–89.

FIGURE 11

Hermann Ende and Wilhelm Böckmann, Justice Ministry, Tokyo, 1888. Photo: *Deutsche Bauzeitung*, 25 (2 May 1891), p. 209.

FIGURE 12

Design for a department store (Kaufhaus) on the Unter
den Linden, Berlin, 1827. Photo: Carl von Lorck,
Karl Friedrich Schinkel (Berlin, 1939), p. 79.

EPIGONE OR PROGENITOR?

After the foundation of the second German empire in the year 1871, Schinkel's esteem noticeably diminished in Germany.[18] He had to be defended against the dogmatism and aridity of his students; he was excused for the limitations of his time, though sometimes even he himself was attacked. The demands for comfort of the Gründerzeit (the Age of the Founders, as the 1870s and 1880s became known) and its need to express its newly gained economic status were no longer reflected in the discretion and frugality of the Schinkel school. The art critic Karl Scheffler only granted to the master the highest "industriousness and intense empathy of an epigone" and to his students only a "bureaucratically correct Greece." The city house façades of late Prussian classicism now seemed puritanical and even boring; the restraint of the brick parochial churches were perceived as "tidy utilitarianism," while the size and discipline of the state buildings were considered to be "monumentality staring with glazed eyes and wrapped in pettiness."[19] Simplicity and meagreness had a provoking effect. Kaiser Wilhelm II's aversion to Schinkel is attested.[20] The art historian Cornelius Gurlitt, teaching in Dresden, considered Schinkel, his sense of duty, and his modesty to be the essence of the Prussian privy councillor, and he claimed that the bourgeois and courtly villas of the "Berlin Hellenes" were "created out of the sense that wealth does not make one happy" and had often led to the opinion that, in art, "poverty does make one happy."[21]

While Gurlitt believed that Schinkel's star was in decline, Arthur Moeller van den Bruck a few years later was already seeing it rise again. His book *Der preußische Stil* was published during the First World War. Where Gurlitt or Scheffler had found only poor routine, Moeller van den Bruck discovered simplicity and reason transfigured into virtues of soldierly asceticism. Poverty was indeed considered a good fortune in art. A new generation, which had tired of the overgrown taste and craving for status of the imperial era, and which in fact held them responsible for the military and political catastrophe of the war, reached back to the style of 1800. Schinkel assumed a central role in Moeller van den Bruck's impassioned sermon ("Prussia must exist!"). In him, "the one who was awakened and called," the "festive balance of purpose and form" had succeeded.[22]

Alongside the Neue Wache (New Guardhouse, 1816 to 1819), the Altes Museum (1822–30), and the Schauspielhaus (Theater) on the Gendarmenmarkt (1818–21) in Berlin, utilitarian buildings also appeared as models for the present, such as the Bauakademie, the lighthouse for the Cape of Arkona on the Baltic Sea island of Rügen (1825–27), the barracks on the Lindenstrasse (1817–18), the portal of the Kalkberg tunnel (1827). Above all, one now referred to the center project for the Berlin boulevard Unter den Linden which was never built (1827; see *fig. 12*). This assignment—a courtyard layout of approximately one hundred individual stores—was designed to meet the needs of the age of the masses. In the making of yet another Schinkel image, that of the modern Schinkel, certain aspects of his work, such as his Neo-Gothic components, had to be omitted. They were now viewed as forgettable concessions that the master had made to Romanticism.

Just before the First World War, then, Berlin architects were rethinking Classicism and at the same time reevaluating Schinkel's accomplishments.[23] None other than the critical Scheffler himself wrote in 1912: "There already are, if one has the necessary fantasy to see them, decidedly modern elements in Schinkel's buildings, in the sense of the present-day utilitarian artist; that is, understated beginnings for a consciously metropolitan functional architecture."[24]

The critic Fritz Stahl in the same year went so far as to proclaim Schinkel as the "future man of our architecture," suggesting that the fame that he had previously enjoyed would be nothing in comparison to his future influence.[25] Schinkel and his epoch embodied a different phase of history, one that had avoided the worst excrescences of historicism and thus offered a means of connecting the torn threads of tradition.

In fact, many participants in the 1912 competition for a Royal Opera House in Berlin had already alluded to Schinkel's Schauspielhaus on the nearby Gendarmenmarkt (see *fig. 13*). For Alfred Messel (1853–1909), Ludwig Hoffmann (1852–1932), or the younger Bruno Paul (1874–1968), the resurrected Classicism was to be found in severely simplified and yet moderately historicizing variations. But these comparatively conservative architects still had to gauge their work to the grander dimensions of the young metropolis and its needs. The fine arrangement and individuality of the forms, which Schinkel and his closest students had nurtured, were lost. But in their systematics, in the repetition of their parts, in their conciseness and precision, the large buildings by Schinkel remained a model of "industrial Classicism."[26] The dignified formulas of the Schinkel period were transferred from Schinkel's cultural buildings to new factories and their administration buildings, and thus they gave the workshops a reflection of cultural legitimation.

One of these "utilitarian artists" was Peter Behrens (1868–1940), who was at the same time a guiding figure of the new and a formal manipulator whose designs achieved great pathos. His contemporaries already drew the connection between his industrial architecture and the Hellenistic antiquity transmitted through Schinkel. With abstract geometries and systematic proportion studies, Behrens had freed himself from the subjectivity of Jugendstil, the German manifestation of Art Nouveau. After his appointment as the artistic consultant for the Berlin electrical company AEG in

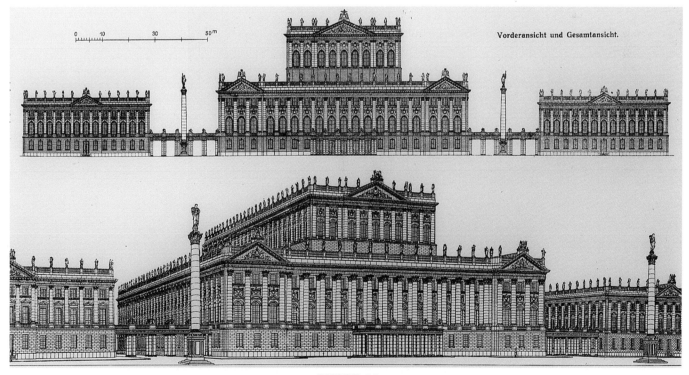

FIGURE 13

Ludwig Hoffmann, Design for the Royal Opera House,
Berlin, entry to the 1912 design competition.
Photo: *Deutsche Bauzeitung*, 48 (14 Feb. 1914), p. 236.

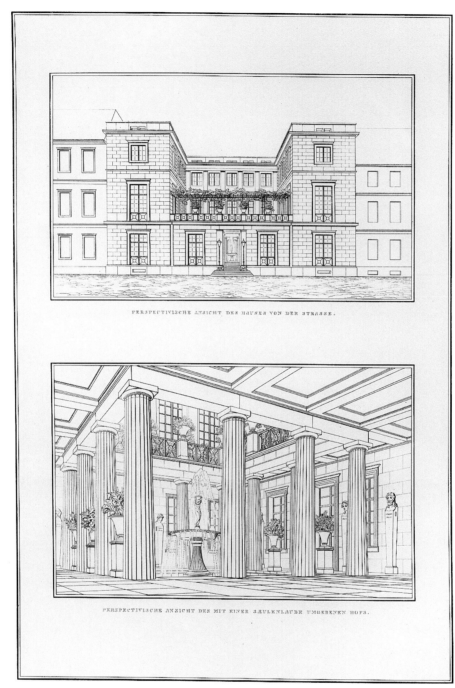

PERSPECTIVISCHE ANSICHT DES HAUSES VON DER STRASSE.

PERSPECTIVISCHE ANSICHT DES MIT EINER SÄULENLAUBE UMGEBENEN HOFS.

FIGURE 14

Design for an urban house, 1826. Photo: *Sammlung architektonischer Entwürfe* (Berlin, 1866).

1907, it was not least of all Prussian Neoclassicism that aided Behrens's buildings to achieve physical presence and monumentality. "If Schinkel were alive today, some of his buildings would resemble those of Behrens in many points."[27] For the house in Berlin-Dahlem, which was commissioned in 1912–14 by the archeologist Theodor Wiegand, Director of the Antikensammlung (Collection of Antiquities) and head of the Schinkel Museum, the allusion is made to one of Schinkel's designs from 1826 for an urban residence (see *figs. 14–16*). Both foresaw an open peristyle. The agreement even extended as far as the suggestion to cover the roof with sheet-zinc.[28]

Above all, Schinkel's influence in Berlin was passed on through memories in the consciousness of the architects, and not only through his buildings. Walter Gropius (1883–1969), for a time an assistant to Behrens and occupied until the First World War with blocklike manor houses, workers' apartments, and manor building in the tradition of rural classicism, grew up in a family in which Schinkel had played an outstanding role. His great-grandfather, his grandfather, and his grandfather's brothers were theater and panorama entrepreneurs, who had already given commissions to Schinkel before his fairy-tale career (see the essays by Kurt W. Forster and Birgit Verwiebe in this volume). Walter Gropius's father remained a fan of Schinkel's architecture. And with the Kunstgewerbemuseum (Museum of Decorative Arts; now the Martin-Gropius-Bau, 1877–81), his uncle Martin had designed a bare-brick building in the best Berlin Schinkel tradition—comparable to the Bauakademie (see *fig. 17*). From Walter Gropius's later days it has been related that for many years he kept on his evening table a reproduction of Schinkel's painting *Blick in Griechenlands Blüte (A View of Greece in its Prime)*.[29]

A FORERUNNER OF MODERNITY

In the 1920s, Schinkel's reputation was established as a forerunner of modernity. "It is high time that Schinkel's services for a new form be appropriately honored," Gustav Adolf Platz wrote in the *Propyläen-Kunstgeschichte*, and he dedicated space to Schinkel in the biographical section of his volume—reserved for the twentieth century—as though Schinkel were an architect of his own era. Leo von Klenze (1784–1864) and Friedrich Weinbrenner (1766–1820) did not receive the same honor. In Platz's words, Schinkel "was the first … to work freely from the essence of the task and the material," an assessment that today one would only accept with great difficulty.[30] Ludwig Hilberseimer, Friedrich

FIGS. 15 AND 16
Peter Behrens, Views of street and garden entrances to the Wiegand House, Berlin-Dahlem, 1912–14. Photos: *Wasmuths Monatshefte für Baukunst* (1918/19), pp. 268 and 273.

FIGURE 17
Martin Gropius and Heino Schmieden, Martin-Gropius-Bau (formerly Kunstgewerbemuseum [Museum of Decorative Arts]), Berlin, 1876–81. Brandenburgisches Landesamt für Denkmalpflege.

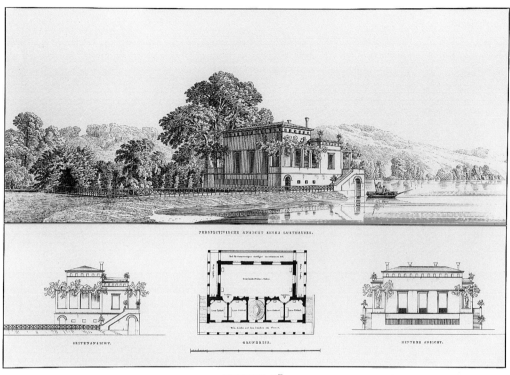

FIGURE 18

Perspective view, elevations, and plan of the Lusthaus,
Potsdam, c. 1825. Photo: *Sammlung
architektonischer Entwürfe* (Berlin, 1866).

Tamms, Oskar Kaufmann, and Bruno Taut, all paid tribute to the patriarch. Taut cited, as an exception, the fantastic aspects of Schinkel's stage pictures, which he, the visionary of the years after the First World War, placed higher than the buildings "in their effect on the formation of an artistic world view." And he asked, "Were the buildings any worse for this?"[31] Schinkel's 150th birthday, which was celebrated in 1931, motivated many modern architects to pay verbal homages.[32]

After the Neo-Gothic Schinkel, now too the Grecian Schinkel was to be sacrificed to the "utilitarian artists." In view of contemporary post-and-beam buildings, critics felt reminded of their progenitor, but "not of the Schinkel of general opinion, the classicist and man of columns, but rather the lesser known one whom we can call the first modernist." Ludwig Mies van der Rohe expressed the estimation somewhat more casually: "Schinkel, the greatest building master of classicism, represents the end of an old and the beginning of a new time. With the Altes Museum he built a waning period. With his boring Gothic churches he was the forerunner of an unspeakably kitschy century, but with the Building Academy he introduced a new epoch."[33]

Instead of the architecture of columns and pointed arches, Schinkel's country houses now received special attention. Realized and unrealized projects like the Lusthaus (Pleasure House) in the vicinity of Potsdam (c. 1825; *fig. 18*) or the Römische Bäder (Roman Baths; see Vogtherr, *figs. 9* and *10*) on the grounds of Sanssouci in Potsdam (1829–40) had been modeled after the appearance of Italian villas and farmhouses. These—along with the reconstruction of the Pliny villas (1833)—were laid out for a charming ensemble effect; they were supposed to create surprising spatial results and offer pleasant views and panoramas. Asymmetry occurred mostly on its own; sometimes, however—as in the depiction of the Lusthaus—it was only seemingly suggested through the view from the upper corner and through the representation of lush vegetation. The layout of these buildings opened up the possibility of further building for future needs, freed from the compulsion of symmetrically ordered sides for representation. "Thus this layout," as Schinkel described the Römische Bäder, "forms a picturesque grouped whole, which ... is capable by its nature of ever continued expansion and enrichment, so that a continual pleasure of production remains in it."[34] This concept stunningly foreshadowed the process-orientation of modern construction, its principle of incompleteness, and its openness to further development based on individual units that can be added, as well as its interplay across the boundaries of interior and exterior space through intermediating forms of covered and open areas.

Mies van der Rohe always professed his faith in Schinkel and has been compared to Schinkel again and again by other authors—from Paul Westheim to Philip Johnson.[35] Until well into the 1920s, Mies's career centered on the replacement of a literal Neoclassicism with a latent Classicism, a Classicism as a way of thinking. Even after such revolutionary projects as the Landhaus in Eisenbeton (Concrete Country House) and the Landhaus in Backstein (Brick Country House)—both from 1923–24—had already been conceived, with the Mosler House (1924–26) Mies began the last of his blocklike closed house spaces, constructed with a flatly inclined hipped roof, dormers, and round or eyebrow windows, and with edged rectangular supports, which bore lintels, balconies, or continuous stone beams for halls of pillars. Some of these villas were created in Potsdam-Neubabelsberg on Lake Griebnitz (see *fig. 19*), directly across from Schinkel's Schloß Glienicke (1824–27).

In the part of his work that began with idealized projects after the First World War, Mies no longer took Schinkel more or less literally; instead, he now sublimated and transposed his influence. In the Concrete Country House, for example, the perceivable elements of classical tradition—such as the flight of stairs, loggia, entrance hall, and a three-wing layout integrated in the core—are brought together to create a formal image that shares only the most fundamental qualities of simplicity and clarity with Schinkel. "Mies, who approached Schinkel and as was common at first took him as a transmitter of a specific formal language, discovered for himself under this classicistic Schinkel that other Schinkel, who had been an eminently objective building master in the sense and with the technical and craft means of his time. This was the Schinkel whose ideal of antiquity had never hindered him from arranging his buildings clearly and sensibly from the determination of their nature."[36]

Mies called Schinkel's Altes Museum *(fig. 20)* a "magnificent building."[37] When he himself had to erect a museum in Berlin, the Neue Nationalgalerie (1962–68), the master of twentieth-century architecture resorted to means that are completely reminiscent of the master of the early nineteenth century: the discipline in binding the axes, the dignified form of the gentle flight of stairs, the templelike

FIGURE 19

Ludwig Mies van der Rohe, Riehl House, Potsdam, 1907.
Photo: *Moderne Bauformen*, 9 (1910).

FIGURE 20

Altes Museum, Berlin, 1822–30.
Landesbildstelle Berlin.

FIGURE 21

Ludwig Mies van der Rohe, Neue Nationalgalerie, Berlin,
1962–68. Photo: Reinhard Friedrich, Berlin.

FIGURE 22

Paul Ludwig Troost, Haus der Kunst, Munich, 1933–37.
Collection of the Library of Congress, Washington.

FIGURE 23

Albert Speer, Decoration of the Lustgarten square, Berlin,
for a Nazi rally, with the Altes Museum in background,
1936. Photo: Rudolf Wolters, *Albert Speer* (Oldenburg, 1943).

FIGURE 24

Hermann Henselmann, View of a highrise and residential
block on the Strausberger Platz, Karl-Marx-Allee, Berlin,
1952–54. Photo: *Hermann Henselmann: Gedanken, Ideen,
Bauten, Projekte* (Berlin, 1978), pl. 33.

raising-up on a building base, the seemingly floating coffered ceiling, and the idea of the city loggia and of the column or pillar walk which was laid before the whole side—or in Mies van der Rohe's eight-pillar construction around the whole building *(fig. 21)*. Comparison with Schinkel's design of a summer residence in Orianda makes the parallel even clearer. In Schinkel's design, a templelike, almost transparent pavilion sits enthroned upon a substructure, which—like the foundation of the Nationalgalerie—could serve as the home of a museum (in the case of Orianda, one for ancient art). The volume of Schinkel's *Werke der höheren Baukunst* that contains the designs for Orianda lay at hand in Mies van der Rohe's studio, according to his collaborator Sergius Ruegenberg.[38]

Even modern architects who demonstrated no closeness to Schinkel professed their belief in Prussia's Oberbaudirektor. Hans Scharoun (1893–1972) developed the principles of an organic, or to use the term of his friend Hugo Häring (1882–1958), an "organ-like" construction contemporaneously with the International Style of modernism and in opposition to it. Häring, like Scharoun, conceived of building as an expression of life, as a "form of performance," as an architecture of processes and not forms. The dynamic was played out against the static, the becoming against the being, the organic against the geometric, the Nordic (and also for a time, the Germanic) against the Mediterranean, for which the name Le Corbusier stood. Häring and Scharoun reclaimed Schinkel for the Nordic tradition. Schinkel had utilized ancient formal material in the Romantic sense, spatially and not physically, spiritually abstract and not sensually concrete.[39]

THE MAN OF COLUMNS

While Scharoun expressed himself in this way about Schinkel, another campaign of glorification was already underway. Scharoun's attempt to claim the Prussian Hellene for the Germanic tradition came even closer to the image of Schinkel within National Socialism. But the National Socialists were not looking for a Nordic Romantic, but rather for the supposed hero, the "man of columns," the "last great building master, who was able to impress his stamp on a whole epoch."[40] The state and party buildings of the Third Reich were praised as the fulfillment and simultaneously the surpassing of Schinkel's work. An edifying text from those years on the "forerunners of the new German attitude towards building" closes with plates of Nazi buildings. Paul Ludwig Troost's portico on the Haus der Kunst (1933–37; *fig. 22*) in

Munich was supposed to appear as the heroicization of the hall of columns on Schinkel's Altes Museum. In addition, the Nazi Ehrentempel (Temples of Honor) on the Munich Königsplatz (1934–35; demolished after the Second World War) were supposed to serve as a continuation of the Berlin Neue Wache. "The true and authentic Schinkel attitude again became the guiding line, but at the same time each previous creation was surpassed."[41]

Clearly, Hitler's own inclination went in the direction of Neo-Baroque displays of magnificence, such as the representational style of the Viennese Ringstrasse and of Parisian grandeur, and not in the direction of Prussian Classicism. Nevertheless, Troost (1878–1934), whom Hitler admired as the greatest building master of Germany since Schinkel, was able to convince him in favor of an arid reductive Classicism. In the living room of the old imperial chancellery used by Hitler, two paintings by Schinkel from the collection of the Nationalgalerie were hung.[42] After Troost's death, the second "building master of the Führer," Albert Speer (1905 to 1981), possessed no greater ambition according to his own admission than to become "a second Schinkel."[43] Speer's teacher at the Technische Hochschule in Berlin-Charlottenburg, Heinrich Tessenow (1876–1950), had found a sensitive answer to Schinkel's valiant Doric style during his remodeling of Schinkel's Neue Wache into a war memorial (1930–31). Speer also had to confront Schinkel in his decoration of the Lustgarten for the Nazi rallies on May 1. In 1936 he covered the walls on the square of the Lustgarten with banners, leaving exposed only the Baroque palace and the peristyle of the Altes Museum, thus misusing them as backdrops (see *fig. 23*). What for Schinkel was to be a cheerful hall of the citizens, open to the garden and the city, Speer transformed into decoration for a marching field. From Schinkel's Neoclassical buildings, Nazi architects borrowed the powerful angular formation, the tendency to leave large sections of wall undifferentiated, and the cubic disposition of mass. Of course, in their treatment of these formal elements they made use of completely different dimensions from those of Biedermeier Berlin. The colossal support placements were interpreted in principle as infinitely continuable parades of columns; the classical orderings, its proportional system, and its relationship to the human dimension were abandoned.

One might think that after the Second World War the earlier invocations of Schinkel's work by such varied protagonists, and especially the claims on him by Nazi Classicism, would have led to a break with his illustrious heritage. But

the German Democratic Republic (GDR), which defined itself as anti-fascist, again turned to Schinkel shortly after its foundation.[44] During an initial phase of discussion, many architects held hopes that Modernism might find a place in their new country, and the newly formed "planning collective" under Stadtbaurat (Municipal Building Councilor) Scharoun (in office from 1945 until 1946) in the still-undivided Berlin presented a radical structural plan along the lines of the Charter of Athens. Despite these efforts, the SED (Socialist Unity Party of Germany) regime soon conceived a national rebuilding plan under the influence of the Soviet Union. Their architectural program, featuring monumental buildings and a "characteristic" formal language that followed historical models, was supposed to protect the architecture of the GDR from the internationalism of their political enemy, just as historicist Stalinist buildings had done in the postwar Soviet Union. A style of building was needed that "was linked to the great building masters of German history ... and corresponded to the feelings of our people," "socialist" in content and national in form.[45]

For Berlin and the former Prussia, the "great building master" of course meant Schinkel. Elements of the Prussian Classical style were used especially in East Berlin's Stalinallee (later, Karl-Marx-Allee, 1952–54, see *fig. 24*) and in the nearby group of buildings on the Weberwiese (1951–52). The East German star architect Hermann Henselmann (born 1905) proved to be the most astute architect, a "forty-year-old madcap," who only a few days after he had been chastised for formalism, presented a design for the Weberwiese "in the new spirit."[46] This "new spirit" was the supposed spirit of Schinkel. In the same year that the high-rise

FIGURE 25

Philip Johnson, Amon Carter Museum of Western Art, Fort Worth, Texas, 1961. Photo: Ezra Stoller, Mamaroneck, N.Y.

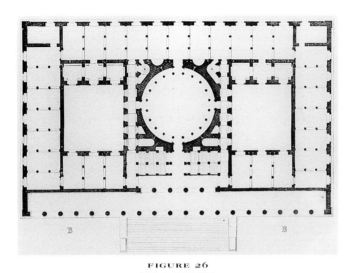

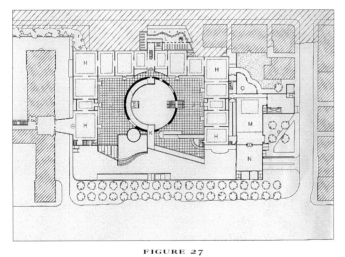

building on the Weberwiese was dedicated as the symbol of the new socialist era, Henselmann published a study on Schinkel. In it, the necessity of a return to Schinkel's forms and principles was justified partly with psychological, partly with political, reasoning. The past had to be studied, because Schinkel's works formed an indissoluble component in the image of the homeland for the people of Berlin. But it was also necessary to claim the Schinkel heritage "in the face of the mortal threat to our national existence by American imperialism," and to bring it into the "embittered struggle … for the unity of our fatherland."[47] The short-term Schinkel renaissance was additionally justified since Schinkel—the architect of kings!—was declared the chosen fighter against feudalism and the representative of an enlightened citizenry.

German reunification under a Socialist banner was still a political goal of the SED leadership in the early 1950s. The care for tradition was rapidly pushed aside when the policy of socialist reunification was abandoned, and Nikita Khrushchev promoted industrialization of the building trades in 1954. The East German leadership adopted this a short time later. In terms of municipal construction, the architects of a regime that was determined to have the effects of large-scale, representative axes and squares could not have found much inspiration in Schinkel. Schinkel had pursued town planning with the construction of individual buildings and in concrete individual assignments, but hardly ever with the aid of far-reaching total planning.[48]

THE CONTINUATION OF HISTORY

In the West, there was renewed interest in Schinkel in conjunction with a very gradual revision of Modernism and a new openness to the diversity and colorfulness of history. Outside of Germany, his name of course was known only to a few experts, completely the opposite of the situation during his lifetime. Philip Johnson was one of his first promoters on the other side of the Atlantic. He knew Schinkel's work not only through the mediation of Mies van der Rohe, but also through his own viewing, and he once wanted to write a book about Schinkel.[49] Johnson even went so far as to maintain that his whole work as an architect was influenced by Schinkel. He pointed to the principle of symmetry without an obvious center, to the additive use of elements, and accentuated corner solutions. As examples from his own work, Johnson cited the Amon Carter Museum in Fort Worth, Texas (1961), with its loggia of columns facing outwardly *(fig. 25)*, as well as the Boissonnas House in New Canaan, Conn. (1957), whose informal arrangement and whose opening into the outer room was indebted to Schinkel's Römische Bäder.[50]

The increasing internationalization of the architectural profession has benefited Schinkel's posthumous reputation insofar as more and more architects from other countries have received the opportunity to see his buildings. The International Building Exhibition (IBA), which was held in Berlin from 1984 to 1987, brought the "jet set" from all over the world to the former Prussian capital city. Since literal citation was now no longer frowned upon, allusions to Schinkel could be found in many of the designs. Among the invited competitors for the former industrial harbor in Berlin-Tegel (1980), both Charles Moore (1925–1993) and Arata Isozaki reproduced in their drawings the nearby Schloß Tegel, which Schinkel had built in 1820–24 for Wilhelm von Humboldt and his collection of antiquities. Even the Spree freight barges, which Schinkel depicted in his published views, are found in various presentation renderings of the IBA projects. That Schinkel had created the character of the small Humboldt palace of quite specific conditions—namely, the inclusion of an older construction with a tower—did not bother Moore or Isozaki any more than did the completely different dimensions that the Tegel Town and Recreation Center required, in contrast to the small Humboldt palace.

Rob Krier also passed over Schinkel's expressed condemnation of "common imitation" and "anxious repetition," when he had to erect a residential complex (1980–83) in the area of Berlin known as South Friedrichstadt.[51] One of Krier's houses came very close to the property where Schinkel had erected a residential house in 1829 for the pottery and tile manufacturer Tobias Feilner—a building that Henselmann had also used as a model for his skyscraper on the Weberwiese. The façade of Schinkel's Feilner House had survived the Second World War, only to be torn down in the redevelopment fervor of the 1950s and 1960s. Krier's house, or more precisely its north façade, is not an actual reconstruction, but rather a sympathetic approximation: different profiles, plaster instead of brick, an additional window axis, and dormers for an additional floor (as, ultimately, the financial calculations of the Berliner Wohnungsbaukreditanstalt [Housing Credit Institution] had to be fulfilled). The rear of the house is done in a completely different style; unity of form was not a priority for Krier. Schinkel spoke of a "lasting, beautiful, and true architecture" in conjunction with the Feilner House.[52] Its imitation, instead, achieves the oppo-

FIGURE 28

Perspective drawing of the rotunda of the Altes Museum.
Photo: *Sammlung architektonischer Entwürfe* (Berlin, 1866).

FIGURE 29

James Stirling, Michael Wilford & Associates,
Rotunda of the Neue Staatsgalerie, Stuttgart, 1977–84.
Photo: Peter Walser, Stuttgart.

site, namely the impression of temporariness, lack of solidity, fraudulence—a passing bon mot.

James Stirling's re-evaluation of Schinkel, on the other hand, went beyond citation. In the Neue Staatsgalerie in Stuttgart (1977–84), Stirling (1926–1992) reconsidered the museums of the nineteenth century and arranged the exhibition halls of the upper floor—as in the older neighboring Neoclassical building—in an *enfilade* around a *cour d'honneur*. As a prototype of the nineteenth-century museum, Stirling named Schinkel's Altes Museum with its ground plan centered on a dome (*figs. 26* and *27*).[53] Schinkel understood his domed hall to be the holy of holies, whose Pantheon-like vault arched over the gaps between the art of the ancient world and the Renaissance, the ancient and modern eras (*fig. 28*). Stirling's rotunda, on the other hand, gapes open; it is overgrown with greenery like a ruin, it remains a vacuum, it negates the concept of the overvaulting unity, which was a central idea of Schinkel's construction (*fig. 29*). The paths are mapped out accordingly. Schinkel's hall is the distributive core of the building, its spiritual as well as its functional center. Contrary to this, Stirling's rotunda is not touched at all by the inner circular tour through the museum. Only an outer, public pedestrian walk winds its way along the cylindrical walls.

What drew Stirling to Schinkel was the attraction of an architecture that was "richer in memory and association" and referred to a "thicker layer of history": the Prussian building official, who in his own century was accused of aridity and pedantry, now appeared—correctly—as a figure with a greater cultural range than the majority of his successors in the twentieth century. Stirling's fascination went so far that in 1980 he proposed the task of "a house for Schinkel" in an annual design competition of the journal *The Japan Architect*.[54] No fewer than 384 participants designed villas that would have satisfied the emperor Hadrian: many of them conceived of a house that contained, in addition to its customary features, a library, gallery, winter garden, servant's wing, swimming pool, tennis court, gardens, and fruit orchards; all of which, to the Prussian official who lived in a government apartment in the Bauakademie, would have seemed like the greatest of royal luxury.

Confrontation with Schinkel was a confrontation with an œuvre that did not offer a monolithic and monumental model. Schinkel worked in a confused time, an age that extended from the Great Revolution of 1789 across the rise of national feelings up to the restoration of a regime that governed by divine right. But at the same time, the epoch also sent towards him the precursors of the industrialized era with its unforeseeable and unheard-of changes. The appropriations of his work proved to be as contradictory as the work itself, and they unfolded in a temporal sequence many varied aspects of his life's achievements, settled-in between dream and duty, between wandering fantasy and calculating discipline. Something "unbound" lay in Schinkel's essence, wrote an earlier author, Hans Mackowsky, in a noteworthy formulation.[55]

Finally, one concern ran through all Schinkel's works, not only his constructed ones, but also his writings: that the chain of appropriation, transmission, and renewal of tradition could break off. This is the concern for the salvation of a history that would be placed in jeopardy both by the slavish repetition of the old and by the bold innovation that "destroys all that came before." Each individual artwork must assure the continuation of history: "Each individual artwork is the beginning of a new history."[56] The question very much remains, whether the reception of Schinkel's œuvre in all its phases—and especially in the latest, postmodern phase—has fulfilled this demand of its protagonist.

NOTES

1. Brentano's remarks are quoted in August Grisebach, *Karl Friedrich Schinkel* (Leipzig, 1924), p. 16; Emanuel Geibel, "Zur Schinkelfeier," in Hans Mackowsky, *Karl Friedrich Schinkel: Briefe, Tagebücher, Gedanken* (Berlin, 1922), pp. 199f.

2. Karl Friedrich Schinkel, "Materialien zum Lehrbuch," in Goerd Peschken, ed., *Das Architektonische Lehrbuch*, in *Karl Friedrich Schinkel: Lebenswerk* (Munich and Berlin: Deutscher Kunstverlag, 1979), p. 150.

3. See "The Author's Preface to the Reader," in Andrea Palladio, *The Four Books of Architecture* (1570), trans. Isaac Ware (New York: Dover Publications, 1965).

4. Schinkel (note 2), p. 150.

5. Karl Friedrich Schinkel quoted in Richard Lucae, "Schinkel im Lichte der Gegenwart" (1865), in Julius Posener, ed., *Festreden Schinkel zu Ehren, 1846–1980* (Berlin: Frölich and Kaufmann, n.d.), p. 56.

6. See Eva Börsch-Supan, *Berliner Baukunst nach Schinkel, 1840–1870*, Studien zur Kunst des neunzehnten Jahrhunderts, vol. 25 (Munich: Prestel, 1977).

7. Schinkel (note 2), p. 146.

8. Mackowsky (note 1), pp. 180f.

9. On this and on the Schinkel reception in the 19th century in general, see Börsch-Supan (note 6), pp. 83f., 196ff.

10. Schinkel (note 2), p. 150.

11. Ibid.

12. Ernst Förster, *Geschichte der deutschen Kunst*, vol. 5 (Leipzig, 1860), p. 337.

13. Georg Niemann and Ferdinand von Feldegg, *Theophilus Hansen und seine Werke* (Vienna, 1893), p. 14.

14. Karl Friedrich Schinkel, *The English Journey: Journal of a Visit to France and Britain in 1826*, ed. David Bindman and Gottfried Riemann, trans. F. Gayna Walls (New Haven and London: Yale University Press, 1993), pp. 41–43, 52, 55, 58, 60, 63.

15. Roula Mouroudellis Geraniotis, "An Early German Contribution to Chicago's Modernism," in John Zukowsky, ed., *Chicago Architecture, 1872–1922: Birth of a Metropolis* (Chicago and Munich: The Art Institute of Chicago and Prestel Verlag, 1987), pp. 91–105.

16. Michiko Reid, "Der Prozeß der Einführung der europäischen Architektur in Japan," in Manfred Speidel, ed., *Japanische Architektur: Geschichte und Gegenwart* (Stuttgart, 1983), pp. 57ff.

17. Posener (note 5).

18. Börsch-Supan (note 6), pp. 19ff, 60ff.

19. Karl Scheffler, *Berlin: Ein Stadtschicksal*, 3rd ed. (Berlin, 1910), pp. 86ff.

20. Walther Rathenau's recording of a conversation with Wilhelm II, in Hartmut Pogge von Strandmann, ed., *Walther Rathenau: Tagebuch, 1907–1922* (Düsseldorf, 1967), p. 133.

21. Cornelius Gurlitt, *Die deutsche Kunst des 19. Jahrhunderts, ihre Ziele und Taten*, 3rd ed. (Berlin, 1907), pp. 216f.

22. Arthur Moeller van den Bruck, *Der preußische Stil*, 3rd ed. (Berlin, 1931), pp. 153, 162.

23. See Paul Mebes, *Um 1800* (Berlin, 1908). On the reception of Schinkel in the first half of the twentieth century, see Christian Schädlich, "Karl Friedrich Schinkel und die Architektur des zwanzigsten Jahrhunderts," *Wissenschaftliche Zeitschrift der Hochschule für Architektur und Bauwesen Weimar* 27, no. 5–6 (1980), pp. 217ff.

24. Karl Scheffler, *Die Architektur der Großstadt* (Berlin: B. Cassirer, 1913), p. 154.

25. Fritz Stahl, *Karl Friedrich Schinkel. 10. Sonderheft der Berliner Architekturwelt* (Berlin, 1912), p. 3.

26. The phrase is Tilman Buddensieg's; see Tilman Buddensieg, et al., *Industriekultur: Peter Behrens and the AEG, 1907–1914*, trans. Iain Boyd Whyte (Cambridge, Mass.: MIT Press, 1984).

27. Scheffler (note 24), p. 154.

28. Fritz Neumeyer, "Zwischen Monumentalkunst und Moderne," in Wolfram Hoepfner and Fritz Neumeyer, *Das Haus Wiegand von Peter Behrens in Berlin-Dahlem* (Mainz: Verlag Philipp von Zabern, 1979), pp. 39–42.

29. Reginald R. Isaacs, *Walter Gropius: Der Mensch und sein Werk*, 2 vols. (Berlin: Mann, 1983), pp. 35ff., 1032.

30. Gustav Adolf Platz, *Die Baukunst der neuesten Zeit* (Berlin, 1927), p. 24.

31. Bruno Taut, "Pro Domo," in *Frühlicht: Stadtbaukunst alter und neuer Zeit*, 1, no. 8 (1920), p. 128.

32. See "Schinkel im Urteil der Baukünstler von heute," *Der Kunstwanderer* (1931), pp. 71ff.

33. Fritz Stahl, *German Bestelmeyer* (Berlin, Leipzig, and Vienna, 1928), p. xiii. See also an undated notebook entry by Ludwig Mies van der Rohe, in Fritz Neumeyer, *The Artless Word: Mies van der Rohe on the Building Art*, trans. Mark Jarzombek (Cambridge, Mass.: MIT Press, 1991), p. 76.

34. Karl Friedrich Schinkel, *Sammlung architektonischer Entwürfe* (28 parts; Berlin, 1819–40). Of the numerous reprints, see that of the 1866 edition, *Collection of Architectural Designs*, trans. Karin Cramer (New York: Princeton Architectural Press, 1989).

35. Neumeyer (note 33), p. 76. Philip Cortelyon Johnson, "Karl Friedrich Schinkel im zwanzigsten Jahrhundert" (1961), in Posener (note 5), pp. 313ff. Under the title "Schinkel und Mies," this essay also appears in Philip Johnson, *Writings* (New York: Oxford University Press, 1979), pp. 165–81.

36. Paul Westheim, "Mies van der Rohe: Entwicklung eines Architekten," *Das Kunstblatt*, 11 (February 1927), p. 56.

37. Peter Carter, "Mies van der Rohe," *Bauen + Wohnen*, 15, no. 7 (July 1961), p. 231.

38. Wolf Tegethoff, "Orianda—Berlin. Das Vorbild Schinkels im Werk Mies van der Rohes," *Zeitschrift des deutschen Vereins für Kunstgeschichte*, 35, 1/4 (1981), pp. 174ff.

39. Hans Scharoun, "Das Wirkbild der Stile, 'der Preußische Stil,' Schinkel," undated essay, in Achim Wendschuh, ed., *Hans Scharoun: Zeichnungen, Aquarelle, Texte* (Berlin, 1993), pp. 96ff.

40. Rudolf Wolters, in Albert Speer, ed., *Neue deutsche Baukunst* (Berlin, 1941), p. 8.

41. Josef Schmid, *Karl Friedrich Schinkel: Der Vorläufer neuer deutscher Baugesinnung* (Leipzig: Oscar Brandstetter, 1943), n. pag.

42. Albert Speer, *Erinnerungen* (Berlin, 1969), p. 132. Translated by Richard and Clara Winston in English as *Inside the Third Reich* (New York: Avon, 1971).

43. Albert Speer, entry for October 2, 1946, *Spandauer Tagebücher*, (Frankfurt, 1975), p. 17. Translated by Richard and Clara Winston into English as *Spandau: the Secret Diaries* (New York: Macmillan, 1976).

44. See the Marxist-Leninist interpretation by Schädlich (note 23), pp. 220f.

45. "Wäre es schön? Es wäre schön! Vorschlag des Zentralkomitees der Sozialistischen Einheitspartei Deutschlands für den Aufbau Berlins" in *Neues Deutschland*, November 25, 1951. See Simone Hain, "Berlin Ost: Im Westen wird man sich wundern," in Klaus von Beyme, et al., ed., *Neue Städte aus Ruinen. Deutscher Städtebau der Nachkriegszeit* (Munich, 1992), pp. 32ff.

46. Rudolf Herrnstadt, "Über den Baustil, den politischen Stil und den Genossen Henselmann," *Neues Deutschland*, July 29, 1951.

47. Hermann Henselmann, "Karl Friedrich Schinkel," in *Über Karl Friedrich Schinkel* (Berlin: B. Henschel, 1952), pp. 6ff.

48. Werner Hegemann, the editor of *Wasmuths Monatshefte für Baukunst und Städtebau*, spoke in 1931 of a "Romantic wildness" in the town planning of Schinkel: "In the important area of town planning, Schinkel had nearly completely failed"; see Hegemann, "Zu Schinkels 150. Geburtstag," *Wasmuths Monatshefte für Baukunst und Städtebau*, 15 (1931), pp. 161f.

49. According to Robert A. M. Stern, in Johnson (note 35), p. 164.

50. Johnson (note 35).

51. Schinkel in Peschken (note 2), pp. 30, 54.

52. Schinkel (note 34), *Sammlung architektonischer Entwürfe* (Berlin, 1831), pl. 114.

53. James Stirling, "The Monumentally Informal. Das monumentale Informelle," in *Neue Staatsgalerie und Kammertheater* (Stuttgart, 1984), pp. 14f.

54. The quotations are from James Stirling, "A House for Karl Friedrich Schinkel," *The Japan Architect*, 55, no. 274 (February 1980), p. 9.

55. Hans Mackowsky (note 1), p. 13.

56. Schinkel in Peschken (note 2), p. 148.

Catalogue

OF THE EXHIBITION

All items are part of the Staatliche Museen zu Berlin, Preußischer Kulturbesitz, Kupferstichkabinett.
Numbers in parentheses denote the Schinkel Archive inventory number.

PART I
BIOGRAPHICAL AND THEMATIC INTRODUCTION

CAT. NO. 1

Self-portrait with his wife Suzanne, c. 1810–15 (H.*24*). Watercolor and body color, *20.1 x 23.5* cm.

CAT. NO. 2

Perspective sketch of classical ruins, signed and dated *1795* (H.*1*). Pen and sepia ink, 10.2 x 13.4 cm.

CAT. NO. 3

Perspective study, after Friedrich Gilly, of Gilly's proposed monument to Frederick II, 1797 (H.3). Pen and ink with watercolor, 13 x 31.8 cm.

CAT. NO. 4

Perspective sketch of the Marsfeld or Champs-de-Mars, Paris, after Friedrich Gilly, c. 1798–1800 (14.39). Pen and ink, 14.3 x 41.2 cm. (Forster, fig. 4.)

CAT. NO. 5

Interior perspective study of the Parisian assembly room, after Friedrich Gilly, 1798–1800 (16.3). Pen and ink with pencil, 23.3 x 37.3 cm.

CAT. NO. 6

Studies of the Parisian assembly room for the Council of 500, after Friedrich Gilly, 1798–1800 (16.2). Pen and sepia ink, watercolor, and pencil, 22.8 x 34.7 cm.

CAT. NO. 7

Perspective studies of two villas on the water, signed and dated 1800 (16.38). Pen and ink, 29.6 x 41.6 cm.

CAT. NO. 8

Perspective study of a columned hall overlooking the sea, 1802 (20c.178). Pen and ink with pencil, 27.1 x 40.5 cm. (Vogtherr, fig. 16.)

CAT. NO. 9

Interior view of the great cave near Corgnale, dated July 3, 1803. (1B.21). Pen and sepia ink with pencil, 33 x 24.3 cm.

CAT. NO. 10

Perspective study of a Roman cemetary, c. 1800–1810 (1B.30). Pencil and watercolor, 22.8 x 41.9 cm.

CAT. NO. 11

Panoramic perspective view overlooking Prague, 1803 (1A.11). Pen and sepia ink with wash, 54 x 73.7 cm. (Plate 1.)

CAT. NO. 12

Schinkel on the summit of Mount Etna with the sunrise in the distance, 1804 (6B.30). Pen and ink with pencil, 49 x 32.4 cm. (Forster, fig. 2.)

CAT. NO. 13

Perspective view of Dresden (as seen through a telescope?), 1803 (1B.17). Watercolor, 29.2 x 30.3 cm. (Plate 2.)

CAT. NO. 14

Bohemian mountains at sunset, c. 1803–05 (2.2). Watercolor and gouache, 21.6 x 35.4 cm. (Plate 3.)

CAT. NO. 15

Perspective view of the ruins of a Gothic cloister and church amidst trees, 1809 (15B.102). Watercolor, 19.3 x 41.3 cm. (Plate 4.)

CAT. NO. 16

Panoramic perspective view of Cologne, signed and dated 1817 (9.24). Pen and ink with pencil and wash, 24.6 x 52.7 cm. (Pehnt, fig. 1.)

PART II
THE DRAMA OF ARCHITECTURE

CAT. NO. 17

Perspective view of an arched bridge with a view of the landscape, signed and dated 1801 (1B.31). Pen and ink with pencil and gray wash, 25.1 x 31.9 cm.

CAT. NO. 18

Panoramic perspective view of a Renaissance tempietto, c. 1805–20 (48c.183). Pen and ink with wash, 53 x 101 cm.

CAT. NO. 19

Perspective view of Pisa Cathedral and Baptistry, c. 1804 (4.13). Pen and ink with pencil and wash, 48 x 54.1 cm. (Verwiebe, fig. 3.)

CAT. NO. 20

Panoramic view of Rome from Schinkel's apartment window, c. 1803–04 (4.56). Pen and sepia ink, 29.5 x 48 cm. (Forster, fig. 1.)

CAT. NO. 21

Panoramic view of Rome, with rooftops in the foreground, c. 1803–04 (54.5). Watercolor over base or underlying color, 33.1 x 52.6 cm. (Plate 5.)

CAT. NO. 22

Gamblers with the Spanish steps and Santa Trinità del Monti, Rome, in the background, c. 1803–04 (4.49). Watercolor and wash, 32.8 x 38 cm. (Plate 6.)

CAT. NO. 23

Perspective view of the Capitoline Hill, Rome, c. 1803 to 1804 (4.58). Pen and ink with pencil, 48 x 54.2 cm. (Verwiebe, fig. 6.)

CAT. NO. 24

Bird's-eye view of a Roman palace complex with a triumphal entry gate, c. 1803–30 (22B.142). Pen and ink with pencil, 25 x 34 cm.

CAT. NO. 25

Perspective view of a palace complex with a bridge, c. 1803 to 1830 (22B.143). Pen and ink with pencil and wash, 24.7 x 53.6 cm. (Van Zanten, fig. 3.)

CAT. NO. 26

Perspective view of a domed cathedral or palace on a hill, overlooking a garden, c. 1803–30 (C.18). Pen and ink with pencil, 29.6 x 41.5 cm. (Vogtherr, fig. 7.)

CAT. NO. 27

Perspective view of the Traunsee from under an arbor, 1811 (1A.9). Pen and sepia ink, 51.4 x 62.2 cm. (Forster, fig. 9.)

CAT. NO. 28

Gothic cathedral behind a massive tree, signed 1810 (54.1). Lithograph, 48.7 x 34.3 cm. (Forster, fig. 6.)

CAT. NO. 29

Perspective study of proposed mausoleum for Queen Luise, 1810 (54.3). Pen and ink with watercolor on an underlying base color, 71.5 x 51.5 cm. (Forster, fig. 5.)

CAT. NO. 30

View from a garden through an arbor to a palace for a Prussian noblewoman, c. 1830–31, entitled *Einsicht* (*Insight*) (15B.121a). Watercolor and underlying base color, 20.4 x 14.9 cm. (Plate 7.)

CAT. NO. 31

Sketch of an elevation for a guardhouse with rounded arches and Egyptian roof and details, c. 1815, possibly a preliminary sketch for the Neue Wache (New Guardhouse), Berlin (20B.116). Pencil, 19.6 x 32.6 cm.

CAT. NO. 32

Perspective rendering of the Schloßbrücke, Berlin, 1819 (23A.64). Pen and sepia ink with wash, 55.7 x 90.3 cm. (Vogtherr, fig. 12.)

CAT. NO. 33

Perspective view of a proposed palace for Prince Wilhelm on Unter den Linden, Berlin, 1832 (33.6). Pencil, 34.2 x 53 cm. (Vogtherr, fig. 11.)

CAT. NO. 34

Rendered elevation of the Altes Museum (1822–30), Berlin, with the fountain in the foreground, c. 1826 (23C.68). Pencil, 22 x 28 cm. (Vogtherr, fig. 13.)

CAT. NO. 35

The Mourning on the Tumulus, Study for a wall-painting in the staircase of the Altes Museum, signed and dated 1832 (D.9). Gouache, 58.6 x 67.8 cm. (Plate 9.)

CAT. NO. 36

Site plan for the redesign of the Lustgarten adjacent to the Altes Museum, signed and dated 1828 (21C. 161). Pen and ink with pencil and watercolor, 43.8 x 49 cm. (Vogtherr, fig. 14.)

CAT. NO. 37

Site plan of the plaza at the Brandenburg Gate, Berlin, with a perspective view of the entrance to the Tiergarten, 1835 (23B.80). Pen and ink with pencil, watercolor, and wash, 53.2 x 66.5 cm. (Plate 8.)

CAT. NO. 38

Interior perspective view of the proposed Gertraudenkirche, Berlin, signed and dated 1819 (26B.11). Pen and ink with watercolor and wash, 22 x 28 cm. (Pehnt, fig. 2.)

CAT. NO. 39

Perspective elevation of a landscaped garden arranged as a hippodrome—project behind the antique villa at Charlottenhof, c. 1830 (34.32). Pen and ink with pencil and watercolor, 16 x 65 cm. (Vogtherr, fig. 8.)

CAT. NO. 40

Site plan and perspective view of Charlottenhof, Potsdam, 1831, from *Sammlung architektonischer Entwürfe* (hereafter called *Sammlung*). Print, 40.8 x 51.2 cm. (Vogtherr, fig. 3.)

CAT. NO. 41

Interior perspective view of a proposed great hall for a palace on the Acropolis, signed and dated 1834. (35B.44). Pen and ink with watercolor, wash, and white highlights, 54.6 x 42.6 cm. (Plate 10.)

CAT. NO. 42

Perspective view of the landscape from the garden of a proposed residence for a prince, 1835 (40C.53). Pen and ink with watercolor, 42.5 x 65.2 cm. (Van Zanten, fig. 2.)

CAT. NO. 43

Perspective view of the terrace of a proposed palace at Orianda in the Crimea, 1838 (35.57). Pen and ink with watercolor and wash, 48.1 x 49.2 cm. (Plate 11.)

CAT. NO. 44

Perspective view of the atrium of a proposed palace at Orianda in the Crimea, 1838 (35.49). Pen and ink with watercolor and wash, 37. 2 x 66.4 cm. (Plate 12.)

CAT. NO. 45

Perspective view of an Italian seacoast with an imaginary villa for Peter Beuth, 1839 (54.8). Watercolor and pencil, 74.7 x 54.8 cm. (Pehnt, fig. 3.)

PART III
THEATERS AND
THEATRICALITY

CAT. NO. 46

Perspective view of the National Theater designed by Carl Gotthard Langhans on the Gendarmenmarkt, Berlin, signed and dated 1800 (H.6). Pen and ink, 13.1 x 21.1 cm. (Schwarzer, fig. 9.)

CAT. NO. 47

Perspective view of the Königliches Opernhaus (Royal Opera House) designed by Georg Wenzeslaus von Knobelsdorff and St. Hedwig's Church, Berlin, 1800 (H.7). Pen, ink, and wash, 17.5 x 27.2 cm. (Schwarzer, fig. 3.)

CAT. NO. 48

Sketches of the elevations and plans of an unidentified theater, c. 1800–1830 (20B.124). Pen and ink, 39.8 x 32.3 cm.

CAT. NO. 49

Perspective views, elevations, details, and sections of a proposed national theater, 1813 (23B.63). Pen and ink with pencil and underlying base color, 49.3 x 54.2 cm. (Forster, fig. 10.)

CAT. NO. 50

Perspective study of the proposed Singakedemie (Choral Academy), Berlin, signed and dated 1821 (21C.141). Pen and ink, 40.4 x 59.2 cm.

CAT. NO. I

CAT. NO. 3

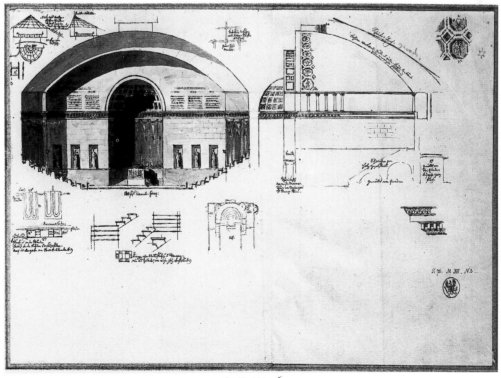

CAT. NO. 6

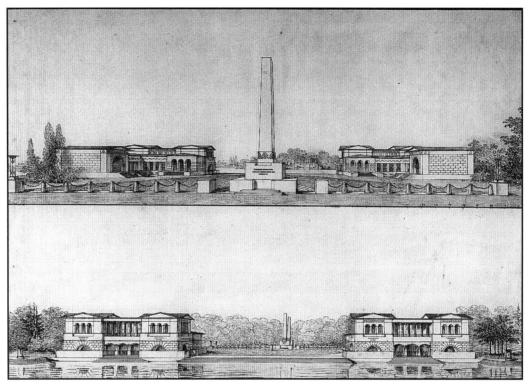

CAT. NO. 7

CAT. NO. 10

CAT. NO. 17

CAT. NO. 18

CAT. NO. 51

Perspective view from the
northeast of the Schauspielhaus
(Theater), Berlin, 1821 (50.11).
Pen and ink with wash and
white highlights, 31.8 x 20.6 cm.
(Forster, fig. 14.)

CAT. NO. 52

Elevation of the main façade
of the Schauspielhaus, 1821, from
Sammlung. Print, 40.8 x 51.2 cm.
(Schwarzer, fig. 11.)

CAT. NO. 53

Perspective view from the
southwest of the Schauspielhaus,
1821, from Sammlung. Print,
40.8 x 51.2 cm.

CAT. NO. 54

Perspective view of the theater
within the Schauspielhaus,
looking toward the stage, 1821,
from Sammlung. Print,
40.8 x 51.2 cm. (Frontispiece.)

CAT. NO. 55

Perspective view of the theater
within the Schauspielhaus, looking from the stage, 1821, from
Sammlung. Print, 40.8 x 51.2 cm.
(Schwarzer, fig. 10.)

CAT. NO. 56

Two sections of the Schauspielhaus, 1821, showing the concert
hall and theater, from Sammlung.
Print, 40.8 x 51.2 cm.
(Schwarzer, fig. 14.)

CAT. NO. 57

Three plans of the Schauspiel-
haus, 1821, from Sammlung.
Print, 40.8 x 51.2 cm.
(Schwarzer, fig. 12.)

CAT. NO. 58

Perspective view of the concert
hall in the Schauspielhaus,
1821, from Sammlung. Print,
40.8 x 51.2 cm.

CAT. NO. 59

Interior elevation of the concert
hall in the Schauspielhaus, n.d.,
(50.8). Pen and ink with pencil
and watercolor, 60.8 x 94.2 cm.

CAT. NO. 60

Longitudinal elevation of the
concert hall in the Schauspielhaus, 1821, from Sammlung.
Print, 40.8 x 51.2 cm.

CAT. NO. 61

Elevation of the entrance façade
of the proposed theater in
Hamburg, 1825, from Sammlung.
Print, 40.8 x 51.2 cm.

CAT. NO. 62

Detail of the elevation of the
proposed theater in Hamburg,
1825, from Sammlung. Print,
40.8 x 51.2 cm.

CAT. NO. 63

Three plans of the proposed
theater in Hamburg,
1825, from Sammlung. Print,
40.8 x 51.2 cm.

CAT. NO. 64

Elevation and sections of the
proposed theater in Hamburg,
1825, from Sammlung.
Print, 40.8 x 51.2 cm.

CAT. NO. 65

Elevation of a proposed, domed,
centrally-planned church
(version IV) in the Oranienburg
suburb near Berlin, 1828, from
Sammlung. Print, 40.8 x 51.2 cm.

CAT. NO. 66

Section of a proposed, domed,
centrally-planned church
(version IV) in the Oranienburg
suburb near Berlin, 1828,
from Sammlung.
Print, 40.8 x 51.2 cm.

PART IV
SET DESIGN:
THE ARCHITECTURE
OF DRAMA

CAT. NO. 67

Gridded perspective sketch of
the Hanging Gardens of
Semiramis, for the Seven Wonders
of the World, an optical perspective picture, 1813 (22.E72).
Pencil, pen, and red ink,
18.4 x 35.4 cm. (Verwiebe, fig. 13.)

CAT. NO. 68

Exterior study for a diorama
of a mine in Calabria, 1812
(22D.179). Underpainted wash,
16.3 x 32.7 cm. (Verwiebe, fig. 10.)

CAT. NO. 69

Interior study for a diorama
of a mine in Calabria, 1812
(22D.180). Underpainted wash,
16.1 x 32.3 cm.
(Verwiebe, fig. 11.)

CAT. NO. 70

Design for a perspective optical
picture, The Fire of Moscow,
1812 (1B.32). Pen and sepia ink
with wash and white highlights,
45 x 64 cm. (Verwiebe, fig. 12.)

CAT. NO. 71

Cut-outs of French soldiers,
related to The Fire of Moscow,
c. 1812 (39D.193). Pen and ink
with wash, 20 x 37.5 cm.

CAT. NO. 72

Grove of the Temple of Isis, a
set design for Die Zauberflöte (The
Magic Flute), 1815 (Th.20).
Gouache, 53 x 75.4 cm.
(Plate 13.)

CAT. NO. 73

Interior perspective view of a
forecourt or grotto, a set design
for Die Zauberflöte (The
Magic Flute), 1815 (22D.96).
Gouache, 29.7 x 37.4 cm.
(Plate 14.)

CAT. NO. 74

Sketch of a grotto, probably for
the entrance to the Temple of
the Sun, Die Zauberflöte
(The Magic Flute), 1815 (15B.51).
Pen and ink, 14 x 19 cm.

CAT. NO. 75

Interior perspective view of the
testing place at the entrance to
the Temple of the Sun, a set
design for Die Zauberflöte
(The Magic Flute), 1815 (22C.119).
Gouache, 52.2 x 74.6 cm.
(Plate 15.)

CAT. NO. 76

Sketch of a pyramid, probably
for the Temple of the Sun, the
final scene in Die Zauberflöte
(The Magic Flute), 1815
(20B.72). Pen and ink with
pencil, 20 x 24 cm.

CAT. NO. 77

Interior perspective view of the
Temple of the Sun with a statue
of Osiris, the final scene in Die
Zauberflöte (The Magic
Flute), 1815 (Th.13). Gouache,
54.6 x 62.5 cm. (Plate 16.)

CAT. NO. 78

Perspective view of a market-place with a fountain, a set design for *Undine*, 1816 (22D.117). Gouache, 34.8 x 50.5 cm. (Plate 17.)

CAT. NO. 79

Interior perspective view of Kühleborn's water palace, a set design for *Undine*, 1816 (22C.173). Gouache, 33.2 x 56.4 cm. (Plate 18.)

CAT. NO. 80

Evening view of Edgar's palace, a set design for *Ariodant*, 1816 (22C.122). Gouache, 45.3 x 63.2 cm. (Plate 19.)

CAT. NO. 81

Perspective view of Jerusalem with Mt. Sinai, a set design for *Athalia*, 1817 (22C.103). Gouache, 35.6 x 54.2 cm.

CAT. NO. 82

Interior perspective view of the Temple of Jerusalem (Temple of Solomon), a set design for *Athalia*, 1817 (22C.104). Gouache, 41.9 x 54 cm. (Plate 20.)

CAT. NO. 83

Interior perspective view of the Temple of Apollo, a set design for *Alceste*, 1817 (22C.124). Pen and ink with watercolor, 45.6 x 57.5 cm. (Plate 21.)

CAT. NO. 84

Entry to the underworld, a set design for *Alceste*, 1815 (22C.123). Gouache, 42.5 x 59.1 cm. (Plate 22.)

CAT. NO. 85

Perspective view of the temple square, a set design for *Die Vestalin (The Vestal Virgin)*, 1818 (Th.10). Pen and ink with watercolor, 39.3 x 57.5 cm. (Plate 23.)

CAT. NO. 86

Interior perspective view of the Temple of Vesta, a set design for *Die Vestalin (The Vestal Virgin)*, 1818 (22D.94). Pen and ink with pencil and watercolor, 30.2 x 36 cm. (Plate 24.)

CAT. NO. 87

Interior perspective view of a hall, a set design for *Agnes von Hohenstaufen*, c. 1827 (22D.176). Pen and ink with pencil and watercolor, 23.7 x 35 cm. (Plate 25.)

CAT. NO. 88

Interior perspective view of a great hall, a set design for *Agnes von Hohenstaufen*, c. 1827 (22c.172). Pen and ink, with watercolor and wash, 23.6 x 37.9 cm. (Plate 26.)

CAT. NO. 89

Perspective sketches of a great hall and arcade, a set design for *Agnes von Hohenstaufen*, c. 1815–20 (H23). Pen and ink with wash, 33 x 21 cm.

CAT. NO. 90

Perspective view of the Peruvian fire temple, a set design for *Fernando Cortez*, 1818 (Th.21). Gouache, 41.3 x 58.9 cm. (Plate 27.)

CAT. NO. 91

Panoramic perspective view of Mexico and the Spaniards' tented encampment, a set design for *Fernando Cortez*, 1818 (22C.149). Gouache, 42 x 58 cm. (Plate 28.)

CAT. NO. 92

Perspective view of the city and Cathedral of Reims, from a Gothic balcony, a set design for *Die Jungfrau von Orléans (The Maid of Orleans)*, 1818. (Th.19). Gouache, 45.6 x 55.6 cm. (Plate 31.)

CAT. NO. 93

Perspective view of the entrance to the Cathedral of Reims, a set design for *Die Jungfrau von Orléans (The Maid of Orleans)*, 1818 (Th.24). Gouache, 47.x 66.4 cm. (Plate 30.)

CAT. NO. 94

A tropical garden, a set design for *Armida*, 1820 (22C.101). Gouache, 27.6 x 40.6 cm. (Plate 29.)

CAT. NO. 95

Perspective view of a Doric temple, possibly a set design for *Olympia*, 1821 (22C.183). Pen and ink with watercolor, 48.4 x 63.9 cm. (Plate 32.)

CAT. NO. 96

Interior perspective view of the Temple of Diana, a set design for *Olympia*, 1821 (Th.15). Pen and ink with watercolor, 48.9 x 64.2 cm. (Plate 33.)

CAT. NO. 97

Perspective elevation of the Temple of Diana, possibly a set design for *Olympia*, or more probably, *Iphigenia*, 1821 (Th.18). Watercolor, 22 x 35 cm.

CAT. NO. 98

Perspective view of an Indian scene, a set design for *Nurmahal*, 1822 (22D.177). Gouache and body color, 23.7 x 37.2 cm. (Plate 34.)

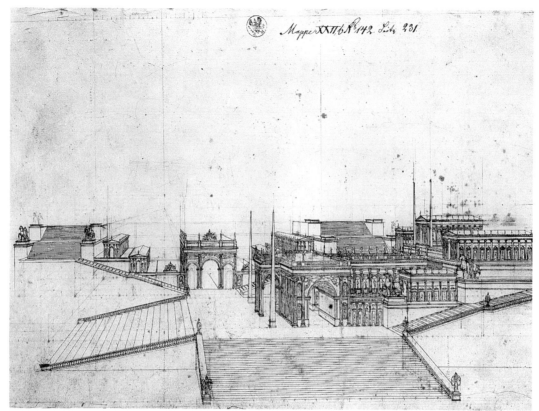

CAT. NO. 24

CAT. NO. 31

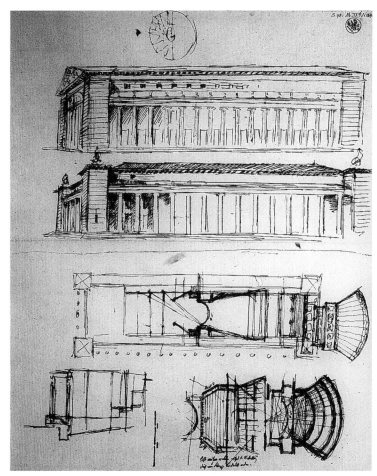

CAT. NO. 48

CAT. NO. 59

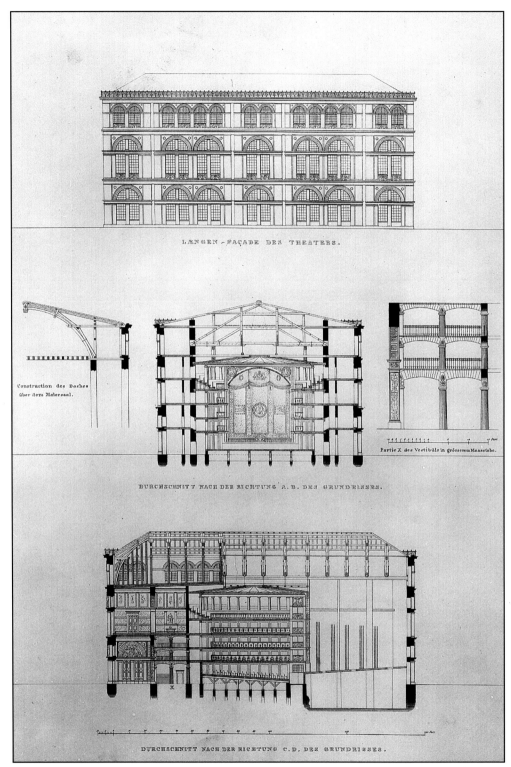

LÆNGEN-FAÇADE DES THEATERS.

Construction des Daches
über dem Malersaal.

Partie X des Vestibüls in grösserem Maasstabe.

DURCHSCHNITT NACH DER RICHTUNG A.B. DES GRUNDRISSES.

DURCHSCHNITT NACH DER RICHTUNG C.D. DES GRUNDRISSES.

CAT. NO. 64

CAT. NO. 81

CAT. NO. 97

STANLEY TIGERMAN

For Karl Friedrich Schinkel, the interrelationship of theater and architecture created an opportunity to utilize the concept of the proscenium stage in his drawings of buildings and opera sets. More often than not, Schinkel established a point of view that allowed him to depict an actual observer of the building, landscape, or spectacle before him. Schinkel's control of the spatial relationship between viewers and the environment rendered in his drawings was influenced as much by principles of theater as by principles of architecture. Unfortunately, this important and engaging aspect of his work proved to be virtually impossible to employ in the large, half-oval racecourse of the architecture gallery at The Art Institute of Chicago (see *fig. 1*). The very shape of the architecture gallery provides an interesting formal counterpoint to Schinkel's theory of spatially planar determinism insofar as one is drawn constantly through the curved space towards a never quite perceivable end that is the perspectival counterpoint to Schinkel's "thin red line" of the proscenium.

Given these restrictions, the decision was made to incorporate into the design of the exhibition space other aspects of Schinkel's architectural and artistic vocabulary, particularly as expressed in two of his most important, extant buildings. Thus, coming into the gallery down a flight of stairs and into an entrance hall, the visitor enters a space that is designed to evoke the Altes Museum in Berlin (see *fig. 2*). One then moves transitionally into and through several chambers that recall the famous Schauspielhaus of 1818–21 and its concert hall (see *figs. 3–5*). Finally, the visitor reaches two "Schinkel-after-Schinkel" chambers that suggest some of the enormous influence that Schinkel has had on architects after his death. The first of these rooms is modeled after a forced collaboration between the National Socialist architect Ernst Sagebiel and Ludwig Mies van der Rohe for a textile industry exhibition, shortly before Mies decided to immigrate to the United States. The second space is a reminiscence of a small section of Albert Speer's project for a new Reich Chancellery building (see *fig. 6*).

Chronologically structured, the installation of the exhibition "Karl Friedrich Schinkel, 1781–1841: The Drama of Architecture" represents an unbroken cycle of design that stretches from the Neoclassicism of the early nineteenth century until the advent of Postmodernism (which ironically coincided with the death of Mies van der Rohe) in the late twentieth century, when theatricality was reintroduced into building design after decades of the detached formalism of International Style Modernism. The dramatic quality of the exhibition's installation—achieved through the use of flattened Classicism (in this case literally painted on the gallery walls)—separates the gallery setting from the present. It creates an appropriately theatrical milieu for Schinkel's original drawings and opera-set renderings.

The theater of architecture and the drama of architecture, architecture as setting and architecture as event, are presented here as mutually self-fulfilling and continually regenerative.

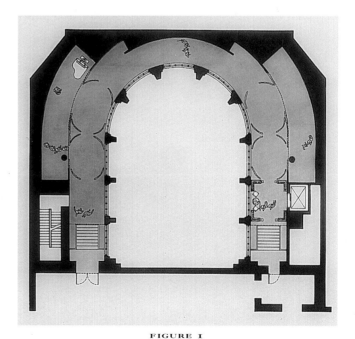

FIGURE I

Tigerman McCurry Architects, Plan of the Karl Friedrich Schinkel exhibition at The Art Institute of Chicago, 1994.

Tigerman McCurry Architects, The Altes Museum,
an installation design for the Schinkel exhibition,
1994.

FIGURE 3

Tigerman McCurry Architects, The Concert Hall
of the Schauspielhaus, an installation design for the
Schinkel exhibition, 1994.

FIGURE 4

Tigerman McCurry Architects, The Concert Hall
of the Schauspielhaus, an installation design for the
Schinkel exhibition, 1994.

FIGURE 5

Tigerman McCurry Architects, The Schauspielhaus
Antechamber, an installation design for the Schinkel
exhibition, 1994.

FIGURE 6

Tigerman McCurry Architects, Schinkel after
Schinkel: From Sagebiel to Speer, an installation
design for the Schinkel exhibition, 1994.

INDEX

All titles refer to works by Karl Friedrich Schinkel unless otherwise indicated.
*Numbers in **bold type** refer to pages with photographs*

All black-and-white and color photographs of works in the exhibition are courtesy of the Staatliche Museen zu Berlin, Preußischer Kulturbesitz, Kupferstichkabinett, Sammlung der Zeichnungen und Druckgraphik; photographs by Jörg P. Anders.

In addition to information provided in the figure captions, the following should be acknowledged for photographs reproduced in this publication:

Jörg P. Anders   23 (7), 26 (11, 12), 27 (13), 37 (1, 2), 38 (4, 5), 39 (7, 8), 41 (9), 43 (14), 84 (1)
Brunzel   48 (22)
Gerhard Döring   64 (15)
Hensmanns   47 (21)
Landesamt für Denkmalpflege, Dresden   64 (16)
Landesbildstelle Berlin   55 (1), 63 (13)
Northwestern University, Evanston, Illinois; Special Collections Department   65 (19, 20)
Stefani Pirolo-Westphal   47 (21)
Stiftung Schlösser und Gärten Potsdam-Sanssouci   21 (3)
Christoph Martin Vogtherr   71 (5, 6)
John Zukowsky   13 (1), 14 (2, 3), 15 (4, 5), 16 (6, 7), 17 (8, 9)